Struct.

Structured Products
Evolution and Analysis

Edited by Clarke Pitts

Published by Risk Books, a Division of Incisive Media Investments Ltd

Incisive Media
32–34 Broadwick Street
London W1A 2HG
Tel: +44(0) 20 7316 9000
E-mail: books@incisivemedia.com
Sites: www.riskbooks.com
　　　www.incisivemedia.com

ISBN 979-1-904339-65-6

British Library Cataloguing in Publication Data
A catalogue record for this book is available from the British Library

Publisher: Nick Carver
Managing Editor: Lewis O'Sullivan
Associate Editor: Alice Levick
Designer: Lisa Ling
Copy-edited and typeset by T&T Productions Ltd, London

Printed and bound in the UK by PrintonDemand-Worldwide

Contents

About the Editor   vii

About the Authors   ix

Foreword   xiii
Gillian Tett
The Financial Times

Introduction   xvii
Clarke Pitts

1   **What Are Structured Products?**   1
Clarke Pitts

2   **History and Evolution: What Happened and Why?**   23
Clarke Pitts

3   **The UK Market**   35
Christopher Taylor
The Investment Bridge

4   **Europe: An Overview**   79
Simon Harris
Mu Capital

5   **The Market in Asia**   95
Angel K. Y. Wu

6   **Japan: Part 1**   119
Hiroshi Wakutsu and Toru Sano
Enzo Co, Ltd

7   **Japan: Part 2**   163
Hiroshi Wakutsu and Toru Sano
Enzo Co, Ltd

8   **A History of the US Structured Products Industry**   207
Scott Mitchell and Daniel Roose
JP Morgan

9   **A Regulatory Perspective**   237
Jeremy Jennings-Mares
Morrison & Foerster (UK) LLP

10 Risk and Modelling   269
    Clarke Pitts

    Index   285

About the Editor

Clarke Pitts worked for Salomon Brothers for seven years in London and New York, followed by Barclays in New York and Tokyo for two years and JP Morgan in Tokyo and London for eight years. His main areas of responsibilities were equities, convertibles and equity derivative trading. Clarke attended the London School of Economics. He is based in London, where he runs a small specialist fund for a group of former colleagues.

About the Authors

Simon Harris is a director of Mu Capital, an investment design and distribution business with a focus on risk-defined investments. Simon has over ten years' experience in structured product markets, including working on the sell side for the UK desk of EFG Financial Products (now Leonteq), a major Swiss issuer. Prior to that, as an editor and analyst for StructuredRetailProducts.com (SRP), Simon helped build the world's leading structured product data source. He joined as SRP's first member of staff in 2003 and went on to help build the firm's European and Asian content, train financial advisers and asset managers, and advise buy-side and sell-side institutions on all aspects of structured products from investment trends to people strategy.

Jeremy Jennings-Mares is a partner in the capital markets group of Morrison & Foerster, based in London. His practice focuses on securities, structured products and derivatives, as well as advising on European and UK financial regulation. Jeremy qualified as an English solicitor in 1993 and has previously practised in Japan, Singapore and Thailand, in addition to the UK.

Scott Mitchell is managing director and heads structured investments distributor marketing for JP Morgan in the Americas. Scott joined JP Morgan in 2004 from CIBC, where he was a director in the US equity structured products group. Prior to moving to New York, Scott worked in equity derivatives for CIBC in London, England and Toronto, Canada. Prior to that, he also he worked in Toronto as a chartered accountant for an international public accounting firm. Scott obtained his BBA from Wilfrid Laurier University in Waterloo, Canada.

Daniel Roose works in the structured investments team at JP Morgan Securities LLC in New York, which broadly has responsibility for the creation and distribution of cross-asset retail structured products in the Americas. Daniel joined JP Morgan in 2006 after a short tenure at a large New York law firm and has worked in a variety of different roles associated with JP Morgan's structured product efforts. Daniel holds a BA from Colorado College.

Toru Sano works as chief operating officer and partner at Enzo Co, Ltd, and is responsible for the company's new initiatives such as the development of a standardised small and medium enterprises mergers and acquisitions market in Japan. Prior to establishing Enzo, Toru was in charge of JP Morgan's fixed income business in Japan. He spent nearly 20 years at JP Morgan, where he held various trading, marketing and structuring responsibilities in fixed income and equity derivatives areas. He holds a BEc from the University of Tokyo.

Christopher Taylor is the founder and managing director of the Investment Bridge Limited. He was previously managing director at Incapital Europe, the London-based affiliate of Incapital, a US-based investment banking firm. Prior to working at Incapital, Chris founded Blue Sky Asset Management, a multi-award-winning boutique investment firm, where he was chief executive from 2007 to 2010. Between 2006 and 2007, he was managing director of the structured investment division of Dawnay Day Quantum, and from 1996 to 2006 he worked for HSBC asset management, the global investment business of HSBC Group, where he was involved in the distribution of actively managed and passive index funds, multi-manager and alternative funds. During this time he was the director of UK structured products distribution for HSBC's structured products business.

Hiroshi Wakutsu works as chief executive officer and partner at Enzo Co, Ltd, and is responsible for the overall management. Prior to establishing Enzo, Hiroshi worked for Nikko Citigroup Securities in Tokyo from 2000 to 2005 as managing director and head of equities derivatives in Japan. Hiroshi worked for Lehman Brothers as managing director and head of global finance for Japan and as co-head of domestic equity sales until 2008. He holds a BSc in mathematics and a CICS from Houston Baptist University.

Angel Wu is the head of products and solutions at ABN AMRO Bank private banking in Asia and the Middle East. She joined ABN AMRO in January 2006, having spent four years running the structured products desk for private clients in Hong Kong before assuming the regional role in June 2010. Prior to that, she was the head of investment advisory at Dah Sing Financial Group. She started her career as an equity analyst covering China B- and H-shares at the

Bank of East Asia. She has also worked in Mees Pierson Securities (Asia) and Citibank Private Bank as an equity research analyst. She holds a Bachelor's degree in economics from the University of Hong Kong. She is a chartered financial analyst, certified financial planner and financial risk manager.

Foreword

Back in the autumn of 2005, during the last credit bubble, I was sitting at my desk in the *Financial Times* in London when I received a phone call. On the line was a senior official at a European central bank with a question: had I, as a journalist, seen any really reliable data on the size of the market in collateralised debt obligations (CDOs)? Or, for that matter, in collateralised loan obligations and bundles of credit default swaps?

I was startled. In 2005, it was already clear to almost anyone watching markets that the world of complex credit and structured finance was exploding in scale and importance. To me, as a journalist, it was also evident that it was very hard for a layman to track that growth, because much of the data on the sector was private, not public. And yet, as I scrabbled away at my job – then head of capital markets at the *FT* – I assumed that there must be somebody "official" who knew what was really going on or, at least, knew how to measure this sector, and its importance to the economy as a whole.

It turned out I was wrong. Two years later, in the summer of 2007, the financial world started sliding towards a crisis when US home owners who had taken out subprime mortgages started to default on their loans, creating a cascade of losses on structured products and derivatives linked to those loans. As the losses piled up, investors, politicians, journalists and regulators alike were startled to discover just how big the market for these mortgage-linked products had quietly become. More important still, they also realised just how integral these structured products were to the financial system as a whole.

That was a surprise: until the summer of 2007, most commentators had tended to assume that structured finance was something of a sideshow to the banking world. Hence, regulators tended to focus much of their attention on the regulated banks and traditional banking operations, leaving much of the structured finance world sitting in the shadows. And journalists tended to echo this focus. On a paper such as the *FT*, for example, the teams of journalists who covered banking or economics had a great deal of prominence in the paper – and in the physical layout of the building; the capital markets team, where I was working, was something of a backwater.

Now, the good news today, six long years after the credit bubble burst, is that nobody in the regulatory or investing world would ever dare to consider structured finance a mere sideshow or backwater. Nor would any senior central bank official struggle to find data on the size of the CDO market, say. In the aftermath of the crisis, policymakers have scrambled to find ways to track the sector, in terms not just of the more visible types of structured financed products (such as collateralised loans) but of the more shadowy elements too (such as synthetic CDOs, insofar as these still exist). Policymakers have even attempted to measure the size of the so-called "shadow banking world", or the parts of the financial sector that exist outside regulated banks. A couple of years ago, for example, a team of economists at the New York Federal Reserve drew up a "map" of the sector, which tries to show how all the different flows in finance interact with each other. These flows are so extraordinarily complex that the map in question had to be presented as a poster – albeit one that is too vast to actually hang on any normal office wall. But while the details on that diagram are confusingly dense, the key point is clear: structured finance is not just an adjunct to the banking world, but is absolutely central to how it operates. Just as 16th-century scholars were forced to revise their world view when Nicolaus Copernicus showed that the Earth revolved around the Sun, not the other way round, regulators, journalists and politicians have been forced to flip their mental map of finance upside down, putting structured products in the central pole.

But while the mental map may have (belatedly) changed, there is bad news too: right now, politicians and financial regulators still seem distinctly unsure about how they want to handle this crucial field. In the immediate aftermath of the financial crisis, there was so much public outrage about the costs of the credit bubble that many politicians were keen to rein the sector in. Little wonder: during the bubble years (between 2001 and 2007) a host of egregious practices flourished, partly because the sector was so complex and opaque. The bundles of securitised sub-prime mortgage debt that were sold on a massive scale in 2005 and 2006, for example, were often badly mispriced, partly because the ratings agencies completely misjudged the risks of default – hence the fact that investors and banks alike were forced to recognise unexpected losses, on a massive scale.

But even as public anger has bubbled up, what policymakers and investors have also come to realise is that the structured product sector plays a crucial role in the wider economy. After all, the initial impetus for structured finance is simply to spread risk; and, at its best, it does this in such an effective manner that it enables credit-hungry institutions and individuals to raise money more easily and cheaply than before. Of course, if structured finance was to disappear overnight, there would be no reason (in theory) why its function could not be replaced with old-fashioned forms of financial intermediation (ie, simple bank loans, bonds or equity finance). But in reality that would certainly push up the price of credit or require that the government step in to replace the private sector, given that banks are being forced to cut loans to meet regulatory standards. And indeed, in the aftermath of the financial crisis, this pattern is exactly what has played out. Since 2007, for example, the private sector securitisation market for American mortgages has effectively collapsed. As a result, state-supported institutions such as the Federal National Mortgage Association (Fannie Mae) and the Federal Home Loan Mortgage Corporation (Freddie Mac) have stepped in – with the result that over 90% of new mortgages that are being issued in the US are now effectively underwritten by the state. Meanwhile, in Europe a sharp decline in the securitisation of corporate loans has hampered credit flows to riskier companies. And this squeeze has been doubly intense, since mainstream European banks have been forced to cut their assets, to meet new capital adequacy standards.

The result, then, is that a particularly bitter irony stalks the Western world: just as structured finance has faced criticism amid a political backlash, it is now needed more badly than ever before, if politicians want to maintain growth. Politicians and investors cannot afford to ignore it, any more than they could ignore the Internet; for good, or ill, the innovation is here to stay. But policymakers, journalists and economists also cannot afford to close their eyes to the potential risks and rewards; if nothing else, they need to understand how the sector works and why it matters. It is just a pity that more books like this were not available in the first decade of the millennium; if they had been, the history of finance might have been quite different.

This book on structured products, edited by Clarke Pitts, is thus both timely and useful, particularly since it covers a range of markets and has been written by practitioners.

Gillian Tett
The Financial Times, London
December 2013

Introduction

This book is a collaboration between me, the editor, and eight contributing authors, each of whom is an expert in their field. It is not intended to be comprehensive and complete in its examination of structured products, as such ambition would be doomed to failure.

Structured products barely existed as recently as the late 1980s, and, at the time of writing, the industry is larger than that of hedge funds, with several trillion US dollars invested in them. While hedge funds are not widely understood either, there is a substantial canon of books on them and they frequently feature in the press. The contrast with structured products could not be more stark. Students (I use the term broadly) of finance are aware that they exist, but very often have little more knowledge or understanding than that.

This book seeks to examine what has happened and why. Along the way, we shall look at the impact of this new industry on other aspects of the capital markets and at some of the most significant events in their history. Crises which were caused by structured products, and in other cases where the catalysts were exogenous but had a major impact on the financial markets via their influence on the structured products industry.

The reader might wonder why, if this industry is so substantial, there is so much ignorance and disinterest and indeed why such a book has not already been written. It might be considered good practice to introduce a premise, produce evidence to support the assertion and then offer explanations and comments. A very large part of the business is entirely opaque and the activity is not widely known beyond the direct participants. Consequently, transactions and the aggregate level of activity are a matter of speculation, and little evidence can be brought to bear. This is a substantial impediment and one, I suspect, which has discouraged other authors and publishers. We shall press on regardless, relying on what we can know and estimating the rest, using whatever evidence and experience we have. It is a weakness that I acknowledge, but if we wait for better information, we may be oblivious indefinitely.

The book is comprised of ten chapters, with the first two, "What Are Structured Products?" and "History and Evolution: What Happened and Why?", written by myself, charting the progress of the structured products markets, discussing how they are defined, delineating different types, expounding upon the structure of each type, and evaluating their scale and scope. Christopher Taylor has produced a thorough account of the UK market in Chapter 3. In Chapter 4 we get an overview of Continental Europe from Simon Harris. In Chapter 5, "The Market in Asia", Angel Wu details the trajectory of the structured products market in Hong Kong, Singapore, Korea, Taiwan and China, from its inception in the 1990s to its state as of 2013, by way of the fall of Lehman Brothers in 2008.

Chapters 6 and 7 take the reader through the evolution of the structured products markets in Japan. The authors, Hiroshi Wakutsu and Toru Sano, were deeply involved in these businesses and can relate this extraordinary account with great authority. Chapter 8, written by Scott Mitchell and Daniel Roose, explains the history of the industry in the United States from 1995, tracing its progress through the trauma of the credit crunch and the recovery thereafter. Jeremy Jennings-Mares, a specialist lawyer, has provided Chapter 9, focussing on regulation and compliance; particularly the recent flood of legislation in Europe. Chapter 10 was written by myself and focuses on risk and modelling issues which have plagued the product providers in the past and are sure to do so in the future too.

ACKNOWLEDGEMENTS

I would like to thank my fellow authors and Gillian Tett for the foreword. We would like to acknowledge the important contribution to the content made by David Stevenson, Ian Lowes, Peter Hargreaves, David Ii, Kyoko Uchida, Wilson Law and Warren Motley. Last but not least, a heartfelt thank you to Emma Dain and Sarah Campbell of T&T Productions Ltd, and to Sarah Hastings, Alice Levick and Lewis O'Sullivan of Risk Books.

Clarke Pitts
October 2009

What Are Structured Products?

Clarke Pitts

This chapter seeks to define what constitutes a structured product, looks at the size of the market and the controversy around the industry and dissects a hypothetical deal in order to show how the mechanics work, before finally delineating between the three major segments of the market.

Over time there have been numerous attempts to define what constitutes a structured product. None are entirely satisfactory and most definitions have been designed with considerations irrelevant to this volume. For our purposes, we shall look at financial instruments that have been created to give investors (holders of the instruments) economic exposure to something through a derivative contract.

The very term "derivative" is itself somewhat nebulous. In this case we shall adopt this definition from the *Financial Times Lexicon*:[1] "A financial instrument whose value is based on the performance of underlying assets such as stocks, bonds, currency exchange rates, real estate."

These instruments are often securities (bonds and warrants, for example) where the redemption and often the coupons are linked formulaically to the performance of an equity price or an exchange rate, etc. They can also be insurance policies or bank deposits, products that many retail and institutional investors might be familiar with. In some particular circumstances, a special contract such as a "contract for difference" or an over-the-counter (OTC) option may be used. These mechanisms (or wrappers) for passing the payoff to the customer are usually carefully designed for investor's circumstances as well as those of the other parties to the transaction. For example, tax efficiency for the investor is often a key consideration, as we shall see later. Other points that matter include the accounting treatment, familiarity for processing and for psychological acceptance. The investment mandate of the client is sometimes a factor.

We now present a hypothetical deal to help elucidate our definition. This is a brief account of the flows of money for a typical transaction: on the trade date, the client pays for a bond, usually buying at it at face value (100%). In this case, let us postulate it is US$3,000,000. The bonds have been newly issued especially for the client after a brief negotiation. Quite possibly, the client is the only holder of this particular issue.

This example bond is a "capital guaranteed note", that is to say that the issuer promises to pay the owner at least their initial investment back after five years, no matter what happens (the guarantee usually depends on the bond issuer remaining solvent until the bond matures) plus any appreciation in their capital if the US stock market as measured by the S&P 500 index is above the then current level (say, 1,500 exactly). The bond issuer has a liability that is linked to the stock market and will mitigate or hedge this by buying a call option from an investment bank. A call option is a contract that pays the option holder, if an asset is above a predefined level (strike) when it expires. In this case the asset is the S&P 500 index, so the payment in the example would be US$2,000 (ie, US$3,000,000/1,500) per point that the index finishes above the strike (1,500). If the asset is at or below that level, then the option holder receives nothing.

The bond issuer has the cash proceeds for five years. The present value of the interest which the issuer will earn on this is put towards fees, costs and the options hedge. When these products started in the late 1980s, interest rates were much higher than they are in 2013. If, on the trade date, the five-year interest rate was, say, 7%, the then "present value" of the obligation to pay the client or bond holder back, five years hence, was 71.3%.[2] This gives the bond issuer 28.7% (100.0 − 71.3%) to pay for options and other costs. Typically, a five-year call option that pays only the price appreciation of the index was worth considerably less than 28.7%. The factors that matter in determining the value of the option include the strike (usually at-the-money, ie, the then current level), the time to maturity, dividends (the expected amount to be paid over the term of the option) and the volatility (a measure of how much the market was likely to move during the life of the option). Note that investor/bondholder does not benefit from the dividends paid, as they do not get incorporated into the index (there is one notable exception – the German Stock Market Index, DAX, includes dividends, and call options on this index are more expensive as a result). If the call option cost 22.0% (US$660,000) and the client was given options on exactly US$3 million worth of equities, then the last 6.7% (US$201,000) went to remunerating the institutions involved and paying some costs, such as legal and licensing (the index publishers, in this case of S&P 500, would normally demand a royalty for using their index in this way).

Whether this represents a reasonable value for the client is a moot point. The client might have invested in an equity fund that would charge over 1% per annum, then underperform the index and expose the client to considerable losses should the market fall materially. (In the late 1980s and early 1990s most equity investors were paying large management fees to invest in equities, usually with poor results to show for it. Twenty years on, their choices are much better, with a wide variety of cheap and efficient index trackers being available. Even so, many are still paying management charges of near 1% per annum and significant trading costs and commissions that are not included in that number. Terry Smith, city doyen, recently suggested that retail investors in the UK were in fact suffering total costs of over 3% per annum.) On the other hand the client would receive the dividends if they invested in an equity fund. Perhaps the most significant problem for everyone was that the cost and value proposition were quite opaque, so the client did not easily understand what they were being charged.

Whether or not structured products are a sensible investment seems to have been a highly contentious issue all over the world. Time and again conventional money managers, journalists and market pundits have railed against the industry and the product has gone from strength to strength despite their protests. Richard Saunders (2008), when he was chief executive of the UK Investment Management Authority (the Investment Management Authority (IMA) is the largest trade body in the UK for conventional asset managers. Its members oversee over £4 trillion according to their website) wrote:

> Now many people – journalists, IFAs and others – have argued that these are not attractive investments, since they guarantee that you will either do worse than a conventional fund or do worse than a deposit account. I will not dwell on that other than to remark that our researches have shown that the National Savings version of the product consistently underperforms by an amount about the same as the equity risk premium. In other words, over time you do not get a stock market return at all, but a risk-free return. Which,

after all, is what you should expect from a product guaranteeing your money back.

This was in follow up to an article in the press attacking structured products.

Peter Hargreaves, founder and then chief executive of Hargreaves Lansdown, a leading wealth management company in the UK took an even stronger line (Hargreaves 2010):

> So as we leave the Noughties and enter the Teenies where there has not been a period of only five years where the market had been lower at the end but a 10-year period where the FTSE was 22 per cent lower at the end. The trouble is that the industry as a whole has run out of ideas. Or is it that the only product you can sell at a profit is something that only benefits the manufacturer and pusher? They certainly have never benefited the client.
>
> Ten years after we discovered that all the platitudes delivered with these products were nothing more than shoddy goods, they still appear. IFAs today are supposed to be qualified, understand the markets and products.
>
> Structured products, guaranteed products, or whatever you want to call them, are a device purely to put commission into unscrupulous salespeople's hands and deliver huge profits for the clever people that devise them.

These examples are relatively extreme but reflect the tone of press, regulatory and other expert comments. While conventional asset management enjoys a halo from coverage of great successes such as Fidelity Magellan and Special Situation funds, the structured product lives in the shadow of the worst mishaps (the Lehman Mini Bonds scandal, for example).

This conflict and the merits or lack thereof for structured products is an interesting topic and one we shall look at again. Certainly, many experts are deeply sceptical, but the industry thrives all the same.

At the end of the life of our hypothetical structured product bond, the investor should get back their investment (US$3 million) and another payment (which can be documented as capital gain or as coupon/interest) determined by the price performance of the stock market.

If the S&P 500 has risen by 50% over the five years (an unremarkable 8.4% per annum), then the investor has made a total profit of US$1.5 million (ie, 50%), which is not particularly compelling

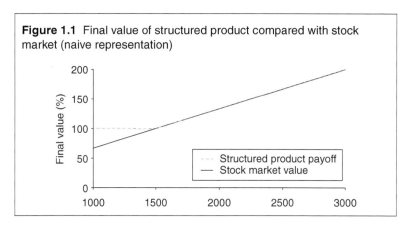

Figure 1.1 Final value of structured product compared with stock market (naive representation)

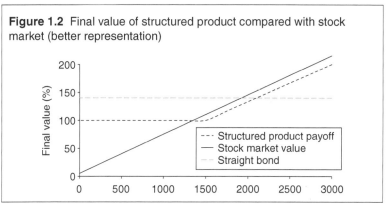

Figure 1.2 Final value of structured product compared with stock market (better representation)

over such a long period. Indeed it is only 10% more than if they had invested in the straight or conventional bond yielding 7% per annum at the outset (this ignores any costs that might be associated with investing in straight bonds). If the client had invested in the stock market directly (so no management fees) and into a diversified basket that tracked the index, (some 500 names at the outset, and then there would be rebalances several times each year as stocks dropped out of the index and others were added) then the client would have benefited from the capital appreciation and the dividends, and would have invested the extra 6.7% (the money set aside for profit, costs and fees) too, so their total yield would have been over 10% per annum, but only if they had been willing to take the capital risk. Again this ignores all the commissions and other dealings costs associated with share dealing; in some jurisdictions there is stamp tax that is neatly avoided in the structured product trade.

If the stock market had fallen by 50%, then the outperformance of the structured product strategy would be more striking. The structured product investor would recover all of their investment, though they would still have missed out on the dividends.

Figure 1.1 illustrates the payoff from our hypothetical "capital guaranteed note" compared with the price performance of the stock market. It has been carefully presented to show that the structured product will yield as much as or more than the stock market. Note, for example, that 75% of outcomes are positive for the investor, and in all cases they seem to do at least as well as or better than the stock market. This kind of misrepresentation has been commonplace; investors and regulators are understandably indignant about it.

A more cautious representation would look more like Figure 1.2.

This is the same product and the same data but presented in a slightly different way. The negative outcomes are presented equally with the positive ones, ie, stock market is up on the right half of the graph and down on the left half, 50% of each (it is not the case that negative outcomes are necessarily as equally likely as positive ones; in fact a 50% drop is much less likely than a 50% appreciation). The return available from an equivalent "straight" bond is displayed clearly. The stock market return includes dividends, in this case of 2% per year, which the structured product investor will not receive, as their asset is linked to an index or share price and ordinary dividends will not benefit them (historically, over long periods, half the "total" return from the stock market comes from the dividends so long as they are reinvested). If a company announces a special dividend, then any index that includes that company is usually adjusted to reflect the value paid out. Similarly, the terms of most derivatives are adjusted to compensate for material distributions of capital other than ordinary dividends.

SOME PROS AND CONS OF STRUCTURED PRODUCTS AS AN INVESTMENT

There are good reasons for choosing to invest in structured products, and there are legitimate reasons to avoid them too. The main positive considerations include the following.

- **Tax efficiency and tax avoidance:** a modest amount of capital risk can lead to a much more favourable treatment of the whole payoff, which is very valuable when capital gains taxes are much lower than interest/income tax rates. By way of example, bonds with capital risk triggered by a 50% drop in the stock market are usually taxed in the UK as if all the return is capital gain or loss, while the actual risk of loss of capital is quite small, as such a drop is unusual. It is difficult for the client and for the Inland Revenue to bifurcate the elements of the product, and this means that the bond and interest elements are treated more favourably for tax purposes.

  There are other tax angles such as the avoidance of stamp tax on transactions. Many early structured products in the 1990s were carefully constructed to comply with government-sponsored tax sheltered savings schemes, such as Business Expansion Schemes in the UK and Plan d'Epargne en Actions in France. Tax rules vary greatly over time and across jurisdictions.

- **Market access:** it can be difficult for clients to access remote or unusual markets, for example, commodities or emerging market equities. This motivation is becoming less relevant, as exchange traded funds (ETFs) are being listed everywhere, with a huge range of investments being made available this way.

- **Payoff transformation:** including the avoidance of downside risk as in the hypothetical case explained above. Another popular strategy is for the investor to "sell the upside", with the investor implicitly deciding at the outset that if the market rises by more than a certain amount, then they will unwind in order to take the profit. The client is therefore "monetising" that commitment by selling the profit potential beyond a certain point (here the client has sold a call rather than bought one). This automatic early unwind is commonly known as an "autocallable" and is extremely popular across the world.

  At the time of writing in 2013, interest rates are very low, and investors looking for yield are using structured products as a way of selling put options, by purchasing structured products that are constructed with a short put option position and taking the value of the option "sold" (ie, the premium) as a coupon stream. In such a transaction, the client will outperform a conventional investment in the underlying asset if the market does not move up a great deal, and will also do well if the market does not go down a great deal. The client has sold options and needs the market to remain comparatively stable. A major move down will precipitate losses, usually comparable to those that they would incur by investing directly. A big move upwards will be profitable for the investor, but much less so than investing directly. If the market does not rise or fall remarkably, then the investor will enjoy a profit and outperformance.

All these things and many others are easily achievable through derivatives and therefore structured products. This will be demonstrated throughout the book.

- **Currency protection:** the derivative and bond denominations are often structured so as to give the investor the returns of a foreign investment in their native currency. To illustrate why this is important, particularly to retail or private clients, we should look at the experience of Japanese investors buying foreign equities. They suffered time and time again when the returns from those investments were offset by the persistent appreciation of the Japanese yen against the foreign currency. If the stock market returns 10% but the exchange rate falls by 10%, then a yen-based investor has not profited at all. Most structured products are sold in the investor's home currency and the returns are paid in that currency. These currency-protected derivatives, called "Quanto" options, are extremely prevalent throughout structured products.

The flip side to these benefits of investing structured products includes the following.

- **Lack of transparency in costs/charges:** this is something that can be mitigated but usually is not, at least for retail investors, who lack the relevant resources to accurately value these investments. It is not in the product providers' or the intermediaries' best interests to be candid about how much margin is being taken out, even if it is a modest amount. Furthermore, any attempt to do so requires a statement of real fair value, which is nebulous. The US regulators are pressing the industry to be more forthcoming at the time of writing, and that may help matters. In the UK, new Retail Distribution Review rules, introduced at the end of 2012, should prevent intermediaries taking commissions except through explicit charges for advice, outside of the transaction. This is explained in greater detail in Chapter 9.

- **An extra layer of risk:** for example, the credit risk of the product issuer, on top of the market risk that the investor was deliberately taking. For the most part, structured products are issued by solid companies that are unlikely to fail, but there have been instances, such as Lehman Brothers, where investors have not received what they were expecting, due to the bankruptcy of the bond issuer.

- **Lack of liquidity:** this does not apply in all cases and does not matter to many investors, but it is a consideration all the same. Usually, salespeople and intermediaries assured clients that they would provide liquidity, if it was needed. That is to say that the client would be able to unwind or sell their holdings at a fair price should they want to. In order to make sure that the price is fair, the market price should be two-sided, ie, both bid and offered, so that the client or another investor could buy more should they so choose.

When the markets turned very nasty in the credit crunch, investors seeking to sell their structured products were often frustrated. In some cases the issuer had folded or at least ceased transacting in those products. Holders of conventional market assets had liquidity problems too, but these were nothing like as severe. A public market for an asset provides not just liquidity but also price discovery. Many products are listed on a public exchange somewhere (often Luxembourg) in order to satisfy client mandates (ie, the clients are managing money for a third party and are required to only buy listed securities), but that listing is rather nominal in nature and there is never any trading on the exchanges. Arguably this is a failure of the exchanges, the lawyers drafting the mandates, the product providers involved and the asset managers that are circumventing their own mandate restrictions.

- **Complexity:** this is a common accusation, particularly by finance professionals and commentators who are adept in the cash markets. They understand and are comfortable with arcane concepts such as "earnings before interest, taxes depreciation and amortization (EBITDA)" and "price earnings growth (PEG)" ratios (for equities) or "Macaulay duration and dollar value of one basis point shift in yield (DV01)" if they are fixed-income specialists, but somehow the idea of derivatives sends them into a spin. Derivatives can be complicated, but then all of finance is susceptible to that charge. In the author's eyes, it is very redolent of the elderly looking doubtfully at a smartphone; it is too new and different and they refuse to engage.

Until the credit crunch and associated market turmoil hit hard, the product providers with the strongest risk management technology, particularly the leading French investment banks, sought to protect the margins in their business by producing new payoffs. The new products were deliberately different in ways that could not easily be broken into established products and so their inventors had a monopoly while other firms raced to catch up (if or when the product became popular enough to make the effort worthwhile). This strategy generated some complicated and messy products that are now mostly defunct. This aspect of the industry has subsided for the most part, for three important reasons.

1. The investment banks were usually left with some very awkward risks that they could not easily hedge. These often ended up costing far more than expected, and in the post-credit-crunch world they tend to attract very high capital charges (for the unhedgable risk).

2. The banks, tired of chasing each other round in circles, created generic pricing engines based on Monte Carlo simulations, so the lead/catch-up time became very short.

3. The clients became wise to the true motivation behind the ferocious level of innovation and were consequently reluctant to buy anything until they could check prices with several product providers.

Regulators have sought to penalise this kind of behaviour with higher capital charges for unusually complex products. It is very difficult to define complexity in this context and most of the compromises proposed thus far have favoured simplicity of concept over effectiveness.

- **Market distortions:** this issue is neither a positive nor a negative in and of itself. However, it is one area that remains very much ignored by commentators and the market itself. The derivative market and the structured product market tend to be dominated by particular trades (at the time of writing, a product called an autocallable bond is very fashionable). This distorts the market price for certain kinds of risk, and the inefficiencies are at once a great opportunity for those that are aware and rather detrimental to those that are doing the fashionable trades. Again, this is something that is best illustrated by example. When the first trades were made in 1988, the main product was very much the sort of thing described above, ie, a capital guaranteed bond with equity upside. As we saw, this involved the investment bank writing (selling) a long-dated (five-year in our example above) call option. This was the only activity in such long-dated derivatives. The main derivative liquidity was on the exchanges for listed options and futures with maturities of six months or less. As a consequence, the price of very long-dated call options became ever higher due to the inexorable demand.

The most convenient way to talk about option values is in terms of "implied volatility". We do not need to understand option pricing for this explanation, but we give a brief summary for the interested reader: in conventional option pricing the value of an option depends on five main factors: the exercise price, the time left until maturity, the prevailing interest rates, the yield, such as dividends paid by the asset, and the amount that the asset moves (in fact, the standard deviation of the natural log of the returns, the return being the change in value each day). The last consideration is known as the volatility. The premiums (prices) are not easy to compare, as the values reflect strike, maturity, interest rates, etc. The "implied volatility" is a more "normalised" way to compare the value across many different options.

A convenient analogy would be to consider corporate bonds from an individual issuer, rather than compare the prices when they have different maturities and coupons; the professionals talk about the yield spread to a standard curve (typically government bond yields). That way they can see that the four-year bond (price is 98.1, yield 3.3%) at 30bp over looks rather rich/expensive relative to the seven-year (107.5, yield 5.1%) bond at 70bp over.

While short-term "realised" volatility remained at, say, 20% and the implied volatility for short-dated options did not vary much from that level, the very long-dated options pushed up to much higher numbers, say 30%. This represented very poor value for the investors. The banks were not happy either, as they had started selling at lower levels before watching the price rise due to large demand and no supply from third parties. So their average sale was at much lower implied volatility than the then current market and they were recording losses. New sales would be at expensive/rich levels, but while they had losses on their books the management is not inclined to give them more capital and may even have made them reduce risk by buying options in the market from other houses with the same problem, which created an ugly squeeze. It was not so unusual, across the period considered, to observe bizarre prices with long-term implied volatility spiking up to 40% or more. This would imply that the derivative market expected the stock market to move 2.5% every day for five years (to be quite accurate it is the root mean square, so the square root of the average of the square of the natural log of daily returns would be over 2.5%); an implausible forecast even in a turbulent market. This mispricing on such unduly expensive levels has been the prevailing market price for many major markets several times in the last twenty years up to the time of writing. These circumstances are a clear opportunity: bold investors can and should capitalise on such grotesque mispricing by writing puts when implied volatility gets very high and by buying calls when it gets very low. Such trades would not constitute an arbitrage but they would offer a very favourable risk–reward trade-off for those that have sufficient insight. It is not just a matter of implied volatility; the same issues arise in correlation between assets, expected dividends and some more subtle aspects such as skewness. (Skewness is an arcane concept that will be explained in greater detail in Chapter 10. In the meantime, suffice to say that it is a measure of how large a difference there is between the implied volatilities of options with different strike prices but otherwise identical terms.)

The resources exist in the industry to make all this more transparent, but a mixture of adverse incentives and well-intentioned but ineffective regulation make such an explanation inaccessible. The mispricing inherent in the derivative markets has made for some excellent opportunities, but investors do not easily recognise them; nor are they advertised and explained as they should be.

TYPES OF STRUCTURED PRODUCTS

This huge and diverse industry can look like a tree, with each branch dividing and subdividing time and again. However beautiful trees are, they cannot be described by listing the twigs and building upwards. Similarly, we need to examine the rather more prosaic world of structured products by starting with the more substantial parts first. There are generically three main groups that need to be considered separately:

1. the privately placed and individually negotiated transactions that are done for a single investor or a very small number of investors;

2. those that are sold to the public through retail networks, such as bank branches or financial advisers;

3. products listed and traded on public exchanges or otherwise widely available to retail investors and institutional clients alike.

In this section, we shall try to elucidate on the market for each of these types, with examples and some basic explanation.

Privately placed and individually negotiated transactions

These are usually incorporated into bonds (typically European medium-term notes from specially created programmes), there are exceptions but we shall not distract ourselves with those for the time being.

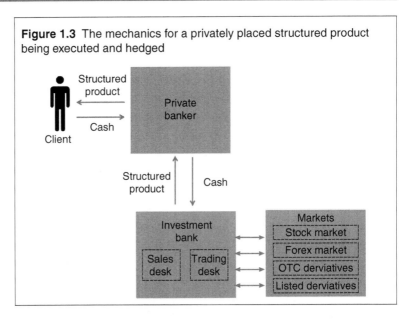

Figure 1.3 The mechanics for a privately placed structured product being executed and hedged

A typical client might be a high net worth individual with an account at a private bank. They have been (collectively) enormous investors on structured products. Whether this is because they have enjoyed profits from investing in them or because of the margins their advisers and bankers have extracted from selling them to the clients is unclear; very likely both are important factors.

The client, or more usually their bank, negotiates with a product provider (typically a major investment bank) that creates a bond with a derivative embedded in it to give the client exposure to whatever they wish, usually equities or equity indexes.

Figure 1.3 shows the process. Note that the private bank and the investment bank are often the same institution. Indeed, some private banks have an explicit policy of dealing mainly or entirely in-house, which seems likely to be detrimental to their clients.

Such transactions are not reported anywhere, so their total volumes are a matter for speculation. Private bank earnings are reported in the financial accounts of their parent organisations. By way of example, Credit Suisse, one of the biggest in the field, has around US$840 billion of assets under management for wealthy clients. It reports gross revenues of US$12 billion per annum[3] from managing those assets. That amounts to 1.4% per annum. No doubt they charge clients for dealing in securities and for advisory services, but the margins in and scale of those activities are unlikely to make up the bulk of the revenues. Their private bankers earn more by selling higher margin products such as structured products and hedge funds. Here the charges are typically over 2%, and can be more depending on the circumstances, both of the product and of the client's willingness to check. Credit Suisse is only offered as an example; they are typical, not exceptional, in this respect. Japanese banks and brokers are far more rapacious with their discretionary clients, charging and churning even more.

These numbers are pertinent, as they give some indication of the scale of the activity in this sort of structured product. The narrative from the private bank accompanying their financial statements reporting the revenues mention that this is a significant part of the business. Wisely they do not reveal a more precise breakdown. If just US$1 billion out of US$12 billion of revenues come from structured products and they are charging 2%, then that is already US$50 billion of structured products being sold into Credit Suisse's private bank clients each year. Credit Suisse manages about 20% of European private bank assets, which suggests that the aggregate size of structured product sales of this type is of the order of US$250 billion per annum. These numbers are extremely imprecise, but they are not out by an order of magnitude. Later, we shall examine other evidence to support this contention.

Private banks are not the only managers of wealthy investors' money; there are thousands of family offices and financial advisers. The European (especially the Swiss) private banks are among the largest, but there are many more in Asia (mainly in Hong Kong and Singapore), and much larger amounts are invested in the biggest in the United States.

Wealthy individuals are not the only ones to invest in privately placed structured products. Institutional investors do so, usually for market access reasons. Corporate treasuries do too, though much less so at the time of writing due to changes in accounting rules, particularly after the introduction of International Financial Reporting Standards accounting rules, which compelled companies to mark such investments to market and to take changes in value directly in their profit-and-loss statements.

In a few cases the volumes have been particularly huge, sometimes with deleterious consequences for one or both parties. In Japan, one product, called Power Reverse Dual Currency (PRDC), became so popular that the hedging activity related to it caused major dislocations of the currency and swap markets. How and why this happened will feature in Chapter 7. It is a startling story and an important one. All the transactions are "private" so no one really knows how big a product it became, but educated guesses run up to US$2 trillion!

Mortgage backed and asset backed securities gave rise to an enormous structured product market – including synthetic collateralised debt obligations (CDOs), then synthetic CDO squared and a slew of other credit linked products – that caused a great deal of stress. Fascinating as this debacle was, we shall gloss over it in this volume. It is the only part of the structured products industry about which a great deal has been written already. Furthermore, this activity was targeted mainly at financial institutions, while other structured products are not. Lastly, their fall from grace was so great that at the time of writing the business is rather smaller and likely to remain that way for a while yet.

Structured products retailed through branch networks

These are the best known and most widely recognised types of structured products. The nature of the distribution process makes them conspicuous. Banks, brokers and insurance companies advertise them in newspapers and in their branch windows to attract investors.

The products are linked to special deposit accounts, or funds or life insurance policies as well as being offered as bonds in the same way as the privately placed products described above.

There have been numerous scandals about appropriateness and the mis-selling of structured products to retail investors. There is some scope for quantifying the level of activity, since all of the deals offered are in the public domain and one consultancy does collate this information in order to resell it back to the industry. Even here though, the data is incomplete and not reliably accurate. That a deal is being offered is a matter of public record, but how much is taken up is not. If or when the product provider offers numbers for the amount they have sold, these numbers are not verifiable and the provider often has good reasons to overstate or occasionally understate the success of a particular deal.

The industry routinely reports annual sales of around US$150 billion per year in Europe. The numbers in Asia (excluding Japan) were very material too, but activity fell off a cliff after Lehman Brothers' demise in 2008, another topic that we shall look at later. Structured products are very popular in Japan (approximately US$50 billion in 2012). The US has had booming sales of structured products but numbers are still lower than those in Europe. The US Structured Products Association (US-SPA) reported over US$50 billion of sales to retail in the US in over 8,000 different products in 2010. A harsh response from the US Securities and Exchange Commission and the Financial Industry Regulatory Authority after mis-selling scandals has depressed volumes since then. Other sources, such as Bloomberg,[4] suggest lower but still very material sales numbers: "US investors bought $25.6 billion of securities last year [2012] that use derivatives to pay yields tied to stock returns, up from $23.1 billion in 2011 and $18.4 billion in 2010, Bloomberg data show." The large anomaly highlights the problems in getting reliable and consistent information. Perhaps the discrepancy arises from structured deposits, which would qualify as a "product" but not as a "security". Neither the US-SPA nor the Bloomberg figures can include the "variable annuity" (structured products sold as life insurance policies) market in the US. Chapter 8 explains more about these. The size of this segment is around three times the size of the securities segment, ie, about US$150 million per annum.

Liquid and listed structured products

This is the fastest growing and most diverse segment. The products are usually listed on stock exchanges and are distributed mainly through secondary liquidity. In the first two generic types of structured product, identified above, the deals are created and sold to meet investment demand. There is usually little or no "secondary" activity in them until they expire or are "knocked out" by some event that triggers early redemption. In this third variety, the market functions in quite a different way. Here product providers list products in the hope and expectation that investors will buy them, and most of the activity occurs after the launch. There are many manifestations and the motivations of investors are fairly distinct.

Some investors use the products to express a directional view with leverage. Good examples of this would include "callable bull–bear certificates" (CBBCs) in Hong Kong and "turbo certificates" in

Germany. The payoff is simple and linear and the client will win or lose up to ten times as much as if they had invested in the underlying asset directly. Losses are capped by "knock out" events, so the client cannot lose more than they invested initially. If the market moves against the client sufficiently, the instrument expires worthless or nearly worthless. This may sound draconian, but it means that the product is cheap and therefore highly leveraged to start with. Effectively, the instrument has a stop-loss embedded in it. CBBC trading (along with conventional warrants) constitutes over 20% of Hong Kong Stock Exchange volume, where the total trading of these securitised derivatives was about US$576 billion in 2011. This product was closely modelled on turbo certificates, which were already extraordinarily popular in Germany and Switzerland.

Another example is the contract-for-difference (CFD). These started as a way to avoid stamp tax on trading in UK shares. Registered market makers in UK shares are exempt from paying stamp tax, a levy on share dealing of 0.5% paid by the buyer of shares. Market makers facilitated the avoidance of stamp tax by buying shares and passing the economic exposure on to clients who wanted to trade actively (rather than buy-and-hold for long periods) through derivative contracts such as swaps. This was extremely popular and led to a standardisation of the contracts and eventually the creation of the CFD market. CFDs and their close cousin "spread betting" became hugely popular, first in the UK and then more recently in Australia, Singapore, Germany and Japan. In fact, they are starting to cannibalise the exchange products that they most closely resemble in some jurisdictions. The UK's Financial Services Agency attributes 30% of London Stock Exchange turnover to hedging related to CFD activity.[5] This is already a huge amount of business. However, the total volume of CFD trading is in fact much larger, as the most popular products include the FTSE 100 index, S&P 500 index, foreign exchange (forex) and commodities, none of which would be hedged on the stock exchange. Only CFDs linked to individual shares are likely to be matched with share trades.

Figure 1.4 shows how simple this really is.

Not all listed and liquid products are leveraged. A significant subset of ETFs are backed by derivative contracts. For a long time, substantially all ETFs created by Deutsche Bank, Société Générale (Lyxor) and those of many other product providers were based on

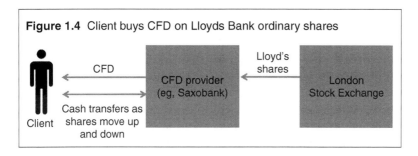

Figure 1.4 Client buys CFD on Lloyds Bank ordinary shares

a derivative contract. For the most part, this was a matter of convenience for the fund manager. The difference between these and the more conventional funds that invest directly in equities (or other products) is slight and only matters when the derivative counterparty defaults – a rare event. However, there are many ETFs that are leveraged, short or have non-linear payoffs; some of these are very popular and they are unambiguously structured products by any reasonable standard. According to research published by JP Morgan in May 2013 (Kolanovic 2013), there are about US$2 trillion invested in ETFs globally at the time of writing, but the vast majority is in linear and straightforward strategies. Some are not though; for example, the Invesco PowerShares ETF linked to the CBOE BuyWrite Index (ticker: PBP) has about US$200 million invested in it. Direxion Daily Financial Bear 3X Shares (ticker: FAZ) has over US$300 million as of June 2013.[6] There are many others with buy–write, which is industry jargon for a strategy where an investor buys an asset and then sells a call option struck at the level where they intend to sell (usually at a higher level than the price at which they have bought the shares). Some are explicitly linked to volatility indexes such as VIX. This strategy tends to outperform simple buy-and-hold investments significantly except when markets are rising rapidly. So it is popular with investors who believe that the market may rise or at least hold up but will not collapse or appreciate dramatically.

CONCLUSION

We have examined the three generic groups of structured products. They have some things in common, but are quite distinct in other important respects. The first two types are mainly created by investment banks and, being predominantly for private clients (high net worth or ordinary savers), a large proportion is equity linked. The gross revenue that the investment banks disclose that is associated with structured products gives us some indication of the aggregate size of this business. This is not public information *per se* but industry studies suggest that the market "wallet" is around US$12 billion (Abouhossein and Lee 2010). In order to guess at aggregate volumes we have to estimate the average margin being made.

When this author started in the business, in the late 1980s, we used to award the salesperson with 7% of the option premium as a sales "credit". At the time of writing the market is immensely more efficient and the bank's margins are such that this business has become significantly loss making for many of the peripheral players. Polling former colleagues who still work in this field, the consensus seems to be about 0.3% of the whole notional is the margin reported as sales credit and therefore the number consistent with the industry total. In which case, the investment banks are collectively executing several trillions of US dollars of structured products transactions per annum. This number is not particularly meaningful and the reader should be wary of reading too much into it. The problem arises as this number includes a broad mix of products and associated margins, so projections are very unreliable. Products that are used to achieve leverage or avoid tax are being traded with a high frequency (and a low margin). Gross sales of these high turnover products are huge, but then a great deal is bought back soon afterwards, so we cannot be confident about using this number to show how much is outstanding at any one time, ie, how much capital is invested in structured products on average. Nevertheless, it does suggest that the extrapolation from Credit Suisse's private bank/wealth management numbers were "in the ball park".

The fund managers who run ETFs and the specialist firms who produce CFDs, for example, are not investment banks *per se* and so are not included in the numbers above. IG Index, the world's largest but by no means only CFD provider, reported gross revenues of £370 million in 2012 from trading with over 140,000 clients. Saxobank, another leader in that industry, reports over US$5 billion of client monies held as collateral against CFD activity.[7]

These are very large numbers by any standard. This industry is bigger (by most measures) than hedge funds and has grown from zero in just 25 years. In Chapter 2 we shall look at how it started and why it has been so successful.

1   http://lexicon.ft.com/term?term=derivatives.

2   Which interest rate is used is important – swap rates were used as an industry standard for a long time as a good approximation. A better and more accurate measure would be the market rate/yield for a conventional bond of the same term from the same issuer. This may not be available nor even exist, so approximations using interpolation and extrapolation and/or proxies can be used.

3   See Credit Suisse Annual Report 2012.

4   See http://www.bloomberg.com/news/2013-02-26/sec-shines-light-on-derivatives-backed-notes-credit-markets.html.

5   The LSE's response to the FSA's consultation on disclosure of contracts for difference is given at http://www.londonstockexchange.com/about-the-exchange/regulatory/response-fsa-consultation-disclosure-contract-difference.pdf.

6   See http://www.nasdaq.com/aspxcontent/etfprofile.aspx?Ticker=FAZ.

7   See the Saxobank annual report for 2011 at http://www.saxoworld.com/.

REFERENCES

Abouhossein, K, and D. Lee, 2010, *Investment Banking Wallet Outlook: All Eyes on Equity Derivatives*, September, JP Morgan Cazenove.

Hargreaves, P., 2010, "Condemned Structures", http://www.moneymarketing.co.uk/condemned-structures/1005255.article

Kolanovic, M., 2013, *Exchange Traded Funds (EFTs): 2013 JP Morgan Global EFT Handbook*, JP Morgan.

Saunders, R., 2008, "Making Sure Things Are Crystal Clear", FT Adviser blog, http://www.ftadviser.com/.

2

History and Evolution: What Happened and Why?

Clarke Pitts

This chapter takes the reader though the conception and evolution of the business.

Using the broadest definition of structured products we would have to include covered warrants, and they probably pre-date the bond variety, though not by long. In the late 1980s the Japanese stock market was enjoying a prolonged and spectacular rally while market pundits (for the most part) feted the rise of the Sun in the East. Any that demurred were dismissed (literally in some cases) as not "getting it", and, while the doubters were vindicated, the wider world did not learn and a similar mass hysteria gripped the investment community in the dot-com bubble ten years later. In 1989, some prescient investors wanted to go short the Japanese market. This could be done using listed futures and options but many investors are unable to cope with the accounts, the margin movements and the hassle, particularly as the Japanese market prohibited "give up" agreements.

This commonplace arrangement allows clients to execute orders in listed futures and options with a broker and to have the trades settle with their own bank or broker. The prohibition of give up arrangements meant that many clients would have had to open accounts with firms they had never dealt with before, a painful and slow process even in those days. Ostensibly the reasons for the ban were administrative and technological but the main issue was and remains protectionism.

Salomon Brothers (and later others) launched "put" warrants on the Nikkei 225 (or Nikkei Dow as it was then known) that were denominated in US dollars and Swiss francs, traded over-the-counter and settled in EuroClear and Cedel to make them very convenient for American and European investors. These warrants were very popular and sold at a furious pace. The secondary trading (market making) in London time involved two full-time traders and hundreds of tickets every day. (The author was one of these traders for a short time; it was a baptism of fire and extremely difficult to cope with. Later, when the author had learned the trade – or more exactly, how to trade – he thought back to those heady times with regret for the missed opportunities.) The price movements of the various warrants each day were used to forecast the likely opening price of the Japanese stock market the next session and this was routinely reported on business news bulletins on television. One of Salomon Brothers' senior equity strategists in the late 1980s was a brilliant if slightly eccentric individual. He was vociferously bearish on virtually everything, but most of all Japan. At that time, research staff were not segregated in the same way as they are now in the post dot-com scandal days and were supposed to drum up business for the secondary equity business. Analysts who are bearish do not encourage clients to invest and are somewhat less effective in this important regard, so they made him redundant. It was not such a bad outcome for him though; he took his bonus and his severance payment and invested that substantial sum in Nikkei put warrants. When the Japanese stock market fell off the proverbial cliff in 1990, he made a fortune.

The Salomon Brothers' Nikkei put warrants were so successful that other investor fads were identified and pandered to in the same way. Salomon had been one of the main underwriters for the launch of Eurotunnel plc (with whom they shared a building above Victoria Station in London). This project had caught the imagination of many and there was interest for clients to express their enthusiasm by going long in a more leveraged fashion, so Salomon launched call warrants linked to Eurotunnel. These were very popular with retail clients and sold in large numbers. Other clients who were more sceptical about the investment prospects wanted to buy put warrants and Salomon could have accommodated them too but it was felt (probably correctly) that the company (Eurotunnel) might not have appreciated that. They would have considered it poor publicity if one of their main underwriting brokers is seen to be facilitating speculators to short their stock in a leveraged way and, as they were an important corporate client, it would be prudent for Salomon Brothers not to raise their ire.

Puts are options that pay when the asset price, in this case Eurotunnel shares, fall below a certain level, the more they go down, the more valuable the put option. They are the opposite of call options and the two can be combined to replicate the asset performance (net of dividends) exactly.

These warrants became more and more popular, Salomon Brothers and Bankers Trust issued and sold warrants on a huge and rather miscellaneous list of stocks, indexes and baskets of stocks. At one point Salomon Brothers was doing thousands of trades per day in these warrants, providing liquidity, leverage and access to investors who were enthused about the CAC 40 in France, baskets of forestry stocks in Scandinavia, Italian banks, German chemical stocks and, perhaps most spectacularly, Ericsson in Sweden. Ericsson became a poster child for the industry; the company was attracting particular attention as a potential winner in the then nascent mobile telephone business. The stock rocketed and investors rushed to participate. They leapt at the chance to get leverage with huge enthusiasm. The Salomon warrants were so widely sold that Salomon Brothers had a notifiable interest in the company in order to hedge the obligation. It traded hundreds of times on many days and eventually the market maker (me) went to Stockholm to meet the chairman of Ericsson for lunch (along with several leading investors from America). Ultimately the company disappointed investors and the stock fell back sharply. When it expired the warrant was out-of-the-money, something that had seemed inconceivable at the height of the bubble. We were astonished when we received an exercise notice saying that an investor wanted to buy the shares at the exercise price, when the stock was trading actively at a much lower level. Warrants are "bearer" securities, so even as the issuer we had no way of knowing who owns them. The notice had come through EuroClear, a major clearing organisation, mainly for bonds but also for warrants, shares and other securities. We pressed them, explaining it was manifestly not in the client's best interest to exercise. EuroClear went back to them but was told that their decision was final. Reluctantly EuroClear confided the identity of the holder who wished to exercise, a leading American investment manager and a fund that specialised in convertible bonds, so they ought to have known better. Armed with this information, Salomon called them directly. They were most indignant to have been approached in this way and insisted on their right to exercise despite our explanation that they could just buy the stock in the market more cheaply. In the end, we had to comply; our frustration was mitigated by our windfall profit of several hundred thousand US dollars.

In 1988–91 there were very few warrant/product providers; two, in fact, at the outset: Salomon Brothers and Bankers Trust. This led to some unusual and interesting problems. Whenever one firm launched a product, the other would copy with a near identical deal that was slightly cheaper. There were no established markets for long-dated derivatives so the fair or market price for such products was a somewhat nebulous concept. The two parallel deals could follow rather different trajectories. In one case, a warrant on Volvo, the Swedish car manufacturer, was materially mispriced by a greedy trader at Bankers Trust who understood that the clients who owned it wanted to sell their positions. One such client noticed that the identical Salomon deal was about 10 points higher and wondered how this could be. In the end, Salomon bought the Bankers Trust warrants from the client and then more from the Bankers Trust market maker – causing a great deal of indignation and ill feeling. Happily for all concerned the market has evolved to prevent such abuses now. Clients have access to pricing tools and specialist firms screen the market for opportunities.

THE FIRST TRADE IN A CAPITAL GUARANTEED PRODUCT

We cannot know for certain who created the first capital guaranteed product but this account has a plausible claim and if another one was done, perhaps in Switzerland, France or even Japan beforehand, then the story is likely to have been very similar.

Midland Bank, then an independent public company in the UK, started a life insurance company called Midland Life plc. The popular products in the late 1980s were life insurance policies, endowment policies (attached to mortgages) and "with profits" policies. The latter product was supposed to provide a diversified investment portfolio with reasonable income and a stable capital value. They have since become mired in controversy over mis-selling and hidden charges as well as poor performance. Midland Life was casting around for ways to break into these businesses from a standing start. A small team of financial engineers who were supporting the bank's foreign exchange derivative trading were brought in to help create products. At the time there was a great deal of press attention given to the role of synthetic portfolio hedging in the 1987 crash. This precipitated a "eureka" moment and the concept of a bond plus option was born. When these options were first proposed to the Midland Life sales team they were sceptical. When first proposed to the Midland Life sales team they were skeptical. Hitherto the stock market had been seen as distinctly risky and recent events (ie, the 2008–12 financial crisis) certainly give such feelings credence. A product that guaranteed your money back and the performance of the stock market might be perceived as too good to be true. The sales team surmised that investors would shy away, fearing a "catch". The first pricing offered gave 100% participation in the stock market and afforded the sales people a very substantial margin but, ironically, to make it more marketable, they diminished the return offered to the clients to just 95% participation and kept the extra profit. The rationale for this was that they could "explain" to the would-be investors that the last 5% of participation was Midland's incentive for entering into the transaction, thereby alleviating the client's doubts. This first deal sold over £20 million worth of policies, which was deemed a great success. The next transaction sold over ten times as much. The ingenuity in these transactions extends beyond the concept of bond plus option. Life insurance companies are taxed on their investment income so the policies held by investors yield "franked" income (ie, a cashflow that has been taxed). However, by using derivatives and offshore entities, they could receive the stock market price return without paying tax inside the insurance company while generating profits for investors that were deemed net of basic rate tax. Once Midland Life had succeeded with these schemes, other insurance companies, including Irish Life, rushed to emulate them. The Inland Revenue in the UK attacked these arrangements; some companies settled, while others went to court and won. Inevitably, the law was changed to prevent this kind of tax avoidance but once again tax had been a catalyst for a new generation of structured products and, once established, they survived the loss of the tax advantage. Insurance companies operate with higher margins and have smaller distribution networks than banks, building societies and brokers; so with the playing field levelled the business migrated back to these types of retail financial institutions. Within a few years, these deals were being sold all over Europe and occasionally further afield.

THE EVOLUTION OF THE MARKET

The common feature of the warrant activity and the early structured products was that clients were buying long-dated options on everything. Naturally this meant that all the major product manufacturers were becoming very short of long-dated options: in the market parlance, "short volatility". New business was being done at expensive (sometimes very expensive) levels, although new product providers started to appear, each with their own capital and willingness to participate, so that helped keep a lid on the pricing to some extent. The investment banks hedged their risk using short-dated options trading on the exchanges; usually this was on very good terms relative to where the structured products were being sold.

In 1990, Saddam Hussein led an Iraqi invasion of Kuwait. When it became apparent that the international community was going to expel the Iraqis using military force, actual volatility in the market became very high. Short-dated options became much more expensive. The hedges that investment banks had bought started to expire and they were collectively left with some very substantial risks. Clients were suddenly bearish on everything and rushed to sell their inventory of call warrants, which helped reduce the bank's exposure but, not easily discouraged by their dramatic losses, clients bought put warrants on the indexes instead. It was hard to go short equities for many clients (some were unable to trade listed derivatives either because their mandates prohibited it, others did not have the necessary infrastructure. Many were wary of listed derivatives but comfortable with warrants despite their being essentially the same thing). Some clients had large equity exposures and selling might trigger tax liabilities. Fortunately for the banks, the first Gulf War was a short-lived affair and the markets stabilised soon after the invasion. Volatility and implied volatility (ie, the level necessary to explain option prices) had spiked to over 50% during the crisis. Business quickly reverted to normal but the banks had learned a valuable lesson – they could not rely on short-term options to hedge and the scale of the business was significant enough that management and control functions were alerted to the scope for meaningful losses. Stricter limits on aggregate exposure were introduced. Senior staff were instructed to find better ways to hedge the risk.

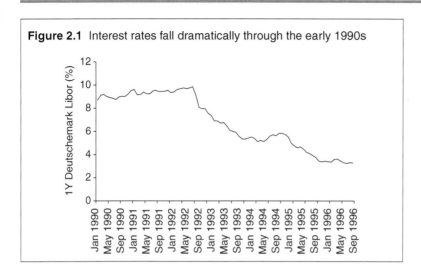

Figure 2.1 Interest rates fall dramatically through the early 1990s

Another important influence on the evolution of the industry was the dramatic drop in interest rates between 1989 and 1992 (Figure 2.1). These two considerations ushered in a new generation of product, the reverse convertible. (There were many names used, this was one of the most popular. The bond plus call structure is very similar to convertible bonds issued by companies as hybrid capital. The new deals were "reverse" in that the equity participation is on the downside not upside (ie, investors became exposed to equity prices if the market went down instead of up).) These structures were similar and yet opposite to the first deals. Investors remained "long" the market, that is to say they profited if the underlying asset (shares, etc) went up in price. They had again bought a zero-coupon bond but rather than buying call options they were selling put options. The premium associated with the sales of the put options were realised as higher coupons paid on the bond. So if the prevailing interest rates were, say, 5% per annum, with a structured product the client might get 9%, the extra 4% per annum being the value of the put option. Usually options are traded and expressed as the present value so if we buy or sell one today the money changes hands that same day. In these structures, the payment was realised over the life of the bond. The drop in interest rates boosted the popularity of this product; investors were acclimatised to a higher return on their savings and were hungry for better yields than they could achieve in the early 1990s.

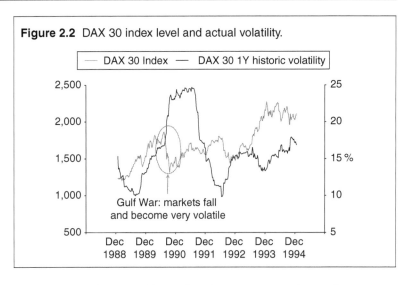

Figure 2.2 DAX 30 index level and actual volatility.

The very high level of long-dated option prices due to the squeeze from large demand by warrant buyers and bond plus call structured products combined with the recent memory of extremely turbulent markets (high volatility) were a great opportunity for the early adopters of the new product, ie, reverse convertibles. They were making an enormous profit by selling long-dated options at far above a reasonable price and so long as the underlying assets held up they recovered their capital at the end. Stock markets were recovering from sharp declines in the Gulf War and these early investors came out of it very well. As is so often the case, you can have too much of a good thing – the great success of the reverse convertible eventually led to a colossal drop of both implied volatility and realised volatility (Figure 2.2). Why this happened is explained in greater detail in Chapter 10.

By the middle of 1992, realised volatility of the DAX (the German stock index) was only 10% and had been for a whole year. The price of options fell sharply and even much longer dated options came down to levels close to 10% implied volatility. Investors had profited from selling options (by buying reverse convertibles) and insisted on pursuing this "proven" strategy. However, this had worked well because volatility had been high and then fell and the stock market was low and subsequently recovered. Selling put options when the reverse is true (ie, the stock market is high and implied volatility is low) should end badly, and of course it did. When the Danes declined to ratify the Maastricht Treaty (June 1992), the currency and stock markets were thrown into disarray, markets fell sharply and volatility shot up. Being short very cheap options provided very little cushion against these headwinds and investors suffered large losses.

This cycle has repeated itself several times since then. That is not to say it is easy to spot when volatility will rise or fall but the investors and their advisers seem to learn these lessons very slowly. They are not helped by the fact that the product's sensitivity to volatility, skewness and interest rates and most importantly equities (or whatever is the underlying asset (foreign exchange, precious metals, indexes etc)) was not disclosed, and still is not. Nor are prevailing levels of implied volatility, correlation and skewness revealed, or historical ranges and averages made available. Either market levels of dividends are not compared against historic payouts or to the forecasts made by the bank's own analysts, or they are but this information is only disclosed to their major institutional clients; retail investors and their advisers are prohibited from seeing this information, lest it confuses them. (In order to qualify to receive "derivative" research of this sort, clients have to certify that they are institutional investors, any that admit to being retail investors or their financial advisers would not normally be allowed to receive such materials – this is mainly at the behest of regulators whose actions are often counter-productive – the irony is writ large.)

In the early 1990s, around the world, banks and brokers were struggling to make money in conventional retail and institutional businesses; deregulation and competitive pressure were compressing margins on agency commissions and on fund management. New legislation and more rigorous enforcement were preventing former "games" such as front running and insider trading.

The margins in these new products were seductive to both the product producers (investment banks) and the distributors (brokers, retail banks and private banks). However, new competitors entered the market at a fierce pace; this compressed margins and took market share from the incumbents. At the same time, staff costs rocketed as new participants sought those with the requisite experience. To boost profitability, the industry sought to increase turnover. There were two obvious routes: first, find more investors and, second, get existing investors to trade more. The latter required some more financial engineering. Locking clients into long-dated products has some drawbacks; they were loath to sell their positions as they suspected (usually correctly) that early exits were not executed on favourable terms from their point of view. It was very difficult to get a third party to validate the price offered; any bank had little appetite for buying expensive products issued by another. How, then, to get the client to take profits in one trade and to enter into another?

The answer was to make the products expire early or "knockout", if a target level of return had been achieved. This was the birth of the autocallable, a fancy term that signified the automatic redemption of a product before its maturity date. These went on to be the most popular products in nearly every jurisdiction; clients were long the market (usually equity index) by selling put options and the whole thing knocked out if the market rallied. The investor makes a bet (mainly) on market direction and if they have made the right call, then the bet is cancelled with some payment to them to make them feel better; wonderful from the product provider and distributor's point of view, rather less so for the client. However, the client will have made a realised profit and have cash in hand and those are key considerations for getting them to trade again.

If the market moves against the client (ie, goes down) then the trade persists, no call or knock out is triggered and the client remains short a put option until either the market recovers or the product expires (usually at a loss to the client).

These products that have an uncertain lifetime and "path dependent" payoffs with market events being triggered at different levels of the stock market severely tested the pricing and risk management technology of the nascent industry's product providers. Early products could be broken down to conventional swaps and options for which rudimentary but tried and tested financial models (such as Black and Scholes) could be used. Simpler products mature and the only market number required to work out the terminal value (or consideration) is the level of the underlying asset at the end. Autocallables and other more sophisticated products are "path dependent" in that the life and value depends on what happens during the life of the bond, not just the final value of the underlying asset but also how it "got" there. The new generation could not be evaluated and risk managed so simply but this limitation did not prevent over-exuberant banks and brokers from doing so, and ugly compromises were made to the detriment of many. A new generation of tools were needed and soon materialised. This is more interesting than it sounds and is explained in greater detail in Chapter 10.

CONCLUSION

The market has grown up, each step was prompted by changes in the environment: low volatility and high interest rates followed by high volatility and low rates. Tax and regulation played an important part too; stamp tax avoidance, income tax avoidance, income to capital gains transformation and use of the life insurance tax structure were all key stepping stones to building an industry that, once established, survived the removal of the tax motivations that had created it.

3

The UK Market

Christopher Taylor
The Investment Bridge

In this chapter we shall focus on the structured product story in the UK.

We start by looking at how and why the concept behind structured investments (defined parameters of risk and return) led to the UK retail structured products industry scaling, at its height, annual sales volumes that exceeded £10 billion and a total market value of £50 billion.[1]

We shall explore the early developments in the market, as it grew from a fledgling industry to one that clearly challenged, and unsettled, the so-called traditional mutual funds world to the extent that the gargantuan and long-established mutual funds industry felt itself compelled to focus on the competition for investor monies that structured products posed. We shall touch on this in more detail in the section on the impact of the press on the industry (see page 64).

We shall also discuss how distribution dynamics shaped the UK market just as much as product manufacturing dynamics and capabilities. In following the industry's journey in the UK we shall consider both fundamental and general issues, as well as specific events, which will be explained in detail, including precipice bonds and the collapse of Lehman Brothers, as well as a "non-structured product event" (the demise of Keydata).[2]

We shall look at the providers, products and practices of the late 1990s and 2000s, and discuss the reaction of professional wealth managers and investment advisers. Importantly, we shall also focus on the reaction of the regulator and their actions, rules and guidance.

The UK industry has reasonably impressive sales levels, if viewed in isolation. However, global industry figures show that the UK market lags other comparable countries in the use of structured products, and since the UK's highest sales point, in the late 2000s, annual sales and the total market in the UK have fallen further still. We shall comment on this in some detail.

The penultimate section of the chapter will provide highlights of the first review of actual performance data (courtesy of research and information portal StructuredProductReview.com) for matured structured products, focusing on those distributed via the UK's professional advisory channel.

We conclude by discussing the rationale for structured products to even exist as an industry, and the place and role of structured products within the investment universe from the perspective of the most important constituent of the investment universe – investors – and consider the future for structured products in the UK.

THE UK INVESTMENT MARKET

The UK has a long-standing investment industry, with the first "traditional" collective unit trust investment fund dating back to the 1930s (according to mutual fund house M&G Investments).

The mutual fund management industry is, as a result, well established in the UK, with annual net retail sales of £14.3 billion in 2012 (Investment Management Association 2013). The benefits of being "first mover" in the investment arena and having been around for some 80+ years are clear. But what if structured products had come first, before actively managed mutual funds? We shall discuss this later.

Alongside active funds, passive funds, albeit challenging the very raison d'être of their active fund cousins,[3] make up the balance of the "traditional" funds sector.

Passive funds emerged at around the same time as the structured product sector in the early 1990s and are also well established in the UK, with certain advisers proud to declare themselves fundamentally passive in their approach and beliefs. The total value of passive funds stood at £71 billion in September 2013 (Reeve 2013).

So, with the UK mutual funds (active and passive) weighing in at £661 billion, and presumably reflecting adviser and investor satisfaction with these mainstay investment propositions, the first question to ask of structured products is "Why bother? Where's the market, investment gap and client need?" The answer, which should apply regardless of which international market the question is raised in, is a basic but irrefutable truth: there are just some things that active funds cannot do and passive funds do not try to do. And that leaves room for alternatives, including structured products.

STRUCTURED PRODUCTS' ENTRY INTO THE UK INVESTMENT LANDSCAPE

As the introduction to this book has already detailed, structured products first surfaced in the UK in the early to mid-1990s, but we suggest that it was the second half of that decade that saw the UK market genuinely develop.

In 1996 structured products brought a new dimension to a somewhat tired and hitherto otherwise unchallenged investment universe, offering advisers and investors something different from the "traditional" investment funds that mutual fund companies had been pushing at them without any major competition.

The structured products industry enjoyed notable success, relatively rapidly. From the early days of some 10–20 providers, raising annual sales of around £1 billion, to an industry made up of close to 100 active providers,[4] issuing nearly 1,000 products and raising nearly £14 billion by 2009 (Currie 2010), which saw the UK retail sales peak (up to the time of writing), suggesting the market has truly come of age.

Before we look at industry-specific events, let us look at what investors themselves want from their investments and what, conceptually at least, they would design for themselves, as investment solutions, if they could. This exercise will highlight why structured product use surged in the UK and globally.

THE FUNDAMENTAL POSITIVES OF STRUCTURED PRODUCTS: MEETING INVESTORS' PRIMARY INVESTMENT CONCERNS AND INTERESTS

Structured investments are not alchemy: they do not make investment risk disappear. However, they can reduce, remove or at least reposition certain investment risks, notably including one of the most important: market/asset risk.

In addition, they can predefine (the parameters of and/or conditions for) returns. Three fundamental items on our investors' wish list are the following. We shall identify how closely structured products match up against these investor-driven points.

- **Remove or reduce investment risks:** no investor takes risk for the sake of it. No matter how cautious or sophisticated the investor, if they could invest without risk they would. Structured products can remove, reduce or at least predefine investment risk (levels and type). This is achieved by formula (by contract) and is not subject to the vagaries of active fund management process or risk. Instead, it is subject to counterparty/credit risk.

- **Predefine/arrange known investment returns:** in addition to removing any downside, investors, of course, want the upside. Structured products can potentially define, and optimise, the investment returns. Again, this is delivered by formula (by contract) and is not subject to the vagaries of active fund management process or risk. In fact, the process risk is carried by the counterparty.

- **Remove (or at least minimise) any charges:** our investors would have no charges in their utopian investment. Structured products, although they do have charges, generally state their returns after any/all charges. Investors' capital is invested without direct deductions.

"Formula driven" refers to the fact that structured investments precisely define risk and return parameters. Critically, both are defined contractually, legally, via the terms of a bond. They are not hopes, aims or promises, as per the active fund management world.

One interesting aspect of structured products is that the entire industry, both in the UK and globally, seems to have done a very bad job of explaining this fact; structured products equate to investing by contract, without investors being exposed to the process involved in generating the returns, which is a risk that is carried by the counterparty.

The investment process and performance risks of a structured product are borne by the counterparty. The bottom line is that if a counterparty is solvent at maturity, they have to deliver exactly what they stated to investors at the outset, regardless of the success or otherwise of their process over the investment term. Investors can simply rely upon the terms of the bond upon which their product is based. Let us prove this important point.

Example 3.1. Imagine that the entire treasury team of an issuer has five years off, from the strike date of a five-year structured product, and no zero-coupon bond is arranged. Imagine also the entire equity derivatives team of the issuer has five years off, from the strike date of the structured product and no derivatives are arranged. Imagine that throughout the entire term of the product the issuer "forgets" to do anything at all behind the scenes: no zero-coupon bond, no derivatives. The risk management team is the issuer and is not there to check that the treasury and equity derivatives team were performing their usual roles and parts of the process.

Q: What will the structured product deliver to investors at maturity?

A: Everything that investors expected at the outset, assuming that the issuer/counterparty is solvent.

The fact is that the process under the bonnet of a structured product hedges a counterparty's exposure to having to deliver the returns of the bonds that they have issued. Investors are not exposed to the "clever stuff" going on. They can simply rely upon the terms of the bonds/securities that their product invests in. The structured products industry has done a very poor job of getting this fundamentally important point across. Yet it is a major point, standing in stark contrast to the investment management and process risk of mutual funds, which are explicitly and fully carried by investors.

Using the words "benefit" and "counterparty exposure" in the same sentence may sound like an oxymoron, after so much scrutiny on the risks of counterparty exposure, particularly after the collapse of Lehman Brothers, but let us consider the benefits, not just the risks, of counterparty exposure.

Firstly, particularly following industry changes, including those imposed upon the industry by the UK regulator, in the years after the Lehman Brothers' collapse, counterparty/credit risk is not hidden by providers – or advisers. Counterparty/credit risk details are explicit in product literature, often on the front cover of brochures, in which the pertinent points of understanding the risk and its consequences are also usually explained extensively. But the most important fact is that counterparties effectively remove or reduce many of the risks that investors want to avoid, remove or reduce but that they have been "educated" to think they must tolerate and accept.

These include market (ie, downside) risk, timing risk and active fund management process risk.

Counterparties define risk and return, via the terms of the bonds that they issue to underpin/back the products that they issue. Some "clever stuff" may go on behind the scenes but this is because the counterparties are hedging their positions, as they, not investors, carry the risks of the investment process.

Contractually and legally, counterparties must deliver at maturity what they promise at the outset, assuming that they remain solvent. In short, the only way that a structured product does not do what it says on the tin is if the issuer/counterparty fails to be able to meet their obligations, which effectively means bankruptcy, or something similarly catastrophic.

Many investors may find it easier to consider whether a major (and probably global) financial institution is likely to be solvent in five or six years than what may or may not happen to the stock market. It is also not unreasonable to suggest that savers and investors can and do understand credit risk, even if they do not know the technical term: most savers and investors generally know that if they place their deposits with a big bank, which does not have major need or appetite for their funds, they might only get around 0.5% pa on that deposit. But, if they want or need a higher return on their deposit, and they deposit with a smaller bank, such as a provincial building society, that wants their funds more, they might be able to get around 3%. That is six times more than the big bank was offering, and is a function of credit risk. Savers and investors intuitively know and understand this, even if not in technical, textbook terms. Many savers and investors also remember what happened with Icelandic banks, the UK's Northern Rock and most have at least heard of or know something about Lehman Brothers.

THE UK MARKET FOR RETAIL STRUCTURED PRODUCTS: A STANDING START IN THE MID-1990s TO £50 BILLION BY 2010

For the reasons explained, the UK (and global) retail structured investment industry achieved strong sales growth rapidly, after it entered the investment arena in the mid-1990s.

Two specific product-driven breakthroughs in 1996 were significant turning points in the UK, which had previously done little in earnest in terms of developing structured products as mainstream investment propositions.

JANUARY 1996: EQUITY-LINKED DEPOSIT ACCOUNTS

The first significant breakthrough arrived on January 2, 1996, when HSBC Asset Management launched the first equity-linked structured deposit in the UK, targeting the Tax Exempt Special Savings Account (TESSA) market.

TESSAs were introduced by John Major (in his only budget as Chancellor of the Exchequer, in 1990) as a low-risk complement to Personal Equity Plans (PEPs), available to anyone in the UK over the age of 18. It was possible to save up to £9,000, via annual limits, over five years. When the first accounts started to mature in 1996, it was possible to invest the maturing sums in a follow-on TESSA, or to start a new TESSA, with the same annual limits amounting to saving £9,000 over five years, if a TESSA had not previously been utilised. Only one TESSA account per saver was permissable.

Prior to 1996, HSBC Asset Management's main proposition, as an asset manager, had been long-only equity funds and passive funds, on the back of the Groups' acquisition of the James Capel funds business. However, Managing Director Alan Gadd and Deputy Managing Director Robin Minter-Kemp took the decision to give free reign to in-house tactical asset allocation and indexation/derivatives expert Bill Maldonado to think through product strategies that could complement their funds offering.

Maldonado's vision was to use HSBC Group's UK banking licence and equity derivatives to develop a deposit account that would have interest calculated by reference to an underlying asset, which, in the case of the innovative and breakthrough HSBC TESSA Plus product, was the UK's FTSE 100 Index.

Offering all the tax breaks and capital security of a normal TESSA deposit account but with potential outperformance of all fixed and variable interest rate returns through the equity link, HSBC.AM ran a nationwide marketing campaign to the independent financial advisor (IFA) channel. The response was positive. Professional advisers embraced the innovation, which gave them an opportunity to add value with their clients, through an equity-linked deposit account, from the asset management arm of a major bank. They also welcomed the commercial opportunity to be remunerated for doing so:

HSBC.AM paid commission on the TESSA Plus in line with normal commission levels on mutual funds – something not seen before, for what was basically a deposit account.

In addition to IFAs, HSBC.AM also courted the "execution only/discount broking" marketing specialists,[5] and the product gained their immediate interest. Prominent firms in the UK, such as Hargreaves Lansdown and Chase de Vere,[6] all undertook marketing campaigns with their clients, with great success.

The HSBC TESSA Plus product, launched on a monthly basis, ran for the next 10 years. At the end of the first five years, ie, at the maturity of the first tranches in 2001, the performance achieved vindicated the product and the decision of advisers and discount brokers/marketeers to promote it: it was the best performing TESSA account in the UK.

One or two other groups with banking licences and in-house equity derivatives capabilities or access to investment banks that could be used for this part of the manufacturing process (eg, Bristol and West and Credit Suisse) also launched equity-linked TESSA accounts. Asset managers without banking licences were simply unable to play, and could do little to target the TESSA market. All that the traditional fund managers could do was look on, and focus on the other tax-free equity product area of the time: Personal Equity Plans.

JUNE 1996: PERSONAL EQUITY PLANS AND CLOSED-END INVESTMENT COMPANIES

The next move, after opening up the TESSA marketplace to structured product competition, was probably the single most important event for the industry in the UK, and was responsible for opening up the mainstream investment market.

Again, it was HSBC.AM and Messrs Gadd, Minter-Kemp and Maldonado that led the way, via PEPs, which had previously been the unchallenged domain of the traditional funds industry.

PEPs were introduced by Chancellor Nigel Lawson in 1986 to encourage saving and wider equity-based investment. General PEPs were originally allowed to invest in qualifying collective investments, ie, mutual funds that were at least half invested in the UK and later the European Union. Eventually, in 2001, the geographical stipulation was removed.

The annual general PEP limit was £6,000 per person. But in 1992 a new type of PEP, called a "Single Company PEP.", was introduced, which allowed investors to hold the shares of a single company. While General PEPs were a great success, Single Company PEPs did not prove particularly popular, because many investors did not want to take the risk of investing in a single company share.

But, following the success of TESSA Plus and wanting to capitalise on the IFA appetite for structured products, HSBC pushed into the PEP market with a further innovation, which this time paired equity derivatives with another product development breakthrough, a Closed-End Investment Company (CEIC): the opposite of the better known Open End Investment Company (OEIC). The beauty of the CEIC was that, while it was technically a single company/share itself, and so qualified for Single Company PEPs, it could invest in, or replicate the performance of, the UK's FTSE 100 Index, ie, it could effectively be a diversified collective investment that could be used for both the General and Single Company PEP allowances. This meant it could facilitate investment of £9,000 per person per year.

This tax wrapper development was innovative in its own right. But, in addition, HSBC.AM designed its new equity-linked structured product, PEP Plus, with 100% protection of capital from FTSE 100 downside and 133% of the upside, without a cap, at maturity. Like TESSA Plus, HSBC.AM's PEP Plus was an immediate success. Following a further marketing campaign to IFAs around the country, with high-level engagement with the leading discount brokers/ marketeers, all of whom were hot for HSBC in the after-glow of the introduction of TESSA Plus, support was exceptional.

Tranche after tranche followed, with variations in payoff terms and strategy along the way. Successful tranche sizes were in the region of £50–100m.

Other companies followed suit, including notable UK brands, such as life assurance company Legal & General and banks such as Barclays. In addition, small and so-called "independent" companies entered the fray, vying for market share against the bigger brands.

THE LATE 1990s INTO THE 2000s: GROWTH PRODUCTS PROLIFERATE BEFORE INCOME COMES TO THE FORE

The majority of the structured products developed and first offered in the UK between 1996 and 1999 were growth based, in a variety of forms. Most were also structured, positioned and marketed as low risk, in terms of protecting capital fully from downside market risk. But, towards the end of the 1990s the pricing environment became challenging, with lower interest rates making the zero-coupon bond element of structures more expensive to arrange while increased market volatility[7] reduced the terms that could be hedged for fully protected offerings, as call options became more expensive to purchase.

In addition, the falling interest rate environment led to increased investor – and therefore adviser – demand for income solutions.

The combination of the pricing environment and investor demand for income was to be instrumental in the first major industry problem: "precipice" income bonds. We shall look closely at precipice bonds later.

One observation on the rise of the industry from the mid- to late 1990s is a simple one: the year-on-year sales growth was demand-led.

No one is forced to invest in structured products. Investors are free to vote with their feet and their funds – and they increasingly chose to invest in structured products.

Between 2000 and 2010, UK sales of retail structured products rose six-fold. A March 2011 *Financial Times* survey of 2,000 investors, found that 40% of them held a structured product in their portfolio: a figure that surprised the FT columnist (indicative of the relatively negative embedded views that the national consumer press seem to have had of structured products over the years).

IMPRESSIVE INDUSTRY DATA FOR THE UK THROUGH THE 2000s: IN ABSOLUTE TERMS BUT LESS SO IN RELATIVE TERMS

Reported sales show that retail structured products gained a foothold in the UK between 2000 and 2010. However, sales in many other countries are known to be significantly higher.

Pinpointing the reasons for the UK's slack utilisation of structured products relative to other markets with any certainty is difficult, but a number of factors appear to contribute to this apparent anomaly.

Unlike many markets, particularly in continental Europe, UK "investor culture" is generally more equity inclined than bond inclined, coupled with a strong and entrenched traditional investment funds industry. Some advisers seemingly consigned structured products to a box labelled "low risk" aimed at and predominantly suitable for cautious investors. This is patently not the case, but to some extent this "box problem" is the industry's own doing, in respect of the "low risk" USP, marketing and messages that have been put out since the early years of the industry's development.

However, the main reason that the UK is behind other markets in its use of structured products is almost definitely a function of distribution dynamics, as opposed to anything product specific.

The pertinent issue is that in the UK investment advice is predominantly in the hands of professional wealth managers and IFAs, as opposed to being the domain of the high street retail banks and building societies (much to their chagrin).

In certain countries in continental Europe it is not unusual for a few major banks to own 80–90% of the investment landscape. But in the UK around 65–75% of investment advice given to investors is through independent advisers. So, while a major bank in Spain might, say, be able to shift a billion euros of a particular structured product in a single tranche, and then repeat this back-to-back throughout the year, this is far from possible in the UK.

In the UK, 20,000–30,000 individual IFAs means that distribution is far from easy to control or even influence. Independent advisers, by definition, form their own views on investment options for their clients, and this includes consideration of investment type, providers and products, and they all have their own individual views and business/client nuances. It has therefore been more challenging to drive UK sales to the levels seen elsewhere, as providers operating in the UK do not control the distribution landscape, and struggle to achieve the same traction and scale (sales volume) per tranche within the IFA channel as providers operating elsewhere can and do.

Furthermore, industry events (including precipice bonds and the demise of Lehman Brothers) have echoed for a long time in the UK, with the media stoking the fire continuously. This has seen opinion on structured products polarise to some extent.

DISTRIBUTION DYNAMICS SHAPE THE UK MARKET: EASY PRODUCTS OR INTELLIGENT INVESTMENTS

We now look at "distribution dynamics" and consider how these have helped to shape the industry. The value and perception of structured products in the UK has often depended more upon the distribution channel in which providers operate than on product manufacturing capabilities, even though some advisers and many commentators and the media have failed to grasp this, and judge the entire industry as if it were homogenous. But this is not the case. The UK market has generally consisted of two distinct types of distribution/provider:

1. high street institutions, with numerous branches, that have big, captive customer bases;

2. providers that do not own any customers and who instead operate through independent intermediaries/Independent Financial Advisory Services (IFAs).

While it was always difficult to ascertain the data accurately, at the height of the market at the end of the 2000s it was thought by most in the structured products industry that 75% or more of the UK's sales were through high street banks and building societies, including the UK state-owned savings and investment organisation, NS&I. The balance (around 25%) was driven by the providers and asset management firms that distributed through IFAs.

The most pertinent difference between the two is the fact that the high street banks and building societies own proprietary distribution, ie, "captive customer bases", numbering anything between 1 million and 20 million customers, plus branch sales staff and so-called advisers. And the bottom line is that, in the 2000s, if you were a bank or building society that owned millions of customers and thousands of branch/sales staff, and were owned by shareholders, the name of the game was simple: profitably sell as much product as possible, to as many customers as possible, as quickly as possible. And repeat, for as long as possible. Post financial crisis and after the implementation of the UK regulator's Retail Distribution Review, this may no longer be the case. Indeed many of the UK's major banks have actually shut down their advisory arms.

During the 2000s, product strategy for the high street institutions could be characterised as a "fast food' product strategy, designed to build scale to sales and profitability. And this meant focusing upon what it was believed customers were most likely to buy and then designing this and putting it in front of them. This might not sound like such a bad thing, but the trouble is that what customers are likely to buy, without good advice or any advice, or with biased or bad advice, can be different from what they actually need or would benefit most from.

Meanwhile, the providers/asset managers owning no customers and distribution, who instead focused on and depended on independent wealth management firms and advisers identifying merit in their approach and product propositions, simply could not get away with a standardised "fast food" product: independent wealth managers and IFAs are research-driven, asset allocation focused and client-centric. Robust due diligence processes are employed to assess investments and to identify integrity, purpose, relevance and suitability, for specific clients.

Independent advisers simply do not care whether a provider maximises their sales or not. In fact, if they perceived that this were the game, they would be likely to avoid a provider altogether.

The reason that all of this is so important is that it is one of the main factors that has determined the type and calibre of products developed by the industry and distributed to investors in the UK. Product integrity and value has often depended upon the distribution channel in which the providers have operated.

Plain vanilla "easy products" are often seen on the high street. Some are or were clearly poor value. Vanilla investments can be a sensible "stepping stone" towards equity-linked investing for inexperienced investors, but low participation rates, low caps on growth or low income and potentially high, hidden charges, which can characterise some products, are clearly not likely to impress professional advisers and advised investors.

One interesting point to think about, however, is whether more "intelligent" structured products, such as those that are put into the independent advisory channel, would maximise sales for high street banks or building societies that own millions of customers. For several reasons the answer is probably not: customers are likely to struggle to quickly and easily pick up on and invest in something that has a slightly more demanding investment story to it. But, more disturbingly, even the advisers or sales staff of the banks and building societies themselves might struggle to readily understand anything more challenging than a plain vanilla offering.

The upshot (or, rather, the downside) of UK distribution dynamics is that some, perhaps many, structured products sold on the high street simply were not of the same calibre as those given to independent advisers. For example, many banks and building societies seemingly had a penchant for "cliquet" products, ie, those that break the investment term down into a number of discrete periods, all of which have their own performance conditions, and which, on the whole, are quite convoluted products to assess. Conversely, independent advisers typically shy away from such structures.

The points made here help to highlight the obvious: not all structured products are the same and not all are virtuous. Differentiation is, therefore, as essential with structured products as it is with any other investment sector, or indeed industry. But differentiation requires industry and product knowledge, which is not widespread (not least in the media) with respect to structured products.

As a result, the whole industry has suffered from the reverberating criticism of the lower grade products often seen on the high street, despite the fact that the products seen in the independent advisory channel have usually been very different and of a higher calibre. Even the independent adviser channel sometimes fails to understand this, with some advisers disliking and not using any structured products because of the negativity surrounding some of the lower calibre products. Clearly this is a loss, not just to the industry but also for investors, who miss out on the "best of breed" structured product providers and products because of the reputation of the worst.

Most wealth managers and independent advisers know that they need to differentiate in the mutual funds world, and do so, highlighted by the fact that few independent advisers use more than 200 funds, out of a universe of 2,000 or more available funds; this is an odd approach, seemingly reserved for structured products. It would be ideal if the same approach, ie, screening and filtering the universe of structured products down to a tight list of the best of breed offerings and using these, was applied to structured products, and there is no valid reason for this not being the case.

SPECIFIC EVENTS AND ISSUES AFFECTING THE UK INDUSTRY: PRECIPICE BONDS, LEHMAN BROTHERS AND KEYDATA

As has been explained, structured products conceptually meet and solve the fundamental concerns and primary interests of investors, probably more than any other investment option. But, despite the positive overall evolution of the industry since its early days, reflected by the sales growth and total market volume achieved, certain specific events have impacted negatively on the UK structured products sector. These include the following.

- **Precipice Bonds:** income products that breached their protection barriers and caused significant capital losses for a significant number of investors.

- **Lehman Brothers:** the unprecedented collapse of the US investment bank hit certain providers and their products, and thus investors in the UK, albeit (fortunately) on a relatively limited basis.

- **Keydata Investment Services:** regulatory intervention in the affairs of Keydata, in relation to its life settlement products, forced one of the UK's key structured product independents and the industry's major third-party plan manager and administrators out of business, creating substantial problems for advisers.

Given the importance of these events we shall focus on each in detail.

Precipice bonds: reverse convertible income products

Let us start with what is undoubtedly the single biggest and longest standing product-specific issue to have affected the UK structured products industry: precipice bonds. The term "precipice bond" was coined by the Financial Services Authority (FSA), as opposed to the media as many people think. The Financial Services Authority (2003a) described a precipice bond as follows.

> [A] product which provides a fixed level of income (or has an income option) over a fixed investment period displaying the following characteristics:
>
> 1. Return of initial capital invested at the end of the investment period is linked by a pre-set formula to the performance of an equity index, a combination of indices or a "basket" of selected stocks (typically from an index or indices);
>
> 2. The customer is exposed to a range of outcomes in respect of the return of his/her initial capital invested;
>
> 3. If the equity index/indices perform within certain thresholds, full repayment of initial capital invested occurs but if the

performance is outside (usually less good than) the thresholds, the customer could lose a substantial part, or even all, of his/her capital invested;

4. Reductions in the amount of initial capital repaid may be geared, eg, 2% of reduction in capital returned for every 1% fall in the related index.

In structured products jargon, precipice bonds are reverse convertibles. For non-industry readers, this means income products where the protection of capital is conditional and usually based on a barrier set at a predefined level of market risk that can be breached in the event of adverse performance in the underlying market/asset, resulting in loss of capital. And the problem for precipice bonds was that market movement was adverse to the extreme.

When these income products were first designed and introduced to the market in around 1997, the FTSE 100 Index had never finished any five-year period lower than its starting level. However, the market story at the back end of the 1990s was basically all about the Internet boom and the euphoria associated with the "new paradigm" of dot-com stocks, before the bursting of this bubble and the markets' subsequent savage correction.

The UK's FTSE 100 Index reached a high of 6,930 points in December 1999, before falling back to a low of 3,230 points in March 2003: a fall of 53%. Similar falls were seen in other major markets, and even bigger falls were seen in certain specialised indexes, such as the US-based, technology-heavy Nasdaq.

The Nasdaq rose by 240% between October 1998 and its climax closing level of 5,048 points (the intra-day high was actually 5,408) on March 10, 2000, before falling back by an astonishing (and eye-watering) 87% by October 2002.

Precipice bond structured income products actually did exactly what they were structured to do: they paid income, often at high levels, but they also lost capital in line with the performance of the underlying market, which was not always restricted to the FTSE 100, or even the Nasdaq, as will be explained shortly.

However, some providers had decided that gearing downside, ie, increasing the magnitude of losses in relation to any fall in the underlying market, was a sensible thing to do, in order to increase the headline rates of the income on offer on their products. Hindsight, of course, proved that gearing downside is far from sensible, especially for products being offered to a wide and unsuspecting audience of retail customers, many of whom were, or should have been encouraged to remember to be, cautious investors.

It is fair to say that precipice bonds say more about the providers and the individuals in those firms than about structured products per se. But the headline numbers involved were big numbers and the fallout reflected on the entire industry. In a memorandum submitted to the Treasury Select Committee of Parliament, in April 2004, the FSA detailed that £7.2 billion of what they had by then labelled "structured capital-at-risk products" (SCARPs)[8] had been sold in the UK retail market between 1997 and 2002, and of that total some 250,000 investors had put in the region of £5 billion into precipice bond income products.

The main headline events falling out of the precipice bonds saga included the following.

- High street bank Lloyds TSB was fined £1.8 million (the largest ever fine by the FSA at the time) for mis-selling its investment subsidiary Scottish Widows' branded products via its branches. It also paid £98 million compensation to 23,000 investors.

- Leading building society Bradford and Bingley, the biggest IFA in the UK at the time, and the fifth firm to be dealt with by the regulator, was fined £650,000 and paid £6 million in compensation to 6,800 investors.

- Two IFA firms, RJ Temple and David Aaron, went into liquidation as a consequence of distributing approximately £320 million of SCARPs/precipice bonds, with the latter also banned by the regulator (after selling the products to some 11,500 investors, according to the appointed administrators KPMG). The ban was particularly notable, as it was the first time the FSA had banned a firm for mis-selling.

The "manufacturing" aspects of precipice bonds

It may be helpful at this point to give a quick explanation of the mechanics of a reverse convertible in terms of the components that make up the structure.

As always, there is the zero-coupon bond, which is effectively an internal deposit arranged by the treasury team of the issuer and counterparty.

In the late 1990s let us say that in the region of 75% of the original coupon was used for the zero-coupon bond element of the structure. So, 25% of the investor's capital remained. Around 6% was taken out to cover the providers set up charges, pay IFA commission and generate a profit.

That left 19%. Let us say that the five-year structure was set up to pay annual coupons of 8% a year. The first 2.5 years of income were actually nothing more complicated than the 19% being given back to investors. But where did the balance of the income stream come from? The answer is that it is a function of the premium obtained from introducing market risk to capital, achieved by the issuer "selling a put option". The premium, say 21%, funds the last 2.5 years of income coupons.

The value of the put is basically a reflection of the risk that it introduces to the structure. For example:

- if a more volatile underlying market, or stocks instead of an index, is used, the put will be more valuable, so the coupons that can be paid by the structure will be commensurately higher;

- if the investment term is shorter, there is a greater risk that the market may be below its starting level at maturity, so, again, the put will be more valuable, and the coupons that can be paid by the structure will be commensurately higher; and

- clearly, if downside losses are geared, ie, the investor will suffer a 2% loss of capital for any 1% loss in the underlying market, the put premium will be increased and the coupons that can be paid will be commensurately higher.

Given the importance of precipice bonds and the noise surrounding them more than a decade after the event, let us look closely at what happened and why, ie, why and how precipice bonds came to be developed, as opposed to just focusing on the symptoms and the aftermath.

Investors looking for income, more often than not, do so as a matter of need. Typically, the need for income is driven by investors who are in (or approaching) retirement, when reliable and maximum income is the obvious requirement: inextricably linked to the imperative of preserving what will usually be hard earned and irreplaceable capital.

Generally, the interest of most income investors is straightforward: yield optimisation coupled with capital preservation. In other words, a decent "return on capital" with "return of capital".

With income products, as we have seen, there will always be a trade-off in balancing the level of income with the level of protection from market risk. The simple fact is that it is not possible to deliver superior income, over and above the risk free rate of the market, without introducing risk to either income or capital, through either market risk or credit risk. This fact should be obvious, but it is often overlooked or forgotten, not least as some providers exhibited the propensity to use "smoke and mirrors" and to neglect to detail risks as prominently as benefits (ie, "hiding big points in the small print"). And that is what happened with precipice bonds.

Up until 1997, as explained previously, the structured products industry in the UK had focused on growth products, quite successfully. However, as the decade progressed, interest rates were reducing and market volatility was increasing in the dot-com bubble. And this mini-cocktail meant that plain vanilla, no-market-risk growth products started to become harder to produce, with alluring headline rates, as had been the case.

At the same time, as interest rates came down, investors and their advisers became increasingly interested in finding income solutions. And this was the backdrop to precipice bonds being conceived.

The rationale for precipice bonds at the time was not so flawed as is seen in hindsight, at least in principle.

The concept involved arranging a structure, linked, say, to the UK's mainstream index, the FTSE 100. Yearly income would be generated by the structure on a fixed and non-conditional basis. But the return of capital at maturity would be conditional, linked to the closing level of the index. However, since its inception in 1984, the FTSE 100 Index had never ended any five-year period lower than its starting level, so the idea of putting capital-at-risk on this basis did not appear too overt or high risk.

Scottish Widows, the life assurance arm of Lloyds Bank, can probably claim the glory of having developed the concept first, in 2008. And its first product was a straightforward affair, offering 8% income a year and capital back if the FTSE 100 Index was at or above its starting level.

The product was developed early in 2008, with a concerted marketing campaign taking place in January and February; the product went live in March. It promptly raised in the region of £250 million (notably, as the industry observed, a multiple of typical growth product sales volume) in the space of just over a week: at which point Scottish Widows was forced to close the tranche early, having run out of hedged assets.

Scottish Widows went on to issue further tranches, raising in the region of £1 billion, varying the structures and underlyings along the way. But other providers wanted a piece of the action, and this is where things started to get interesting: if you are not the first company launching a product, but are instead the second, third or fourth company launching a similar product, how do you compete? You need to beat the product already in the market in some way, and in terms of income products the thought process of the day was simple: beat the headline rate of income on offer.

Enter the second provider. It wanted to take market share from Scottish Widows and decided that it would do this by producing a higher fixed-income coupon. But how did it achieve this? Higher returns must be a function of higher risk, either market risk or credit risk. And precipice bonds were all about market risk (leaving aside credit risk for discussion regarding the end of the next decade, and the story of Lehman Brothers).

So the second provider, which thinks it needs to beat 8%, decides that it can offer 9%, by making the five-year term a four-year term. That simple step created more value in the "down and in" put option being sold, because the shorter term carried an increased risk that the market could end the term lower than when it started. More risk is now on the table but, so far, things are still relatively sensible.

However, a third provider is waiting eagerly in the wings, watching the sales being raised. Its executives decide they want a piece of the action. But how will they compete with the 9% coupons now in the market? Simple, make the four-year term (that was originally a five-year term) a three-year term: and, hey presto, we have 10% income.

Now, quite clearly, things are starting to get a little bit "stretched" in terms of what would normally be considered a reasonable time horizon for a stock-market-linked investment. But the headline rate is the best in the market, so prudence is abandoned. So, we have now moved from 8% per year fixed income to 10%. But the worst precipice bonds ended up with coupons as high as 13%, or more. How do you get from 10% to 13%? There are a number of ways, all of which clearly depend upon increasing the investment risk.

The first step is to swap the underlying index from the mainstream FTSE 100 Index for the more volatile EuroSTOXX 50 index. The extra volatility makes the structure more risky, which is reflected in the value of the put options being sold, and anything extra on the value of the put, giving the structure more risk, lifts the coupons higher. So, now we have three-year structures and we have swapped the FTSE 100 Index for the EuroSTOXX. What is our next step?

We are in a tech bubble, with all the volatility in the TMT stocks, so the next provider swapped the EuroSTOXX for the Nasdaq, which was already rapidly approaching its all-time high. That took coupons to even higher double digit territory.

But how did providers in the UK get to the heady heights of more than 13%? Indexes were exchanged for baskets of stocks and down-side risk was geared so that, if the underlying was, say, 30% lower than its starting level at maturity, the loss of capital that investors suffered would be twice this, ie, 60%. In fact, the worst precipice bonds paid an extra high income but then failed to repay any capital to investors, because falls in the underlying markets and assets, geared by the structuring, wiped out 100%.

The "distribution" aspects of precipice bonds

Structured products gained significant traction with IFAs in the UK in the latter part of the 1990s. The number of distributors, including independent financial firms and advisers, ran into the thousands.

However, according to the FSA, in its April 2004 submission to the Treasury Select Committee, their review of the sales of the 25 largest distributors of SCARPs, covering both direct offer (ie, execution only/discount brokers) and advised sales, identified that these firms sold approximately £3.2 billion of the total £7.3 billion invested in SCARPs between 1997 and 2004.

An important aspect of understanding the issues surrounding precipice bonds is understanding that the distribution channel that was most responsible for the sales was "direct offer" (the term used by the FSA), more commonly known as "execution only" or "discount" brokers.

Discount brokers are often part of a normal IFA firm, but operate very differently. Their interaction with investors is often via "direct offers", eg, mail shots and newsletters. These are sent to large databases of prospective investors/clients, highlighting products that they might like to invest in, without any form of advice. An incentive (some form of discount) is often offered, and this is usually a function of some of the commission that would be generated by the purchase being rebated back to the investor.

The IFA firms behind the marketing faced high numbers of complaints from consumers, some of which were then dealt with by the regulator's ombudsman; many complaints were upheld, on grounds including

- suitability of the products,

- the covering letters, marketing documents and accompanying providers financial promotions (ie, product brochures), and

- poor systems, controls and complaints handling.

"Execution only" firms generally believed that they could not be held liable for advice, as they made it clear to investors that no advice was being offered or implied in the marketing communications sent to them.

But the regulator took a different view in assessing the role of IFA/discount brokers in respect of precipice bonds. While their services did not fall under the rules pertaining to advice, the FSA/Financial Services Compensation Scheme (FSCS) instead held them responsible and accountable for ensuring that their marketing communications were "clear, fair and not misleading" and treating customers fairly.

Lehman Brothers: the other major issue to have affected the UK structured products sector

Structured products expose investors to risk, even when these may be different and potentially reduced compared with other investments, and even when some providers, especially in the earlier days of the industry's development in the UK, might have let their marketing teams overstate the references to capital protection and low market risk.

One consequence of precipice bonds, after 2003, was that all eyes were on the market risks, ie, the risk of losses that could follow poor performance in the underlying. This had been starkly evident in precipice bonds in relation to high income products, with geared downside, etc.

The FSA issued numerous updates, guidance notes and fact sheets during the precipice bonds saga. These started in December 1999, with the regulatory warning "High income products: make sure you understand the risks", which was on the regulator's website, drawing specific attention to the FSA's concern that consumers needed to understand that their capital may be at risk with structured products. In February 2000 this text was produced as a consumer fact sheet, and further alerts were issued in March 2001, August 2001, August 2002 and December 2002. In February 2003 an FSA Guidance Note even stipulated that firms (providers and advisers) must send the fact sheet to investors.

Finally, the FSA produced a supposedly all-encompassing fact sheet, "Capital-at-risk products", in which it carefully detailed the risks of structured products but in which it completely omitted the other main risk, ie, counterparty/credit risk.

Interestingly, following the collapse of Lehman Brothers and all of the work that the regulator did over the year that followed, culminating in its output of September/October 2009, the fact sheet became very difficult to find, perhaps because it highlighted that the regulator itself had not carefully considered and accounted for the risk of a major issuer/counterparty collapse and the consequences of such in respect of retail structured products.

But this serves to highlight the fact that, prior to the unprecedented global financial crisis of 2008, nobody – governments, central banks, regulators, fund managers, wealth managers, advisers or investors – had seriously considered the failure of any of the world's major banks. But that, of course, is what happened on September 15, 2008, when Lehman Brothers, the fourth largest investment bank in the US, filed for bankruptcy.

The good news is that even though the collapse of a major counterparty is a catastrophic event, Lehman Brothers was actually (luckily) a contained event in terms of its impact upon structured product investors in the UK.

This is not to down-play the importance and severe impact of the event upon the investors affected. It is, instead, a factual reference to the numbers involved. In 2008, the UK retail structured products industry saw gross annual sales of around £6 billion. However, according to the FSA, only around £100 million was invested in Lehman Brothers-backed retail structured products, by approximately 5,500 investors.

Relative to other markets, the UK's exposure to Lehman Brothers was low

Lehman Brothers had not been a mainstream issuer in the UK market, during the early to mid-2000s. In fact, its issuance in the retail sector was virtually non-existent prior to 2007, a year before its collapse. In that year, it self-promoted its own products and it also issued securities to back the products of a small number of the independent firms that promoted products to the IFA channel.

In April 2009, as a result of the impact of Lehman's collapse, the FSA announced a "Thematic Review" of the UK structured products industry, in which it focused on the entire industry to identify who did what business, with whom and how.

In May 2009, the FSA also agreed a "Wider Implications Review" with the Ombudsman. Investor complaints related to Lehman Brothers structured products were suspended pending the outcome of the reviews.

In October 2009, three months later than expected, the FSA released the findings of its review. It was a substantive and detailed output that demonstrated a good level of understanding of the industry, its providers, the processes and products.

Regulatory Review findings: advisory firms

As part of its root and branch review, the regulator looked closely at a range of advisory firms, and advisory failings were identified. They looked at 11 firms and 157 individual client files, all of which were linked to Lehman, accounting for 24% of the total Lehman exposure in the UK.

Their assessment of the client files that they looked at was that 31% were deemed to have been suitable, 46% unsuitable and 23% were unclear.

This, clearly, was not confidence inspiring and, as a result, prescriptive rules and guidance for advisers were issued by the regulator, including, for example, guidance that advisers should carefully consider the appropriateness of placing more than 25% of any clients' portfolio in structured products and/or more than 10% with any individual issuer/counterparty. This was only ever a threshold, above which the regulator expected advisers to more carefully consider the rationale of placing more than these levels, but many advisers incorrectly believed that it was a hard-and-fast rule.

It is important to note, having highlighted that advisory failings were found as a direct result of the firms' or advisers' use of Lehman-backed products, that many of the failings were generic and would have emerged had the review been for any investment product type: for instance, the manner in which advisory firms categorised their clients' attitudes to risk, their approach to portfolio diversification, and the use of tax wrappers.

Regulatory Review findings: providers

The regulators' review of the industry included contact with all providers, not just those that had used Lehman-issued securities.

It is instructive to understand what the regulator took issue with, and what it did not, and why certain plans were in line for compensation scheme protection when others were not, in respect of the independent plan managers that promoted Lehman-backed products, including the plan manager that Lehman itself used to promote its own products.

Critically, the regulator announced that it had found serious deficiencies in the financial promotion material, ie, the product literature, of three independent companies: ARC Capital and Income; NDFA and DRL. A fourth independent provider, Meteor Asset Management, was found to have explained the counterparty risks appropriately/adequately for investors, but the failings in the brochures of the other three companies resulted in these firms going into administration.

The most important point to make is that counterparty credit risk is a performance issue and the FSA does not regulate performance if (and it is an important "if") the risk and consequences of the risk are adequately detailed, in a clear, fair and non-misleading manner. This was the issue that caught the three providers that were put into administration: their product literature was not deemed good enough in terms of clearly detailing the risks and consequences of the risks.

Conversely, it is also important to note that providers that use an issuer/counterparty that defaults are not put out of business, if they have complied with regulatory rules and expectations.

Similarly, advisers are not deemed at fault for using a structured product where the counterparty defaults, if they have fulfilled their professional responsibilities appropriately in identifying and explaining this risk to prospective investors.

The regulator found that 15 "capital secure" products (as opposed to the capital-at-risk structures) from ARC, DRL and NDFA had mis-led investors, who were subsequently covered by the FSCS, because this meant they were victims of mis-selling. Investors had been led to understand that their capital was not at risk.

However, investors in the "capital-at-risk" products received notification from the FSCS that the counterparty risk was deemed to have been adequately explained, and for that reason they would not get compensation. But, one or two committed advisers and investors managed to find reasons why compensation should apply, in respect of certain plans.

In the case of the DRL Kickout Performance Plan Issue 1, the brochure stated the issuer/counterparty would have a Standard & Poor's (S&P) rating of A+. What it did not mention was that S&P had downgraded Lehman Brothers to A during the offer period, before the strike date, and DRL did not tell investors. Investors thought they were buying an investment with a counterparty of A+, but actually it was A, which was deemed mis-selling.

With regard to the NDFA Fixed Income plan, NDFA did advise investors of the downgrade, but its letter to investors said that they still considered "the counterparty to be strong". What they did not detail, however, was that when S&P downgraded Lehman their report was quite negative in its outlook. This was enough for the NDFA letter to be deemed misleading.

And the third case was that of the ARC Capital and Income Fixed Plan. The reason that compensation was available to investors for this product is an indictment of the provider and people involved: the counterparty bank, ie, Lehmans, while not named, was stated to be a "major UK bank", which, clearly, Lehman Brothers was not.

In concluding this section it is important to highlight that before the collapse of Lehman Brothers and the subsequent FSA review and its subsequent findings, new rules and guidance, it was normal for providers not to name counterparties – at least not before the strike date. Various reasons were cited for this, most notably the belief that Prospectus Directive rules prevented such a disclosure.

But since October 2009 all structured products promoted in the UK have explicitly stated details of the counterparty and offered extensive information regarding the credit risk and how to assess it.

In fact, the collapse of Lehman Brothers was the catalyst for significant improvements to the industry and the way it operates and is advised upon.

Keydata Investment Services

We now discuss the structured product event that was not a structured product event – despite swathes of people confusing it with being one, including some advisers and commentators and possibly even the regulator, as well as professional indemnity (PI) insurers to advisory firms.

In June 2009 the UK regulator forced Keydata Investment Services (a firm that everyone identified as a structured product provider) into administration, as a result of various alleged irregularities. But the demise of Keydata was nothing to do with structured products, and the events surrounding its demise actually highlight a significantly positive aspect of structured products in the way that they are arranged and work.

Keydata was a well-known independent "provider" of structured products, in the UK.[9] In addition, it was also what was known as a third-party plan manager and administrator, offering its services to other providers, including securities issuers and other independent firms that did not possess or want to set up all of the regulatory permissions or infrastructure needed.

But, following its implosion, it became clear that Keydata was not what everyone had understood it to be. Its third-party plan management and administration services were, in fact, the major part of its business. At the time of the regulator placing Keydata into administration, it had investment assets of some £2.9 billion. Of this, circa £2.2 billion was in respect of its third-party plan management and administration clients. The other circa £700 million was split into two distinct areas.

First, Keydata's own structured products, backed by various securities issuers/counterparties and promoted to IFAs. As of June 2009, this part of its business made up around £200 million of its £2.9 billion total book. This was far less than anybody realised. Everybody believed that Keydata was a major, multi-billion pound structured product provider.

Second, it became clear that Keydata had offered a specific range of products that many people had thought to be structured products (as that was the business that Keydata was in) but that were actually "life settlement" products. But life settlement products are not structured products, even when the provider of them is thought to be a structured product provider. Making matters worse the "story" around the Keydata life settlement products turned into an astonishing scenario, with details of alleged fraud emerging, £105 million unaccounted for, etc: a tale worthy of a good fiction writer.

However, the good news was that within two weeks of Keydata going into administration, the appointed administrators, partners in PricewaterhouseCoopers, clarified that all of the Keydata structured products were unaffected by any of Keydata's wider issues and were all accounted for, sitting in ring-fenced client-money accounts, with investors exposed to the major financial institutions that were the securities issuers/counterparties involved. This highlighted a unique strength of structured products: even when the "provider" fails, investors are not exposed to this problem and are instead exposed to the solvency of the counterparty backing the products.

The events surrounding Keydata, especially because of the dramatic details, including the regulator involving the Serious Fraud Office, were noisy, to say the least. And many commentators, ie, media and some advisers, simply labelled Keydata a structured product provider, and plastered "structured product failings" all over their press coverage, failing to distinguish between the structured products that were safe and unaffected and the life settlement products that were a toxic mess.

It is possible that some commentators did not understand the difference, at least initially. But it is concerning that the regulator appears to have contributed to the misunderstanding.

In its Final Notice to building society Norwich & Peterborough (N&P), in April 2011, regarding the life settlement products that they had sold their customers, the FSA referred to "complex structured products". N&P had sold £53 million of the Keydata products to 3,200 customers, and was fined £1.4 million by the FSA, and forced to pay £51 million to affected customers.

Regulatory stance and actions

We have already detailed many of the actions of the UK regulator in relation to structured products over the development of the industry, including the significant regulatory scrutiny following precipice bonds and Lehman-backed products: the two most important and far-reaching and deeply impacting events.

Now, let us also comment on additional actions and areas of focus for the regulator (the Financial Conduct Authority (FCA) took over from the FSA in April 2013) and consider the purpose and aims of the regulator.

In April 2010, six months after its work on Lehman Brothers, the FSA produced the findings of its review of structured deposits. In November 2011 and March 2012 it issued guidance consultation and then finalised guidance papers, specific to structured product providers. And, more generally, in 2013, the regulator's "Retail Distribution Review" (RDR) made it mandatory for advisers in the UK that wished to position their firms as "independent" to consider all investment options for their clients, as opposed to only offering a restricted set of propositions. The FSA stated, in the run up to the implementation of RDR, that it would specifically expect independent advisers to understand that "whole of market" included structured products, and that advisers would need sufficient knowledge of structured products to either competently advise upon them, or competently decide not to, based upon specific client circumstances and objective views of structured products.

Has the regulator, through all of its actions and focus, achieved its aim: to protect investors? Despite some shortcomings in demonstrating an intimate knowledge and understanding of the sector at certain points, the regulator deserves credit for its work and recognition of the fact that it has clearly come up the curve significantly in its working knowledge of the industry, providers, their processes and practices and their products.

It has certainly got closer to its aim through its actions and interventions in the industry and through the rules and detailed guidance that it has produced and enforced, for providers and advisers.

Financial promotion/marketing material, ie, the brochures for structured products, are significantly improved across the industry. It is understood by providers that they must

- be clear about where money is invested, ie, in the bonds/ securities issued by a single institution,
- be clear about relevant counterparty risk, including details of the specific counterparty;
- prominently state that capital is at risk,
- use language investors can understand,
- not describe a product as "protected" or "guaranteed" if this is inaccurate or misleading,
- explain the circumstances when FSCS coverage applies, and when it does not.

And one of the most positive upshots of everything has been the "New Normal": counterparty information is always explicitly disclosed and carefully explained.

In addition, providers must meet the regulator's stringent expectations of products being based upon robust product development processes that include demonstrable identification of the target audience, modelling that assesses back-tested performance and stress tests forecasts of performance in a full range of possible market environments.

In summary, it is fair to suggest that, at the time of writing, the UK structured product sector is probably now more tightly regulated than any other part of the investment universe, to the extent that commentators, advisers and investors should be confident that the industry operating today does so with client-centric integrity and prerequisite product development expertise, skill and care.

THE IMPACT OF THE MEDIA AND COMMENTATORS UPON THE INDUSTRY

Despite the retail structured products sector having soared to a £50 billion value in the UK at its height, the fact is that sweeping statements, often founded upon specific industry events, have coloured and characterised the views of the media and many commentators, including the professional advisers whose views are often sought by and featured in trade and consumer publications.

Structured products have endured many years of (what appeared to be, at least to those in the industry) criticism levelled at the industry as a whole, often based on worst-case examples, without clarification or distinction. Common sense alone should be enough for the press and commentators to realise that the UK structured investment industry is anything but a single uniform market. For instance, in 2009, nearly 100 providers actively issued nearly 1,000 products, raising nearly £14 billion.

Of course not all providers or products are the same. But, one-size-fits-all comments surround the structured products sector. The key word missing always has been "differentiation" – between providers, processes and/or their products. However, differentiation requires an understanding of the subject matter, which was and often still is missing when it comes to structured products.

There have only ever been two major negative incidents from which the UK retail structured products industry cannot defend itself.

- The precipice bonds debacle: even though the scale was major, precipice bonds were an indictment of the providers and individuals involved, as opposed to the structured products industry itself or structured products themselves. Not all providers issued precipice bonds.

- Lehman Brothers: unlike precipice bonds, Lehman and its fallout did not occur on a major scale in UK retail structured products. The volume involved was around £105 million in 2008, a year in which the total structured product issuance was around £9 billion.

But the fact is that the worst incidents have been used to castigate the industry as a whole. And, this is something of a "special" approach by the media that stands in contrast to its approach to traditional mutual funds.

The mutual funds industry seems to benefit from a more aspirational stance that focuses on the best aspects of the industry and the best potential of its providers and their funds – as highlighted by the term "star fund manager", used in reference and deference to the doyens of the sector, such as Fidelity's Anthony Bolton and Invesco Perpetual's Neil Woodford.

This phenomenon is akin to "halos versus shadows", which succinctly refers to the way in which the worst incidents, worst products and worst providers have cast shadows over the structured products sector, while the best examples, best managers and best funds cast halos over the realm of mutual funds.

Let us take a look at the reverberating and favoured "facts" from media articles that seek to warn and "educate" readers about the perils of structured products. Over the years, these have included the following:

- they are complex;
- the charges are too high;
- dividends are an important part of the total return;
- they cap the upside;
- there is no liquidity – investors are locked in;
- you cannot have your cake and eat it too;
- you cannot have equity returns without equity risks;
- risk can be controlled through diversification and time;
- structured products and derivatives are a zero-sum game;
- the only people that win are the investment banks;
- it is "the wrong time in the cycle" to buy protection;

and the media's all-time favourite,

- if it looks too good to be true it probably is.

But the main fact that about this list of "facts" is that actual facts need to replace what is best described as "faction".

Any of these points and criticisms above can be valid for some structured products, but none are valid for all of them, despite some of the points sounding like hard-to-argue-with "truisms". Much of the criticism that the industry has faced is outdated and misguided. It is also the case that much of the criticism emanating from financial advisers, which finds its way into various press articles, comes from those who simply have not kept up with the industry and the advances that it has made over the years. These commentators are often respected individuals, in good businesses, with plenty of credentials, but when it comes to structured products never has so much been said by so many people who know so little.

It is also the case that some of the negative comments come from firms or organisations with commercial reasons for not wanting to see the structured products sector flourish. These include certain discount broking firms (such as Hargreaves Lansdown) that rely upon annual commission (known as "trail commission") from traditional mutual funds. Structured products do not usually offer such commission. Importantly, it also includes the trade association of the mutual funds world, known as the Investment Management Association (IMA).

The IMA first started commenting on structured products in 2008. A brief look at mutual fund sales between 2006 and 2008 is all it takes to see what motivated them. Net retail sales of mutual funds in the UK fell 75% in this period: from around £15 billion in 2006 to around £9.5 billion in 2007, to around £3.9 billion in 2008.

The IMA's vested interest criticisms of the industry caused some ripples for the structured products industry. The IMA is a respected organisation. But, the points the IMA made were based upon the worst possible examples of structured products, and used to make sweeping and generalised comments on the whole sector. Something that the IMA itself would, no doubt, have objected most fiercely to if the reverse had ever applied, ie, if the structured products sector criticised the whole of the mutual funds world based upon its worst performing funds.

Without doubt, the structured products industry in the UK (providers, products and advisers) raised its bar and advanced its approach, its integrity and its value for investors as it evolved. In addition to the regulatory intervention, the industry acted of its own accord to evolve collective best practice, not just meeting but exceeding regulatory rules, guidance and expectation.

In 2009, the UK's leading structured product companies, including the major issuers and independent providers, established the industry's own trade association, the UK Structured Product Association (UK SPA). UK SPA is not a commercial entity. Its creation was a unified response by the industry to the problem of structured products being misunderstood and misrepresented.

In addition to the formation of UK SPA, in 2009, one of the UK's leading independent advisory firms, Lowes Financial Management, launched StructuredProductReview.com, a dedicated research service conceived, created, developed and maintained to help professional advisers engage with the structured products sector and to aid the identification of providers and products that may be suitable for their clients.

StructuredProductReview.com (SPR) has grown strongly in terms of both the providers and the number of advisers using the service. In November 2013, more than 8,500 individuals were registered users of the site.

It is a simple truth that no investment is perfect: none are. But structured products offer investors propositions that active mutual funds cannot and that passive mutual funds do not.

Investors should diversify: not just in terms of their asset allocation but also in terms of investment type and approach, ie, they should include and align "best of breed" solutions from the active funds, passive funds and structured products sectors.

The media needs to better understand this. In particular, it needs to recognise some of the significant and unique positives of structured products, particularly the "best of breed" examples, and the advances that the industry has made such that it includes more positives in its coverage of structured products.

The structured product sector in the UK is now tightly regulated. It operates with integrity and value with client-centric providers and it is well-advised upon: with the "advised" percentage of the market (as opposed to execution only and/or high street non-advised) markedly up since the late 2000s: from what is believed to have been less than 25% in 2007 to more than 50% in 2013.

Structured products have increasingly been embraced by wealth managers and advisers in the UK because of the value that they can add within portfolios, alongside other investment types. These wealth managers and advisers identify "best of breed" products based on objective views, like any other area of the investment universe. In fact, the UK's regulatory regime introduced in 2013, after the Retail Distribution Review, makes objective views of the industry mandatory. This can only better serve investors' best interests. It would be very positive to see the UK media demonstrate that they appreciate this.

UK PRODUCT DYNAMICS: PLAIN VANILLA AND FTSE 100 DOMINATE

Choice is a good thing. As is innovation. And the structured products industry is rightly recognised for providing both. Structured products can be constructed to provide investment propositions, for growth or income, on virtually any investment/asset allocation theme, offering enhanced risk–return profiles.

Propositions can be developed and launched exceptionally quickly, in response to market conditions, potentially opening up and facilitating unparalleled asset allocation access and scope.

However, despite the industry's scope to innovate and enhance advisers' and investors' asset allocation options, product issuance in the UK has remained predominantly plain vanilla and UK-centric, not least in the use of the main UK index, the FTSE 100.

This has particularly been the case on the high street. But even in the professional advisory space the industry has struggled to open up solid interest or, more pertinently, solid support for anything other than FTSE 100-linked products with simple and usually low/lower risk payoff strategies. The most impressive sales scale has always been at the no risk/low/lower risk and simple end of what has been possible.

Structured deposits, which do not present any risk to capital, have seen the greatest sales flow. In addition to the high street banks and building societies, this has also been the case for the providers that distribute products through the independent advisory channel. One particular reason for this has been the compensation scheme safety net that is in place for qualifying deposits in the UK, which as of 2013 covered investors against losses to a maximum level of £85,000 per person, per institution.

Next along the product curve, in terms of risk, after deposits, are no-market-risk structures. While a fully protected structure potentially allows a product to be launched as a deposit, if the issuer is a licensed deposit provider or deposit taker, any returns generated by a deposit are deemed interest and are therefore taxed as interest, at income tax levels (as opposed to being deemed capital gains and taxed at capital gains tax levels, which in the UK have been considerably lower). So, there is demand for no-market-risk structures, which could be launched as deposits, to be launched as investments. It is also the case that not all issuers are licensed deposit takers in the UK. It is important to note that only deposits ordinarily have recourse to FSCS protection, in the case of the default of the counterparty.

No-market-risk, protected growth structures, offering no market downside and potentially unlimited upside are hard to argue with,

Table 3.1 Summary of autocall (kickout) strategy

Description	Investment applications
• Products are usually launched with a five- or six-year tenor. The level of the underlying market/asset is monitored and, on a pre-agreed frequency (eg, annually, semiannually, quarterly), if the level of the underlying market/asset is at or above a predefined level (often the initial level), the structure is "called", ie, closes automatically, repaying capital and the total accumulated return, at the first trigger opportunity.	• Investors can generate potentially high fixed returns, even if the underlying market/asset(s) performance is flat, or, for defensive structures, even if it has fallen. • Autocalls are used by wealth managers/advisers as innovative tactical investments, in uncertain markets.

if participation rates are strong and any caps on maximum returns are high enough.

In the UK, dividend levels on equities are generally higher than elsewhere in the world, so high participation rates are necessary, as the FTSE 100 Index is a price-return index, ie, it does not take dividends into account in its calculation.

Capital-at-risk structures have also been popular in the UK, particularly in the independent advisory channel. Moving a structured deposit or no-market risk-structure to one that includes market risk is usually done through the use of a barrier that provides protection from a defined level of adverse performance in the underlying. Commonly, such protection has been based upon barriers set at 50–60%, ie, the underlying market/asset can fall by 40–50% before capital may be lost due to market movement.

Historically, the UK's main blue chip index, the FTSE 100, has never breached a 50% barrier level when set up on a "European" basis, ie, when the barrier is only monitored at maturity, on the final day of the investment term, including back-testing all five-year periods dating back to the inception of the index in 1984.[10]

Similarly, on a daily close "American" basis, ie, when the barrier is observed at the closing level of the index every day during the investment term, the FTSE 100 Index has only ever breached such a deep level of protection on three specific days.

Let us highlight a couple of specific structures that are normally issued with contingent protection, ie, capital-at-risk:

- "Turbos" or "super-trackers" (geared growth) products offer returns as high as, say, 10 times any movement in the underlying index, to a capped maximum return, often in the region of 50–75%, over five or six years.

- "Digitals" generally offer the simplicity of two possible outcomes: a decent fixed and predefined return, based on the index simply being at or above its starting level, or repayment of capital if the index is below the starting level, with protection of capital unless the index is more than 50% below its starting level. The returns have been as high as 75%, over five or six years, based on no growth in the underlying. Understandably, "digitals" attract good support, both on the high street and in the independent advisory arena.

The structure that has dominated the UK for much of the latter 2000s and early 2010s has been the autocall/kickout.

- Autocalls (Table 3.1) are usually launched with five- or six-year terms but offer automatic early closure, with full repayment of capital and accumulated coupons, at the first anniversary (or predefined point) during the investment term, based on the underlying markets/assets simply being at or above their starting levels, or a similar predefined condition.

No market/asset growth is required. Defensive structures even allow markets/assets to fall. If the strategies do not autocall at the first anniversary, the coupon/growth payment is "rolled up", ie, accumulates, and is paid at the first subsequent anniversary, based upon the original market/asset condition, ie, the market/asset must simply be above its original starting level.

Because the strategies often successfully "call", ie, close early, at the first anniversary, the growth payments of such strategies have been looked on by some advisers and investors as "quasi income", with the benefit of being taxed as capital gains (this benefit is significant, especially given the high coupons/growth being generated).

Autocall coupons were as high as 15–18% per year, or more, in the late 2000s, based upon the prevailing pricing environment. After the volatility created by the financial crisis dissipated, coupon levels gradually trended down to 10–12% per year, with 6–10% more the norm, as market volatility decreased further in 2012–13.

- Lastly, for investors seeking income, structured products have been able to provide various strategies, either within a deposit-based structure or within an investment environment. Income can be fixed, with return of capital dependent upon the performance of the underlying market/asset, or conditional, dependent upon the performance of the underlying (for example, if the underlying trades within certain parameters).

Structured product performance data for products in the UK Professional Adviser channel

In 2013, SPR presented the first review of actual maturity data, for structured products in the UK. Due to their position, as a service provided for professional advisers, the data that they collect and analyse only covers products designed for and distributed through independent advisers. All of the figures given below, therefore, refer only to those structured products distributed through independent financial advisers.

SPR analysed all such products to have matured since November 1, 2008, on the premise that this covered products that could have been launched up to six years earlier, ie, back as far as 2003, giving a total period of a decade for the review.

The analysis was conducted on a similar basis to the accepted approach of the mutual funds industry, separating results into quartile rankings, to highlight not just average performance but also the top and bottom performers.

Underlyings

In terms of underlyings, the data from SPR highlighted that, out of all the maturing products, 74.8% were FTSE 100 Index based.

Annualised performance of all FTSE 100 linked structured products

The first headline result (Table 3.2) detailed the performance of all FTSE 100 linked structured products, including deposits and investments and no-market-risk and capital-at-risk.

Table 3.2 Annualised performance of all FTSE 100 linked structured products

Quartile	Performance (%)
1st	10.47
2nd	6.47
3rd	2.97
4th	0.98

Source: StructuredProductReview.com.

Table 3.3 Annualised performance of all capital-at-risk FTSE 100 linked structured products

Quartile	Performance (%)
1st	12.29
2nd	9.18
3rd	7.33
4th	2.65

Source: StructuredProductReview.com.

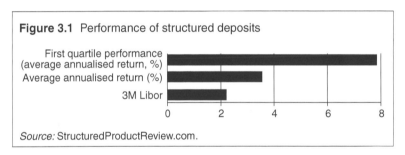

Figure 3.1 Performance of structured deposits

Source: StructuredProductReview.com.

Annualised performance of capital-at-risk FTSE 100 linked structured products

The second data set (Table 3.3) produced isolated the performance of the capital-at-risk structured products, excluding any deposits or capital protected products.

Annualised performance of FTSE 100 linked structured deposits

The performance of structured deposits came next (Figure 3.1). It is interesting to consider the performance of structured deposits (which are sometimes considered as a cash alternative) against the actual performance of cash.

As a cash proxy, SPR used three-month Libor, finding that over the same terms as the matured FTSE 100 linked structured deposits three-month Libor displayed an average annualised return of just over 2%, more than 1% below the average annualised return of the structured deposits, and well below the average annualised return of the first quartile of these products, which was nearly 8%.

Annualised performance of capital-at-risk structured products

The study broke its analysis down to a more granular level, with regard to capital-at-risk structured product performance.

By definition, this excluded any structure that protected all of an investors' capital from market risk, investments and/or deposits.

Impressively, SPR found that of all the FTSE 100 capital-at-risk products to have matured since November 2008 less than 1% had matured with any loss of capital due to market movement. Equally impressively, only just over 8% matured with nothing more than return of invested capital, and, in comparison to these products, which did what they said on the tin in terms of providing protection from a defined level of market downside, the average FTSE 100 Index loss was 6.3% for the same time periods.

Most impressively, over 91% of all the FTSE 100 linked capital-at-risk products to have matured, over the time period of the study, delivered positive gains for investors, whether as income or capital growth.

Annualised performance of capital-at-risk FTSE-100 autocall products

Splitting the capital-at-risk products down by product strategy/ type, the first subset analysed was the doyen of the industry, autocalls. Of all the capital-at-risk, FTSE 100 linked, autocall products to have matured, 97% delivered a positive gain, and the average annualised gain was an impressive 9.19%.

Just 3% of the autocalls that matured failed to deliver any gains, but notably no FTSE 100 linked autocall products to have matured resulted in any capital losses.

Annualised performance of capital-at-risk FTSE 100 linked digital growth products

Looking at capital-at-risk digital growth products, SPR found equally compelling performance statistics. The average digital product delivered 6% annualised return. The average of the top quartile delivered over 10%.

Perhaps the most compelling aspect of the analysis of digital product performance identified, however, was that none of the products would have been outperformed by the performance of the FTSE 100 Index itself.

Annualised performance of capital-at-risk FTSE 100 linked "super-tracker" (geared growth) products

Lastly, the geared super-trackers data showed similarly impressive actual performance.

The average capital-at-risk, FTSE 100 linked, super-tracker delivered close to 6% annualised, with the average of the top quartile delivering nearly 12%.

Again, notably, similarly to the digital products, where the cap of these super-tracker products had been reached, the FTSE 100 Index had never outperformed the returns generated.

The comparable FTSE 100 Index performance over the same time periods as those of the maturing digital and super-tracker products showed only 4% annualised gains, highlighting the strong outperformance delivered not just by the best structured products but even by the average product.

CONCLUSION

The structured product proposition for investors, in the UK, is a strong one. The concept and principles of structured products meet the fundamental interests of investors. Performance has been good, but the fact is that it has not been plain sailing for the industry, up to the time of writing, in the UK.

Structured products offer investors solutions that active mutual funds cannot and passive mutual funds do not. Structured products solve the most fundamental interest of many investors, removing or reducing exposure to unnecessary risk, ie, market/asset downside. Critically, structured products also do what they do as a contract, as legal obligations. This is all positive. So, why the hard journey for structured products?

The embedded position of the mutual funds industry in the UK is definitely one factor. Its position is mostly a function of the fact that it came first. But, imagine if structured products had come first: if, instead of launching the first unit trust in 1931, M&G had launched a structured product.

In addition, specific industry events have echoed loudly for a long time, fundamentally colouring and dividing the opinions of commentators, advisers and investors. These isolated incidents have cast shadows over the industry, and it is hard to rebut the perception (and perhaps the reality) of structured products used by UK high street banks and building societies, particularly in respect of structured deposits and the calibre of advice. The perception has not been good, and this has long been a thorn in the side of the industry.

But the innovation potential with structured products is unparalleled by any other investment option, including "traditional" funds.

The performance offered and delivered, as evidenced by the first performance review to have been conducted on the sector, is compelling and should be persuasive. The performance data also highlights that structured products bend and break the relationship between the markets' risk and returns and investors' risk and returns. They can generate predefined returns for predefined levels of risk, and do so with no active fund management process risk.

Further, their unique selling point is that they provide investment propositions based upon legal contractual obligations, precisely delivering exact stated levels of returns for the exact stated levels of risk. This is absolutely compelling, but has been poorly understood in the UK.

Greater understanding of the structured product sector in the UK would clearly be positive. More transparency regarding actual past returns, highlighting the superior risk–return profiles of structured products, would be good news, and proof of the value of structured products.

The industry needs to do more to promote itself, but it must also continue to do more to raise its own bar. If the future looks anything like the past, for the industry, we can speculate about what can be expected: will it be a case of "the more things change, the more things will stay the same"? That is, opinion will continue to be polarised, resulting in fragmented recognition of the industry's positives and its value and therefore limited support for and sales of its products.

On the other hand, if the industry can continue to evolve and collectively get it right, and gain widespread recognition for its credentials, approach and proposition, it will increasingly enjoy strong support and have the bright future it deserves.

1   See http://www.StructuredRetailProducts.com.

2   The demise of Keydata technically should not be covered in this chapter, but as it was confused by so many people with being a structured product event, we explain what it actually was. The irony is that it proves one of the major benefits of structured products once it is properly understood.

3   Many passive funds are offered by the same houses that also run active propositions.

4   Some provider groups accounted for more than one provider entity, eg, a global group may have issued products via its asset management brand as well as its life company and its retail bank, ie, could be counted as three providers.

5   Discount brokers are firms that do not provide advice but instead provided discounts to investors that are "self-directed", ie, make their own decisions about what they want to invest in (often in response to marketing).

6   Chase de Vere was not a discount broker, but used to operate a very successful centralised marketing arm.

7   The market scaled new heights, driven by the technology, media and telecoms (TMT) boom that was later to become a bubble and that burst.

8   Financial Services Authority (2003b) introduced this new product label, which added to their previous definition of "precipice bonds".

9   This point is actually a bone of contention for IFAs, as Keydata was actually categorised by the regulator as an intermediary, resulting in compensation scheme levies eventually landing on advisers, as opposed to providers.

10   Data from www.StructuredProductReview.com.

REFERENCES

Currie, M., 2010, "Structured Products Sales Soar", *Investors Chronicle*, January 25, URL: http://www.investorschronicle.co.uk/2012/02/22/structured-products-sales-soar -0GoWF4aT3G RgNgvyp0yhVI/article.html.

Financial Services Authority, 2003a, "FSA Guidance Note 7", February 19, URL: http:// www.fsa.gov.uk/pubs/guidance/guidance7.pdf.

Financial Services Authority, 2003b, "Clarification and Revision of Financial Promotion Rules and Guidance", Consultation Paper CP188, July, URL: http://www.fsa.gov.uk/ pubs/cp/cp188.pdf.

Investment Management Association, 2013, "Retail Sales: Last 10 Years", November, URL: http://www.investmentfunds.org.uk/fund-statistics/retail/?what=graph&show= 12.

Reeve, N., 2013, "Passive Funds at Record Levels in UK", *Financial Times*, URL: http:// www.ft.com/cms/s/0/65e4c046-1497-11e3-b3db-00144feabdc0.html#axzz2mzgSYwjt.

4

Europe: An Overview

Simon Harris
Mu Capital

This part of the book charts the evolution of the structured product markets in mainland Europe. It is the story of that continent's varied financial markets, which, despite attempts to homogenise them, from the introduction of the unified currency in 1999 to countless centrally originated (but locally implemented) regulatory and fiscal directives, have remained steadfastly idiosyncratic.

THE EARLY DAYS

Back when this author was an editor for the website StructuredRetail Products.com, a number of providers were keen to give Dr Robert Benson (at Midland Bank) a run for his money for having written one of the first structured products. Here the fact that there is no formal definition of what constitutes a structured product comes into play.[1] Vito Schiro's UBS office sent over a scan – the earliest documented claim – of an advertisement for Guaranteed Return on Investments Units in the SMI, launched by UBS forerunner Swiss Bank Corp (SBC) in January 1991, some six months later.

Indeed, SBC appears to have beaten Société Générale to first place in continental Europe, though Société Générale claims that the first European structured fund, Franvalor Variance, was launched in 1991 through the Société Générale retail network, with subscriptions open until March 1992. The capital-guaranteed fund was linked to the performance of France's Cac40 stock index.

"Other banks had launched capital-guaranteed products, but they did not use a fund format," said Ron Oman, then head of communications for the global equities and derivatives solutions business at Société Générale Corporate and Investment Banking. "The idea that retail networks could be important distributors of equity derivatives

Table 4.1 The European structured retail products market (as of year-end 2012)

Country	Outstanding amounts (€ bn)	Market share (%)
Italy	204	27
Germany	134	17
France	81	11
Belgium	79	10
UK	59	8
Spain	42	5
Others	170	22
Total	769	100

through funds was very new. We accessed new clients with low competition because US banks were targeting asset managers as clients, not retail networks."

So, in 1999, amid the optimism of the new European currency and the approaching new millennium, structured products had already started to make their presence felt across the continent, albeit somewhat under the radar, hidden in local "wrappers", the work of banks' quantitative structuring desks presented to retail, private clients and institutions as funds, deposits, life insurance contracts, trusts, medium-term debt programmes of banks, special purpose vehicles – the whole spectrum of legal instruments to raise pooled funds from investors.

By 2004, research firm Capital Markets Daily conservatively estimated that issuance of structured medium-term notes in that year was US$171 billion for 14,300 issues, compared with US$161 billion for 13,000 issues in 2003. Significantly more than half this amount is understood to have been sold in Europe, as the US private banking and retail markets were slower to adopt structured products at a mass market level. In total, at least €111 billion of personal savings were invested in structured products in 2003, up from €96 billion in 2002 and €85 billion in 2001, suggested reports from BNP Paribas, Merrill Lynch and StructuredRetailProducts.com.

By the end of 2012 (Table 4.1), there were around €769 billion invested in publicly issued retail structured products, according to European Securities and Markets Authority (2013). Italy reigned as the largest market in Europe, followed closely by Germany, France, Belgium and then the UK and Spain. In 2012 sales fell to their lowest since 2004, with around €100 billion of sales, compared with around €250 billion at the market's peak in 2007.

By looking in more detail, we will try to understand a little more clearly what characterises some of the publicly visible aspects of these markets and provide a snapshot of their state at the time of writing and suggest where they are headed.

ITALY

Perhaps surprisingly to some, Italy stands out as the largest retail market on a size basis, with in excess of €200 billion under management. The market is dominated by large bancassurance groups Intesa Sanpaol and Unicredit and cooperatives like Banco Populare and the post office (Poste Italiene). At the height of its retail market dominance Poste Italiane raised over €1 billion for two tranches of its Reload2 product, a six-year capital-protected product linked to a basket of indexes (DJ Euro Stoxx 50, S&P 500, Nikkei 225, SMI, Hang Seng), which began in the second half of 2005. The diverse underlying basket in this product is representative of another notable feature in this market.

Although Italian issuers choose to link investments to local index, the FTSE MIB and the Euro Stoxx, investors have tended to be happy buying access to a wide variety of international markets. This contrasts with other markets such as the UK where it is very difficult to market retail products linked to anything other than the local index (FTSE 100). What is it that makes Italian investors so open to underlyings they are likely unfamiliar with? One banker at Unicredit told me that in Italy, especially before 2008, investors trusted the distributor implicitly, and so it was not a problem that the underlyings were not familiar. Indeed, in some deeply traditional (and often wealthy) communities structured products were bought with as little as possible being said about the product details. "A coffee would be drunk, a signature discreetly written. The deal was done."

The relationship manager was trusted to invest in international markets. In the UK, investors have a less personal relationship with distribution and so require products whose underlyings they are more familiar with.

Interestingly, since the collapse of Lehman Brothers in 2008, with increased regulatory scrutiny and the growing trend for listed products, the market has become more parochial or at least more vanilla in terms of its underlying markets. Gone are the baskets of commodities and the international index baskets that used to be marketed to mass audiences by Poste Vita, the post office's life insurance arm. At the time of writing the market has become increasingly similar to others, with Euro Stoxx and MIB dominating the underlying assets for mass-marketed bonds and life contracts, while local and well-known international blue chips dominate the listed market underlyings.

Indeed, the market has changed a lot since the late 1990s, which saw mostly capital-protected structures within life insurance products. This evolved throughout the next decade with increasing numbers of capital-at-risk structures, increasing sold directly via bonds, as issuers started to seize the opportunity to meet their funding needs more cheaply. The market continued to grow with a tendency towards bond-based issuance in spite of setbacks such as the failure of Parmalat and Cirio, both of which left retail bond holders with billions of euros in losses. By 2007, Lamberto Cardia, then president of the Italian regulator Consob, noted the proliferation of structured bonds and the necessity for new rules and regulations in line with the implementation of the European Mifid directive, on November 1, 2013:

> The importance of the retail investor's participation in the structured bond market is emphasized by the number and volume of products offered to the investors. Consob, from May 2006 till now, has approved over 1,000 prospectuses. Another 350 prospectus[es] have already been deposited and are waiting for approval at the moment. Over 40% of these products are structured and we are observing a rising number of products, above all bonds with a high level of complexity. For a long time Consob has been committed to preventing problems regarding the difficulty found by investors in understanding the products and their risk levels. These activities, which have at times caused the disappearance of some product types, will be monitored using quantitative analysis models.

Italy has gone on to become one of Europe's most progressive quantitative disclosure regimes, where all products are reported to the regulator with independent third-party valuations as well as rigorous back-testing, stress-testing and scenario analysis. Additionally, in recent years the market has shifted to a listed products market with issuers listing on Sedex the structured products-dedicated compartment of Borsa Italiana, which launched in 2005.

Although there are now many more structured products issued on exchange than structured bonds issued directly to investors, the volumes of the over-the-counter (OTC) bonds (often sold via life-assurance contracts) continue to outweigh listed issuance.

GERMANY AND SWITZERLAND LISTED MARKETS

The visible structured retail product markets in Germany and Switzerland have evolved in very different ways from most of the other European markets being dominated by listed warrants, notes and certificates, traded mainly in Stuttgart and Frankfurt (for Germany) and in Zurich (for Switzerland). The fact that it is easy and cheap to issue listed certificates on an automated "on exchange" way has led to very high levels of product launches with several hundred new products offered each day.

Over the past 10 years the German and Swiss markets have grown rapidly.

Germany

In Germany, the Deutscher Derivate Verband (DDV), the German Derivatives Association, is the industry representative body for the 17 leading issuers of derivative products in Germany. It was established in February 2008, with offices in Frankfurt am Main and Berlin. The largest association of its kind in the world, DDV serves as a political interest group in Brussels.

DDV's members are among the most important certificate issuers in Germany, representing about 95% of the total market. The association's work is supported by 10 sponsoring members, which include the stock exchanges Stuttgart and Frankfurt am Main, finance portals and service providers.

Once again, wider cultural factors seem to have influenced this market. The nature of the German-speaking markets corresponds to the (positive) Teutonic stereotypes of high efficiency and careful taxonomy. Both Swiss and German markets have developed a precise map of product types.

These are split between shorter term leverage, directional speculative products akin to warrants and contracts for difference, and more long-term investment products. The latter are closer to what the retail structured product market sees in other countries. Investment products are divided into fully capital protected (with coupon/cap and uncapped) and capital-at-risk products, such as express certificates (known elsewhere as autocallables or kickouts), reverse convertibles, discount certificates, bonus certificates and credit-linked notes. Discount certificates are very popular with German investors, accounting for around a quarter of turnover, according to the DDV. The products, which tend to have terms of under a year, will typically link to a blue-chip stock and pay a fixed coupon provided the underlying is above a certain level at maturity. If the stock is below that level, then the investor will take physical delivery of the share or a cash equivalent.

According to figures released by the DDV in mid-2013, the association's estimate of the overall outstanding volume in the German market was €92.2 billion, based on data provided by the 16 participating banks. This figure does not include fund-wrapped, pension and OTC products.

A chief characteristic of the German structured product market is that it tends to be much more "story" driven. That is to say, investors need to understand the investment case behind the product. This explains the predominance of local shares as underlyings; favourites include BASF, BMW and of course the local DAX index. Oil and gold are also popular. It is also indicative of another feature of the German market in that products tend to be "bought" rather than "sold". Investors are much more likely to know what they want and look to find an appropriate product to match their needs rather than simply being sold one of a very small range on offer from their local bank. With so many products in the market, banks need to compete using these stories.

This author remembers asking a German banker, Siegfried Peel, then at Sal Oppenheim, why it was that structured products were so popular with retail investors in Germany. He described the huge fairs where retail investors would turn up to meet providers and find out about the latest investments. The big difference, it seemed, is that German investors are interested in their investments. The German media reports regularly on the latest products, not questioning the

Table 4.2 Investment products

Country	2012 Q2	2012 Q3	2012 Q4	2013 Q1	2013 Q2	Δ2012 Q2(%)*	Δ2013 Q1(%)**
Austria	13,400	13,600	13,500	13,300	12,900	−3.73	−3.01
Germany	92,082	93,501	90,631	89,797	86,886	−5.64	−3.24
Switzerland	139,376	138,026	127,309	131,763	124,871	−10.41	−5.23
Total	244,858	245,127	231,439	234,861	224,658	−8.25	−4.34

* Percentage change between 2013 Q2 and equivalent last year quarter 2012 Q2. ** Percentage change between reporting quarter 2013 Q2 and previous quarter 2013 Q1. The German figures are sourced from the 16 issuers assembled under the umbrella of Deutsche Derivate Verband (DDV) and entail assets from the sales of listed note-based structured retail products to customers based in Germany. The 16 issuers cover about 95% of the German market in these products. The Swiss figures are sourced from the Swiss National Bank and represent all assets in listed note-based structured retail products held in Swiss depots of issuers domiciled in Switzerland. The figures therefore also include, to a small extent, assets from product sales of these issuers outside Switzerland.
Source: EUSIPA.

value of structured products in a generalised manner as in other countries but rather looking at the merits of one product versus another.

The leaders in the German market are mostly local players. DDV figures from 2013 show that Deutsche Bank once again achieved the top ranking (Table 4.2), with a market share of 16.5%, followed by Commerzbank in second place with a share of 15.9%.[2]

Landesbank Hessen-Thüringen retained its third ranking of the previous quarter with a share of 14%. In fourth place was Deutsche Zentral-Genossenschaftsbank, which achieved a market share of 13.5%, while Hypo Vereinsbank occupied fifth place with a share of 9.9%. As is the case in so many markets, the top few players take a disproportionately large share, in this case the top five occupy more than 70%.

It is worth noting that, although money was lost by German retail investors throughout the financial crisis, the bad publicity and accusations of mis-selling surrounding structured products that have dogged other markets have not been so marked thanks in part to the open nature of the listed market. "As the products were listed, pricing remained transparent throughout the crisis and so although investors lost money they didn't lose confidence that the products would not do as they said", suggested structured product director, Carmine Meoli, of Vontobel, a Swiss issuer of listed products.

From November 14, 2013, the DDV has asked its members to become the first to insist that issuers publish the issue price of their products, so that investors can see the margin the banks expect to make on products.

Switzerland

The Swiss market for structured products is dominated by private banking distribution, with the pure retail market being a much smaller part of the business. As in Germany, the Swiss issuers are represented by a large association.

The Swiss Structured Products Association was established on April 4, 2006, to represent the shared interests of issuers. The size of the Swiss market has been estimated at around Swfr166 billion (€134 billion), according to the Swiss National Bank, which monitors the breakdown of client accounts.[3]

Dominant providers include international names like UBS and Credit Suisse but also local private banking issuers such as Julius Baer, Vontobel, Leonteq and ZKB. In terms of distribution outside the larger banks, Switzerland has armies of independent asset managers who act on a discretionary basis on behalf of investors. These self-regulated distributors are often key to the distribution of products in Switzerland, with over 2,000 players and around 11% of the Swiss financial services market worth over Swfr600 billion. The Swiss Association of Asset Managers (SAAM) is the leading industry association of independent asset managers in Switzerland.[4]

The nascent Swiss market being an international centre of private banking and also until the mid-2010s quite opaque, individual deals were rarely seen. Early products, appearing as early as 1995, were often capital-protected notes offering exposure to hedge funds. This gave way to a trend for constant proportion portfolio insurance (CPPI) products, also often linked to hedge funds. These replicated option-like strategies using dynamic asset-allocation techniques: essentially, investors' money is moved between cash-type "safe assets" and the underlying fund or "risky assets". The proportion in risky or safe assets is determined by a formula that calculates how much needs to be held in cash to guarantee the investors' capital at maturity. The problem with the early versions of these strategies was that if the risky assets performed badly early on, then the capital was allocated to safe assets for the remainder of the term, thereby losing the potential for higher returns. This is known as being "locked in". During the bear market of 2000–2 a number of CPPI products became locked in, frustrating many investors, especially those who had borrowed to invest in the products and then had to continue to pay the interest on the loans.

The structured products market was revived in 2003 by the introduction of conditional capital protection, which gave the investors in this market what they wanted, ie, capital protection with full participation. This led to the issuance of callable yield notes on indexes, bonus coupon notes, equity yield notes and capital-protected reverse convertibles, with a knockout on the capital protection, all of which have continued to grow in popularity.

As in Germany, there is an agreed taxonomy or "map" for naming structured product payoffs, also split into leverage (warrants, sometimes with stop losses) and investment products, which are split into capital protection, yield enhancement, participation and investment products with reference entities (linked to the credit of an entity other than the issuer).

With regards to underlyings, products linked to local shares tend to dominate, although interest rates, currencies and bonds all feature in the extensive listed market. Investment periods tend to be short (less than two years) and products are generally quite simple. Reverse convertibles massively dominate the numbers of issued investment products, although capital-protected and participation products do attract large sizes according to the Swiss National Bank, which sees a fairly even spread across all product types in terms of volumes (Swiss Banking 2011).

Swiss products are overwhelmingly issued as debt directly to investors and (as noted above) often on the local exchange, Scoach. In response to the financial crisis in 2008, the Swiss Stock Exchange (Six) developed a collateralisation mechanism. It was worried that counterparty risks would scare investors off structured notes and so created a mechanism called collateral secured instruments (COSI), which allows issuers to mitigate counterparty risk by depositing collateral with the exchange in the form of securities or cash deposits. The collateral is marked-to-market on a daily basis. Additionally, the value of the COSI product itself is evaluated daily by two independent fair-value providers. Based on these prices, the necessary amount of collateral is deposited by the issue, generally in the form of investment-grade bonds specified by the Swiss National Bank.

BELGIUM

With around €79 billion outstanding, the Belgian market is considered the largest in Europe on a per capita basis, with structured products representing well over 8% of household assets in Belgium (ESMA report, July 2013).

Belgium is a highly concentrated market with three main players (KBC, Fortis/BNP and ING) taking between 70% and 80% of the market. Competition between these providers is intense, with new structures being offered on a regular basis and popular products being copied quickly.

Most Belgian structures tend to be sold via unit-linked life insurance contracts or via funds reflecting the domination of large bancassurance distribution. The trends as to whether fund or life wrappers dominate are often dictated by regulatory or tax regimes.

In 2013, for example, a tax on life-wrapped products has been increased from 1.1% to 2%, while fund managed products suffered from regulatory pressure in 2010 and 2011. A smaller but significant part of the market, the 30% or so that is not dominated by bancassurance groups, is issued as direct securities.

One example of a unit-linked life product is MI Security EMU Consumers 1, being sold in November 2013 by KBC Life. It is a 5.5-year structure issued by KBC Bank that offers a return based on a basket of 20 shares. It pays 100% of any rise in the average price of the basket capped at 80%. If the basket falls, however, the investor's maximum loss is capped at 10%. The final basket level will be the average of monthly readings taken over the last 12 months of investment.

In the early days of the Belgian market, life-wrapped growth products dominated and, starting from the mid-1990s, Belgium's CGER Assurances, the life arm of a private banking group, half owned by Fortis, issued a very popular series of products offering capital-protected exposure to the local Bel20 index. Products tended to have long durations of between 8 and 12 years in order to benefit from tax advantages for this wrapper.

By 2005, the market had grown dramatically and income products started to gain traction too, with over a quarter of all products issued being linked to interest rates in one form or another. These products tended to use steepener payoffs. A typical example is Fortis's B Fix 2006 Bond 13 Spread Coupon, a 12.5-year capital-protected income fund (Sicav) linked to the euro swap rate.[5]

For the first four years the product pays a coupon of 4.5%. Then in the following years it pays three times the difference between the 10Y EUR swap rate and the 2Y EUR swap rate, subject to a minimum of 2% and a maximum of 8%.

Throughout 2005 and 2006 capital-protected growth funds and life contracts and steepeners linked to rates gathered significant assets for all the major providers in the Belgian market.

Leading up to the financial crisis in 2008, Belgian banks, along with many others, struggled to maintain liquidity, thereby affecting secondary market valuations of structured products. Subsequent changes in the financial services landscape included the sale of Fortis Bank, which was first partly bought by the Belgian government in 2009, then fully purchased by the government and sold to BNP Paribas, which initially took a 75% stake but completed the purchase in 2013. KBC took bailouts in 2008 and 2009.

Although things have improved dramatically since then, the Belgian regulator, FSMA (the Financial Services and Markets Authority), has responded with perhaps the most dramatic reaction to the crisis in terms of the structured products market.

In June 2011, the FSMA called upon the financial sector not to distribute to retail investors structured products that "are considered unnecessarily complex".

The FSMA made it clear that this meant that firms signing up to the moratorium should not sell any products that had limited upside but no limit on the downside, such as reverse convertibles, it also said that digital options, barrier options and conditional capital are overly complex for retail investors. Additionally, it said that not more than three mechanisms should be used within one product. It defined retail as clients with a net worth of less than €500,000.

Perhaps unsurprisingly, following the announcement of the moratorium, the issuance of capital-at-risk products fell significantly. In 2013, however, the phoenix-like market started to register a growing number of issuers catering to investors outside the moratorium.

Since August 2012, when the moratorium officially came into effect, almost all distributors have signed up voluntarily, with the exception of Commerzbank, Natixis and a number of independent financial advisers, including Alternea and AIK Group.

By summer 2013, the FSMA hailed the project a success, saying it had led to a simplification of the market. "Since the introduction of the moratorium, seven out of ten structured products use a maximum of two mechanisms to calculate the return," said Jean-Paul Servais, chair of the FSMA at the launch of authority's annual 2012 report. "Before the moratorium some products counted seven mechanisms or more".

The FSMA said that, of the 556 products launched since the moratorium, 413 complied with the strict rules of the moratorium and reported an increase, both in the number of newly issued structured products and in sales volumes.

FRANCE

France has always been considered one of the key structured products markets in Europe as well as a training ground for financial engineers. Once again, a story of nurture as much as nature, the structured product market reflects the country's focus on engineering as well as a financial services culture that is dominated, as in Italy, by state owned institutions such as the post office (La Poste) as well as large mutuals such as Banque Populaire. The engine of the industry is certainly centred at Société Générale and rival BNP Paribas, while the distribution power within France lies with the state-backed savings banks such as Caisse D'Epargne.

During the early part of the market's evolution, SG and BNPP targeted retail fund managers with captive mutualised and state-owned distribution. These managers, such as Federal Gestion, the asset management arm of Arkea Mutual, a mid-tier cooperative of agricultural communities in Brittany and the Massif Centrale would invest in assets in order to offer capital protection as well as a growth strategy, generally linked to the local Cac40 index. The early products were generally eight years long in order to fit in with the typical minimum tax-efficient term of a life assurance contract. They had simple descriptive names like "option guarantee actions" and "protected equity options".

The market grew rapidly as fund management houses took up the innovation that allowed capital-protected defined returns with minimal active management (as with most structured products, assets that provide the return are purchased for the whole term from day one) but with investors who paid annual fees, similar to any other managed fund. SG and BNPP themselves developed large asset managers within which they could distribute products through their own branches.

As the market developed throughout the late 1990s, the underlyings grew more diverse, the payoffs grew more exotic and so did the names. Also, the terms were split clearly between life products, which were eight years, and direct investments (six years) that could be held in the PEA, a local tax-free wrapper.

Unfortunately, this period of growth in the structured products market coincided with the growth of the dot-com bubble and as products matured in the early 2000s investors began to see disappointing returns. The investor with the highest profile was perhaps "l'affaire Benefic". The Benefic products typified the way in which large French distributors, in this case the post office and its asset management arms (Sogeposte), had embraced structured products and started to market them en masse, with glossy posters and big public launches.

The Benefic product, whose capital was not guaranteed, was sold to 300,000 customers at the end of 1999 and the beginning of 2000. The result? When the product matured three years later, the savers saw their initial capital eroded by between 12% and 36%, depending on which tranche of Benefic they invested in. It is not the only product of its kind to have ended in disappointment. The Caisse D'Epargne, with its Ecureuil Europe 2003, or Carrefour, with Millennium 3, in particular, met the same fate.

The 2000s were littered with stories of legal action and accusations of mis-selling, and by 2005 the outcry over the sale of Benefic prompted the Ministry of Finance to commission a report into the sale of financial products in France. The report made various proposals in regards to the marketing of structured products. This author spoke to the French regulatory chief at that time, Pauline Leclerc Glorieux, who said that proposition underpinning a product should be explained in plain French, and that its risk–reward profile should be made clear, and demonstrated with examples of the product's potential and actual performance:[6] "It should be clear that a product forgoes dividend and part of the upside of the market in order to provide protection."

Following the regulatory fallout of the early 2000s, the French market saw very few capital-at-risk products, although structures continued to include exotic names and esoteric payoffs. A classic example is Al Dente 7. Launched in 2006 by state-backed manager Ecureuil Gestion, this eight-year fund was linked to a basket of 15 shares. At maturity, the performance of each share in the basket is measured, with a minimum performance per share corresponding to a 40% rise for the five best-performing shares, a 40% fall for the five worst-performing shares and 0% for the five remaining shares. The product offers a minimum capital return of 100% at maturity, plus 90% of the average of all share performances in the basket.

As in all markets, the financial crisis of 2008 took its toll on all investor products, and accusations of mis-selling continued as product returns failed to meet investor expectations. Regulatory scrutiny increased and the retail market saw volumes decline. The result of these changes was the evolution of the landscape of the financial services market, which has, in turn, affected the structured product space. Distribution via financial advisers has grown significantly and, perhaps counter-intuitively, so have capital-at-risk products. Fund-wrapped products have lost their dominance in the post-crisis years, and notes wrapped in life assurance wrappers have become more possible, probably as they are cheaper and, arguably, more transparent. More foreign issuers, such as Barclays, Credit Suisse and Deutsche Bank, have joined the public offer market, leveraging the growing independent distributors, and the burgeoning listed market has, as in other countries, attracted growing support from investors and issuers alike. Although the large bancassurance networks such as Credit Agricole continue to dominate distribution, a polarisation seems to be occurring between those very retail product producers and the emerging independent financial adviser market. It will be interesting to see how this develops.

CONCLUSION: PRODUCT MATURITY

As can be seen from this whistle-stop "grand tour" of the continental markets, there are as many differences as there are similarities in the key structured product market, and although there are some trends that transcend borders, such as increased and centralised regulatory control and a trend towards listed, liquid and transparent delivery mechanisms, the differences are also significant. Market structures and distribution networks are key to the shape of each individual market, as are factors such as the tax regime and the history and culture of investing that has defined investor tastes. It will be fascinating to see how technological and regulatory developments such as improved harmonisation affect the market over the coming years. One thing for sure is that the multi-faceted and endlessly flexible way in which structured products can appear will ensure their survival.

1   "It is very much a question of definition of what a structured product is in the end, but we have a good case to make", said UBS's European head of equity derivatives, Vito Schiro, in 2000.

2   For more information regarding 2013 Q2 see http://www.derivateverband.de/DE/MediaLi brary/Document/PM/02%202013%20Marktanteile,%202.%20Quartal%202013,%20EN.pdf.

3   See data for 2013 Q1 on page 8 of http://www.svsp-verband.ch/download/news_content/ 851_market_report_sspa_october_2013.pdf.

4   See http://www.swissbanking.org/en/20110107-bro-vermoegensverwaltungsgeschaeft-rva .pdf.

5   See http://services.bnpparibas-ip.com/doc/pros/FOBF06_FP_DUT_BE_1105.pdf.

6   StructuredRetailProducts.com, October 6, 2005.

REFERENCES

European Securities and Markets Authority, 2013, "European Economic Report on Retailisation in the EU", Report no. 1.

Swiss Banking, 2011, Wealth Management in Switzerland: Status Report and Trends", URL: http://www.svsp-verband.ch/download/news_content/851_market_report_sspa _october_2013.pdf.

5

The Market in Asia

Angel K. Y. Wu

The booms and busts in the Asian structured products industry have been associated with key market events such as the Asian financial crisis in 1997–98, the Severe Acute Respiratory Syndrome (SARS) outbreak in 2002–3 and the fall of Lehman Brothers in 2008. This chapter covers the structured product trend in five Asian markets: Hong Kong, Singapore, Korea, Taiwan and China.

HONG KONG AND SINGAPORE GET BACK TO BASICS AFTER GROWING COMPLEX

Hong Kong stood out among its Asian peers (excluding Japan) in structured product development in the 1990s. This could be related to the size of its stock market – the second largest in Asia after Taiwan in 1991 and the biggest from 1992–2000 (based on statistics from the World Federation of Exchanges) – which positioned itself as the pioneer to provide deposit and equity alternatives. In the early 1990s, currency deposit certificates, equity bonds, covered warrants, guaranteed products, equity swaps and over-the-counter (OTC) options were mainstream structured products offered to private banking and institutional investors.

The currency deposit certificate was first introduced to Hong Kong private banking investors in the late 1980s, but it did not become popular until the mid-1990s. As time went on, the currency deposit certificate became known as the dual currency deposit (DCD) or premium deposit (PD). The underlying of this instrument is a currency pair (for example AUD as the base currency and USD as the alternate currency) for which an investor can earn a higher yield than the base currency deposit rate subject to the risk of converting the base currency to the alternate currency at an unfavourable exchange rate. In Singapore, this instrument has been offered to private banking investors since the early 1990s. In the late 1990s, banks in Hong Kong and Singapore began to actively market this product to retail investors.

Equity bonds are issued at a discount to par. If the price of the underlying equity is above the cap price (usually plus or minus 10% from the initial spot price of the underlying) of the bond, the bond will be redeemed at par. During 1992–93, the equity-linked note (ELN) – an evolution of equity bonds – was introduced to institutional and private banking investors. An investor holds the view that the underlying equity will be range traded over the life of the product and purchases the note for yield enhancement. If the price of the underlying equity does not fall below the strike price at maturity, the investor will get back the notional amount at par. Otherwise the investor will receive the underlying equity at the strike price, incurring a loss. The equity-linked deposit (ELD) is the deposit form of the ELN and is widely accessible to retail investors.

The issuance of equity bonds or ELNs grew in tandem with the size of the covered warrants market. A covered warrant gives an investor the right (but not the obligation) to buy or sell the underlying equity at a specific price. A covered warrant is issued by a financial institution and not by the company of the underlying equity. The warrant is "covered" as the issuer owns some of the underlying equities. An issuer profited from selling expensive options through covered warrants issuance and buying cheap options from equity bonds or ELNs. Covered warrants could fetch a higher premium as they were targeted to retail investors who were less sensitive to option pricing. Following the relaxation of the requirements of minimum market capitalisation and free float for covered warrant issuance in Hong Kong, the number of covered warrant issuers jumped from three during the period 1991–94 to more than twenty in the period 1995–97 (Arumainayagam 1997).

During 1995–96, Jardine Fleming launched a number of guaranteed products linked to, eg, the Nikkei, USD/JPY and Hang Seng index (Arumainayagam 1997). However, guaranteed products only started to gain traction after the Asian financial crisis in 1997–98. The Hang Seng index tumbled to a low of 6,544.79 points in August 1998 (Figure 5.1). Likewise, Singapore's Straits Times index also plummeted from its 1997 high (Figure 5.2). In an unstable market environment, investors sought deposit or equity alternatives with lower volatility.

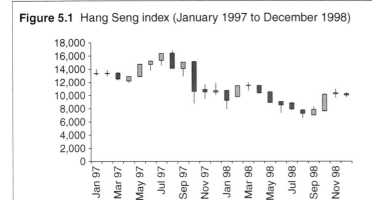

Figure 5.1 Hang Seng index (January 1997 to December 1998)

Source: Bloomberg. Highest: 16820.31 on August 7, 1997. Lowest: 6544.79 on August 13, 1998.

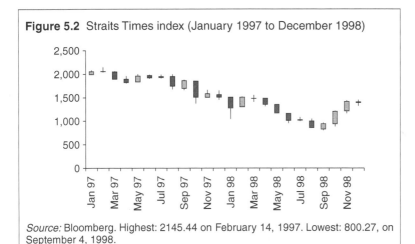

Figure 5.2 Straits Times index (January 1997 to December 1998)

Source: Bloomberg. Highest: 2145.44 on February 14, 1997. Lowest: 800.27, on September 4, 1998.

Singapore and Hong Kong have since then proceeded very much along the same lines with regard to structured product development. Cross-border or offshore booking arrangements, the inclination to have a regional hub in either jurisdiction with the same operational standards, as well as the similarities of legal and regulatory frameworks, are key drivers of such a phenomenon. The behaviour of investors is also similar. This can be explained by having the same dominant ethnic group in both locations. According to its Census and Statistics Department, Hong Kong's population is predominantly Chinese (93.6% in 2011). In Singapore, Chinese people formed

74% of the resident population as of the end of June 2012 (information from the Singapore Department of Statistics (2012)). Owing to proximity, Singapore is also the preferred location for wealthy Thais, Indonesians and Malaysian Chinese to set up offshore banking accounts.

Guaranteed products are commonly based on a combination of the payouts of a zero-coupon bond with that of an option. Index-linked, currency-linked, interest rate-linked, equity-linked and commodity-linked products are available to investors. One popular instrument is callable USD London interbank offered rate (Libor) range accrual note. An investor receives a coupon if the USD Libor rate fixes within a pre-defined range. A conditional coupon is accumulated on a daily basis. The note is callable usually quarterly or semi-annually. The investor receives 100% of the notional amount at maturity or when the note is redeemed early. Other popular products include dual range notes (coupon is linked to the fixing of two underlyings), constant maturity swaps (CMS), steepeners (the coupon is linked to the CMS spread), snowballs (first coupon is fixed; subsequent coupons are dependent on the payout in the immediately preceding period), wedding cakes (there are different coupon-setting ranges, and the conditional coupon is dependent on the range in which the fixing lies), target redemption (the note will be redeemed early once the preset accumulated coupon target is reached) and inverse floater or leveraged inverse floater (performance is linked to a decrease in interest rate). Constant proportion portfolio insurance (CPPI) is also widely used. It provides a capital guarantee by dynamically allocating between the risky and the riskless assets. The strategy allocates to a risky asset with a pre-defined multiplier. There is a protection floor or cushion. When the value of risky asset falls, the strategy will allocate more to the riskless asset and will stop investing in the risky asset for the remaining tenor of the product if the portfolio value drops to the protection floor.

Investment banks and asset management companies began to tap the retail market in the 2000s. In 2000, CMG First State Asset Management launched a Technology, Media and Telecommunication (TMT) Guaranteed Fund in Hong Kong; UOB Asset Management launched the United Capital Guaranteed Funds, the first Central Provident Fund (CPF)-approved, Singapore-dollar-denominated capital guaranteed unit trust in Singapore.

In December 2001, the Securities and Futures Commission (SFC) of Hong Kong eased the placement requirements of derivative warrants at launch and introduced liquidity providers, contributing to the jump in the number of listed derivative warrants from 22 at the end of 2001 to 1,304 at the end of 2005 (Hong Kong Exchanges and Clearing Limited 2006). The need for hedging by warrant issuers planted the seeds of the tremendous growth in structured products in the 2000s. It is important to note that Hong Kong equities with larger market capitalisation and better liquidity are also commonly used as underlying equities of the structured products offered in Singapore.

In 2003, the outbreak of SARS, a respiratory disease that killed a significant number of people in Asia, resulted in a downturn in both the Hong Kong and the Singapore economies. Nevertheless, the quick rebound in the markets created a new scene for structured products. Investors became unsatisfied with guaranteed structures given the upside was not as high as direct investment of the underlying equities.

In the private banking sector, non-principal protected callable range accrual notes linked to an index, an individual equity or a basket of equities became popular. On average, a private bank distributed US$10 million to US$30 million worth of callable range accrual notes on a daily basis. The coupon was usually guaranteed for the first observation period. The conditional coupon was accrued on each exchange business day when the price of the underlying security is at or above the coupon accumulation strike price. An investor will get back 100% of the notional amount when the note is redeemed early by the issuer or if the embedded option is not exercised at maturity. If the underlying security is a basket of equities and the option is exercised at maturity by the issuer, the investor will usually receive the worst performer of the equity basket. Best-of-option (the investor receives the best-performing underlying security in the basket) may also be used, but is not as popular as worst-of-option, which can be offered at a lower note price.

During 2002/3, the first equity accumulator (originating in the foreign exchange market) was introduced to private banking investors. The equity accumulator is a combination of barrier call and put options. An investor is able to accumulate the underlying equity at a price lower than the initial spot price, subject to the knock-out event when the price of the underlying equity is at or above the knock-out price (which is higher than the initial spot price). On the other hand, the investor needs to continue to accumulate the equity at the strike price even if the share price falls below the strike price. The investor will also miss the upside opportunity of the underlying equity due to the knock-out event. The most common knock-out level is 103% or 105% above the initial spot price. Accumulation is commonly on a daily basis but settlement is either monthly or every two weeks. The knock-out event may happen based on the closing level of the underlying equity or at any time on an exchange business day. The contract can be leveraged, meaning the investor will be obliged to purchase twice (or sometimes three times depending on the contract) the daily number of shares if the share price on the relevant exchange business day is lower than the strike price. A leveraged accumulator has a lower strike price than a non-leveraged accumulator.

Example 5.1 (Illustrative example of an accumulator).

- **Underlying:** Stock A listed on the Hong Kong Exchange.
- **Initial spot price:** HK$100.
- **Tenor:** 1 year.
- **Strike price (or accumulation price):** HK$95, 95% of the initial spot price.
- **Knock-out price (or early termination price):** HK$105, 105% of the initial spot price.
- **Knock-out event (or early termination event):** daily closing price.
- **Daily number of shares:** 100.
- **Leverage factor:** 2 times.
- **Settlement:** monthly (assume 20 accumulation days in the first month).
- **Knock-out settlement:** knock-out day + 2 exchange business days.

Scenario 1: If, on the tenth accumulation day, Stock A closes at HK$106, the contract is knocked out or terminated early, and the investor is obliged to purchase 900 shares (being 100 shares per day × 9 days; no accumulation on the knock-out day) at HK$95 per share, on condition that Stock A has never closed below the strike price. As the contract is knocked out or terminated early, the investor bears no further obligation or liability under the contract.

Scenario 2: If no knock-out event has occurred, and in the first month Stock A has closed below HK$95 for 10 exchange business days, on the first-month settlement date the investor is obliged to purchase 3,000 $(3,000 = (100 \times 20/2 \times 1) + (100 \times 20/2 \times 2))$ shares, at HK$95 per share.

A lot of investors were attracted by the opportunity to profit (due to a lower accumulation price than the initial spot price) in a short period of time (thanks to the knock-out feature). For instance, under scenario 1 above, when the accumulator is knocked out or terminated early, an investor earns HK$11 (= HK$106 – HK$95) per share, in 10 days, compared with a profit of only HKD 6(= HK$106 – HK$100), from outright stock purchase. As the chance of making short-term gain is high during a bull market, the accumulator quickly became the most popular structured product among private banking investors. The average daily notional amount offered by a private bank was estimated to be US$10 million to US$30 million. The contract size of an accumulator for some corporate investors and family offices could even reach US$100 million.

Some investors were not satisfied with a too-soon-to-occur knock-out event in a bull market as they could not continue to enjoy accumulating the underlying equity at a favourable strike price when the contract was knocked out or terminated early. The guaranteed accumulator was introduced to provide a guaranteed accumulation period for an investor regardless of the occurrence of a knock-out event during the guaranteed period. Based on scenario 1 of the illustrative example above, under a non-guaranteed accumulator contract, an investor purchased 900 shares at the strike price after the occurrence of a knock-out event. If accumulation is guaranteed for the first month, the investor would be able to purchase 2,000 shares (ie, 100 shares per day × 20 accumulation days) at the strike price.

The earlier the contract is knocked out, the higher the effective yield of the investment, and this is further magnified by buying the contract on a margin or leveraged basis. Most investors do not need to maintain 100% of the contract notional amount with the bank.

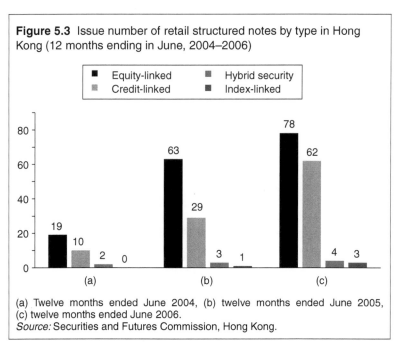

Figure 5.3 Issue number of retail structured notes by type in Hong Kong (12 months ending in June, 2004–2006)

- ■ Equity-linked
- ▩ Credit-linked
- ▩ Hybrid security
- ■ Index-linked

(a) Twelve months ended June 2004, (b) twelve months ended June 2005, (c) twelve months ended June 2006.
Source: Securities and Futures Commission, Hong Kong.

The initial margin is usually 20–40%. If the contract size is US$1 million and the initial margin is 30%, an investor is only required to maintain US$300,000 cash with the bank when the contract starts. Maintenance margin fluctuates with the spot price of the underlying equity during the life of the contract.

In the summer of 2007, Bear Stearns' US subprime mortgage exposure set alarm bells ringing, triggering the beginning of the global financial crisis. Decumulators, the reverse of accumulators, were introduced in light of demand for bearish products. Decumulators enable an investor to sell the underlying equity at a strike price higher than the initial spot price, subject to a knock-out event. The knock-out level is usually 95% of the initial spot price. A leveraged decumulator is also common. An investor can dispose of the equity at a higher strike price subject to the risk of selling twice the daily number of shares if the price of the underlying equity is higher than the strike price. Some investors use decumulators as a hedging tool against an accumulator with the same underlying equity. However, when the accumulator is knocked out while the decumulator is not, the investor ends up facing the risk of buying shares at an unfavourable price in order to settle the decumulator obligation –

the contractual agreement to sell the underlying equity at a fixed strike price, even if the market price is above the strike price, until maturity or early termination of the contract. There is also a more complex structure that enables an investor to accumulate and decumulate simultaneously by netting out the difference in the two strike prices, subject to knock-out.

In retail banking, the development of structured products has been equally strong. In Hong Kong, the number of retail structured products jumped from 31 in the 12 months ending in June 2004, to 147, or HK$9.8 billion (equivalent to US$1.26 billion), in the 12 months ending in June 2006 (Securities and Futures Commission of Hong Kong 2006). On October 14, 2003, Cheung Kong (Holdings) Limited announced the set-up of a HK$10 billion (or US$1.29 billion) Retail Note Issuance Programme. In the company announcement, it was cited as "the first of its kind in Asia". On March 5, 2007, Standard Chartered Bank announced the offer of non-principal protected ELN in Singapore. In the bank's press release, it stated the bank was the "first retail bank in Singapore to offer choice of five international markets". The five markets are Singapore, Hong Kong, the US, the UK and Japan.

Callable bull/bear contracts (CBBCs), introduced in June 2006, are another key retail product in Hong Kong. CBBCs are an alternative product to derivative warrants with a knock-out feature. They are in-the-money instruments. Trading of CBBCs will be ceased (a mandatory call event) if the warrant is knocked out. There are two categories of CBBC: category N has the same call price as the strike price, while category R has a call price higher (bull contract) or lower (bear contract) than the strike price. Category N CBBCs are rare in Hong Kong. Volume started to pick up after the 2008 global financial crisis as the supply of volatility was lacking. Investors trade CBBCs as they are more like a delta-one product and less affected by implied volatilities. According to Hong Kong Exchanges and Clearing Limited, as of June 17, 2013, there were 1,145 CBBC issued on the Hong Kong Exchange, versus 24 at the end of 2006. In the first half of 2013, CBBCs accounted for about 10–15% of daily market turnover.

On the corporate side, owing to the family-led predominance (which is a cultural phenomenon for Chinese-owned enterprises), a lot of corporations have a loose dividend policy and tend to reinvest their cash. On October 20, 2008, Hong Kong-listed CITIC Pacific

Limited announced a mark-to-market loss of HK$14.7 billion (or US$1.89 billion) due to hedging of the Australian dollar to settle an iron ore mining project. The loss was incurred by the use of leveraged foreign exchange contracts, including target redemption forward contracts.

As investors became hungry for yield, demand shifted away from equity-linked products towards credit-linked products. Investors obtain a higher yield from credit-linked products but are exposed to loss if a credit event of the underlying credit is triggered. According to the Securities and Futures Commission of Hong Kong (2006), the number of credit-linked notes (CLNs) increased from 10 in the 12 months ending in June 2004 to 62 in the 12 months ending in June 2006 (Figure 5.3). Likewise, in Singapore, CLNs gained traction. The heavy exposure to credit-linked notes by retail investors has had a prolonged effect on not only structured product development but also the banking industry in both locations.

The collapse of Lehman Brothers on September 15, 2008 was a key watershed moment. According to the Monetary Authority of Singapore (2009) there were 7,800 retail investors who bought Lehman Brothers' Minibond programme notes through nine distributors. Together with DBS's High Notes 5, Morgan Stanley's Pinnacle Notes (series 9 and 10) and Merrill Lynch's Jubilee Notes (Series 3 Link-Earner notes), about S$520 million (or US$364 million) worth of the notes was sold to retail investors (Monetary Authority of Singapore 2009). The Hong Kong Monetary Authority had received 21,868 complaints of Lehman-related investment products as of September 27, 2012 (Hong Kong Monetary Authority 2012). A total of around HK$20.2 billion (or US$2.61 billion) worth of Lehman-related structured products, of which HK$6.2 billion (or US$0.8 billion) was private placement, was distributed by banks (Legislative Council of the Hong Kong Special Administrative Region 2012). Annual gross sales of structured products in Hong Kong were estimated to have reduced from US$29.5 billion in 2008 to US$6.3 billion in 2009. In Singapore, the number decreased from US$4.8 billion to US$3.2 billion during the same period.

Investors lost confidence in structured products after the fall of Lehman Brothers. Litigations against banks or distributors by private banking, corporate and retail investors were common. Investors and the media gave the nickname "I kill you later" to accumulator

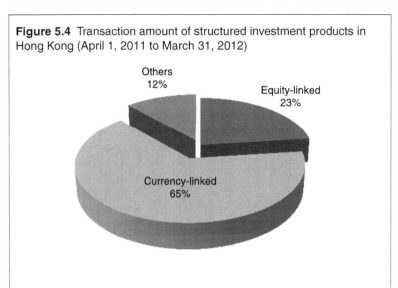

Figure 5.4 Transaction amount of structured investment products in Hong Kong (April 1, 2011 to March 31, 2012)

Others
12%

Equity-linked
23%

Currency-linked
65%

Source: Securities and Futures Commission, Hong Kong.

and "they kill you later" to decumulator. Protests outside retail branches have become a common street scene in Hong Kong. Since the fall of Lehman, demand for complex products or product innovation has become weak. Currency-linked investments have become the most common type (Figure 5.4) of structured investment products (Securities and Futures Commission of Hong Kong 2012). On the equity side, ELN, ELD or equity-linked investment has regained its importance.[1] Short-dated fixed coupon notes (FCNs), which are similar to ELNs but with a guaranteed coupon and a callable feature, started to dominate. Investors also purchased twin-win structures. If the underlying equity or index is knocked out (the knock-out level is above the initial spot price), an investor will get a coupon plus the initial investment amount. If the underlying equity or index is not knocked out, and the knock-in event (the knock-in level is below the initial spot price) has never occurred, the investor will be able to gain from either the up or the down performance of the underlying equity or index.

The regulatory regime has become more stringent. Investor protection is the focal point. In Hong Kong, for instance, "health warning", "cooling period", "key fact statement" and "fee disclosure" are enforced. According to the Securities and Futures and Companies Legislation (Structured Products Amendment) Ordinance

2011, the safe harbour rule that refers to "the minimum HK$500,000 denomination (or approximately US$64,000–65,000) in the form of shares or debentures" and "no more than 50 persons" exceptions for the offer of structured products is no longer available (Securities and Futures Commission of Hong Kong 2013). In Singapore, under the Private Banking Code of Conduct, the Client Advisor Competency Standards (CACS) exam took effect from September 2011 to raise competency of private banking professionals. From January 2012, the Monetary Authority of Singapore has introduced additional guidelines, under the Securities and Futures (Amendment) Bill 2012 and Financial Advisors (Amendment) Bill 2012, for the sale of more complex investment products such as, but not limited to, restrictions on advertisements and prohibition on use of the terms "capital/principal protected" to retail investors (Monetary Authority of Singapore 2012).

Due to lower risk appetite, many investment banks have closed down their derivatives businesses in Hong Kong and Singapore. The industry, however, has not become less competitive as the decline in demand has made the pie smaller. As structured products have become commoditised and every bank is finding ways to cut costs, using an electronic platform to sell structured products will become a new trend in the industry.

SOUTH KOREA WAS ONCE THE FASTEST GROWING STRUCTURED PRODUCTS OR DERIVATIVES MARKET IN ASIA

South Korea was one of the hardest hit countries during the Asian financial crisis of 1997–98. The turmoil took a heavy toll on the economy, with both chaebols (local business conglomerates) and financial institutions being dampened severely. Regulations of financial institutions were loosened as a trade-off of the support package from the International Monetary Fund. The market evolution ended up with increased foreign capital participation, such as the acquisition of Korea First Bank by Standard Chartered Bank and Citibank's purchase of KorAm Bank.

Deregulation and financial reform have been attributed not only to higher foreign capital participation in the banking sector, but also to the rapid growth of the securities and the asset management industries. As of December 2012, there were 61 securities companies and 84 asset management companies in South Korea, according

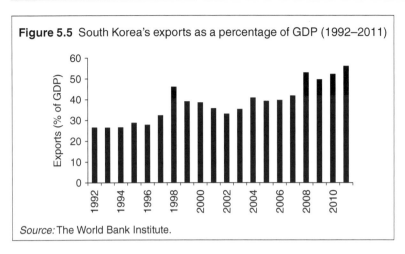

Figure 5.5 South Korea's exports as a percentage of GDP (1992–2011)

Source: The World Bank Institute.

to the statistics related to the "status of financial companies" provided by the Korea Financial Investment Association (KOFIA), compared with 36 securities companies as of the end of 1997 and 28 asset management companies at the end of 1999 recorded in the Financial Supervisory Service (FSS) 1999 Annual Report. Intensified competition has triggered the need for product development.

On the demand front, South Korea's export dominance supports the growth of currency-linked instruments. The country has adopted an export-oriented growth strategy, with exports making up 56% of 2011 GDP, versus 27% in 1992 (Figure 5.5). Currency knock-in–knock-out (KIKO) is one of the most popular products. On expectation that the KRW would remain strong, many exporting companies invested extensively in this product between 2006 and 2007 (Ko and Moon 2011). The investor is able to profit from KRW/USD trades within the knock-in and the knock-out levels. If the knock-out event occurs (ie, the KRW appreciates more than expected), the investor's right to sell USD at a favourable exchange rate ceases to exist. If the knock-in event occurs (ie, the KRW depreciates more than expected), the investor needs to sell USD at an unfavourable exchange rate, resulting in a loss. In 2008, investors incurred substantial losses due to the depreciation of KRW. Nearly 140 lawsuits against the banks regarding the KIKO issue had been filed with the Seoul Central District Court (Yulchon 2011).

The first KOSPI 200 futures contract was introduced in 1996, followed by the listing of the first KOSPI 200 option contract on the Korea Stock Exchange in 1997. Foreign investors got access to the

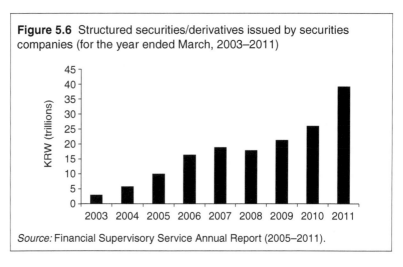

Figure 5.6 Structured securities/derivatives issued by securities companies (for the year ended March, 2003–2011)

Source: Financial Supervisory Service Annual Report (2005–2011).

local equity market mainly through the purchase of one- to three-year USD participation notes. However, the equity-linked structured products market had not been sizeable until equity-linked warrants (ELW) and over-the-counter (OTC) equity-linked securities (ELS) were developed.

According to the Financial Supervisory Service (FSS), structured securities issued by securities companies jumped from W3 trillion (or US$2.57 billion) in 2003 (FSS Annual Report 2005) to W39.2 trillion (or US$34.8 billion) in 2011 (FSS Annual Report 2011) (Figure 5.6). Despite its short history, South Korea's derivatives exchange became the most active in the world (based on the number of contracts) in 2011 (Table 5.1).

Note that the value of contracts traded/cleared in each exchange may vary. An exchange with the highest number of contracts traded/cleared may not necessarily be the largest exchange by contract value, and vice versa.

Equity-linked securities (ELSs) first appeared in 2003, when they, together with warrants and other new instruments, were classified as securities, and companies with an OTC derivative licence were allowed to distribute such products.

The most popular ELSs are the "two-stock autocallable", also known as "two-stock step-down trigger", which is a hybrid instrument with a combination of a debt instrument and options. A two-stock autocallable structure will be terminated early or autocalled if the closing level (ie, the average closing price of at least three days

Table 5.1 Top derivatives exchanges ranking (2011)

Rank by number of contracts traded/cleared
1 Korea Exchange
2 National Stock Exchange of India
3 Multi Commodity Exchange of India (includes MCX-SX)
4 Zhengzhou Commodity Exchange
5 United Stock Exchange of India
6 Shanghai Futures Exchange
7 Dalian Commodity Exchange
8 ASX Group (includes ASX and ASX 24)
9 Osaka Securities Exchange
10 Taiwan Futures Exchange
11 Tokyo Financial Exchange
12 Hong Kong Exchanges & Clearing
13 Singapore Exchange (includes AsiaClear)

Source: Annual Volume Survey, Futures Industry Association, April 17, 2012.

prior to maturity or the volume-weighted average price on the maturity date) of the worst performing stock (ie, the stock with the worst performance against the initial spot price) fixes at, or above, the relevant strike level on the relevant early termination valuation date, and the investor will receive the pre-agreed coupon and the initial investment amount.

If the ELS is not terminated early or autocalled and the closing level of the worst-performing stock is at, or above, its final strike level on the final valuation date, the investor will receive a pre-agreed coupon plus the initial investment amount.

If the early termination event does not occur, and the closing level of the worst performing equity is lower than its final strike level on the final valuation date:

- if a knock-in event has never occurred (ie, the closing levels of all basket underlyings are never lower than the relevant knock-in level on any exchange business day during the tenor of the structure), the investor will receive the pre-agreed coupon and the initial investment amount; or

- if a knock-in event has occurred, the investor will receive the notional amount times the performance of the worst performing equity.

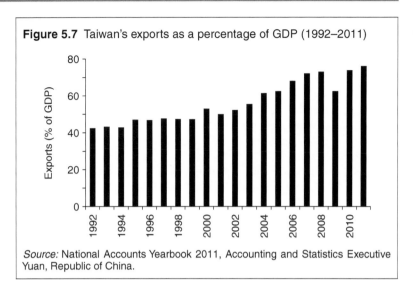

Figure 5.7 Taiwan's exports as a percentage of GDP (1992–2011)

Source: National Accounts Yearbook 2011, Accounting and Statistics Executive Yuan, Republic of China.

The introduction of ELWs in December 2005 added a new page to the history of derivatives development in Korea. An ELW is similar to a plain vanilla option that gives investors the right, but not the obligation, to buy or sell the underlying equity at a predetermined price on or before the expiry date. Retail investors bought ELWs because the instrument allows them to gain exposure to the market with a small investment amount. The knock-out barrier (KOBA) ELW was introduced in September 2010, and Korea bypassed Hong Kong to be Asia's largest warrant market, with an average daily trading value of about W1.6 trillion (or US$1.4 billion) at the end of 2010 (Hong Kong Exchanges and Clearing Limited 2010; Korea Exchange 2011). KOBA ELWs can be terminated if the underlying security reaches the predetermined price level, ie, a bull ELW will terminate earlier if the underlying equity has dropped to a predetermined level, and vice versa for a bear ELW, ie, a bear ELW will terminate earlier if the underlying equity has risen to a predetermined level.

ELWs, being a hedging platform for the OTC positions, has grown hand-in-hand with the ELS market. In a stable and bull market, the investor is able to enjoy an ELS coupon without incurring any loss of the initial investment. In 2007–8, however, when the global equity market was hampered by the breakdown of Lehman Brothers and the subsequent financial crisis, the knock-in level kicked in and a lot of investors suffered from losses.

Aiming to lower volatility in the market and clamp down on "scalpers" – high-frequency traders who profited on small price fluctuations – new regulations such as mandatory education require-ment, minimum deposit rule for investors and quotation restrictions for liquidity providers, were introduced (Jung-yoon 2012). A man-date was also issued to apply a one-day "cooling period" for elderly investors (aged 65 years or above) purchasing derivatives (Mi-ju 2012).

The Asian financial crisis triggered reforms in South Korea, fol-lowed by robust growth in the financial industry. While it is too early to conclude how the collapse of Lehman Brothers and the new reg-ulations have affected industry growth, it is true that the momen-tum in what was once the fastest growing derivatives market in Asia has decreased significantly. According to KRX Fact Book Korea Exchange (2011), average daily trading value of ELWs plunged to W241.6 billion (or US$0.22 billion) at the end of 2012, from its peak of W1.6 trillion (or US$1.4 billion) at the end of 2010.

TAIWAN WAS SEEN AS THE "TESTING GROUND" OF STRUCTURED PRODUCTS

During the early 1990s, despite having one of the largest stock ex-changes in Asia excluding Japan, Taiwan's derivatives market was relatively immature as futures or options exchanges were absent and local financial institutions were not allowed to trade OTC derivatives. Local stocks represented the largest portion of a typi-cal investor's portfolio. Taiwan's onshore derivative products were mainly composed of foreign exchange contracts and interest rate contracts.

The dominant role of exports, which account for two-thirds of GDP (Figure 5.7), supports the demand for foreign exchange deriva-tives in Taiwan. According to the statistics provided by the Bank-ing Bureau of Taiwan's Financial Supervisory Commission (FSC), as of March 2013, foreign exchange contracts accounted for about 55% of the notional amount of outstanding derivatives for domestic banks (including branches of foreign banks), of which more than 99% were for trading purposes. As in most other Asian countries, Dual Currency Investment (DCI) is popular. On top of that, bar-rier options (single or double), digital options and second gener-ation exotic options such as fader (where the notional amount is dependent on the currency fixings that fall within the preset range), target redemption (where an investor is able to sell a currency at a preset strike price, and the option is knocked out when a preset profit threshold is accumulated) and range accrual (where return is dependent on the number of currency fixings that fall within the preset range) are also used.

Interest rate-linked derivatives grew strongly during the between the late 1990s and 2009. Before the Lehman Brothers collapse, investors did not consider that an issuer could go bust, and were active in doing long-dated (usually 10-year) principal protected structures linked to interest rate. The callable USD Libor range accrual note is a typical structure that investors were interested in. Other products, including exotic structures known as snowballs, wedding cakes and CMS steepeners, were also common.

The launch of Japan Capital Guaranteed Trust (CGT) by Jardine Fleming in 1995 instigated a new chapter in the history of structured products. With a minimum investment amount of less than US$400, the product was launched successfully to retail investors. Subsequently, more issuers moved into the market, creating a pool of different varieties of structured products (Chen *et al* 1998).

The collapse of Lehman Brothers has changed the picture. According to a September 15, 2008 press release from the FSC, domestic financial institutions (including banks, securities companies, trust companies and insurance companies) had an estimated exposure of about NT$40 billion or US$1.25 billion in investments and transactions relating to Lehman Brothers. For individual investors (mainly wealth management customers), Lehman Brothers-related structured products also amounted to NT$40 billion or US$1.25 billion (Financial Supervisory Commission 2008). The FSC urged banks to take initiatives to settle investors' complaints, conducted a "special examination" for banks with a large number of disputes or product exposure and indicated rejection of any related applications from banks that failed to resolve disputes at a reasonable rate.

Subsequently, the FSC issued new directions for banks trading in financial derivatives. The new directions define professional and non-professional investors, assign rules on "cooling periods", make the product approval and review processes stronger, and provide guidelines related to marketing and advertising materials. Guidelines for a salesperson's compensation are also provided. Moreover,

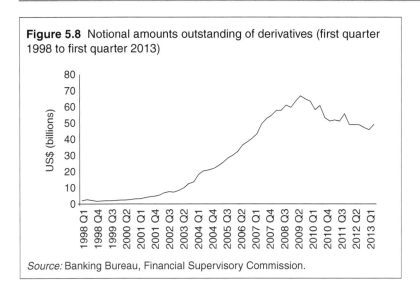

Figure 5.8 Notional amounts outstanding of derivatives (first quarter 1998 to first quarter 2013)

Source: Banking Bureau, Financial Supervisory Commission.

a master agency system was established, under which issuers of offshore structured products are required to maintain an on-shore presence (either a local branch or a local subsidiary, or a local branch or a local subsidiary of a product guarantor as its master agent) to assume relevant legal responsibilities.

The loss in confidence in structured products and the new regulations have resulted in a reduction in the size of the derivatives markets (Figure 5.8). However, given low interest rates, demand for interest rate linked products, in particular fixed-to-float structures (the coupon is fixed in the first few periods and will be linked to a floating rate thereafter) and cap-floor floater (the interest rate is linked to a floating rate subject to a cap and a floor) are relatively popular. Meanwhile, investors have shown interest in long-dated high-yielding AUD- and NZD-linked structures, such as NZD-denominated TOPIX linked notes.

The structured product market has evolved from an "extensive mode" to a "dedicated mode". In January 2013, The FSC amended the "Directions for Banks Conducting Financial Derivatives Business". Banks who want to offer derivatives financial products involving Taiwan and the Mainland China can file the approval application with the central bank directly (Laws and Regulations Database 2013). It will not be surprising to see more new products linked to renminbi (RMB).

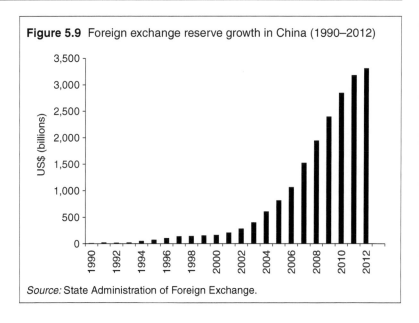

Figure 5.9 Foreign exchange reserve growth in China (1990–2012)

Source: State Administration of Foreign Exchange.

EMERGING GROWTH OF WEALTH STRUCTURING PRODUCTS IN CHINA

China's derivatives history can be traced back to 1990, when the first experimental futures market, the Zhengzhou Commodity Exchange, was opened. Since then, the government has been gradually relaxing measures to open up the derivative market. According to state administration of Foreign Exchange, foreign exchange reserves in China jumped from US$11.09 billion in 1990 to US$3,311.6 billion in 2012 (Figure 5.9), which has driven the need to hedge against foreign exchange and interest rate risks. In 2005, the People's Bank of China published the "Notice on Issues Regarding Expanding Designated Banks' Forward Sale and Purchase of Foreign Exchange Business to Customers and Launching RMB Swaps against Foreign Currencies". Before that, only the four state-owned commercial banks and three joint-stock commercial banks were licensed to engage in currency forward transactions. The notice extended the permission to almost all commercial banks. In 2006, the People's Bank of China promulgated the "Circular of the People's Bank of China on the Relevant Matters Concerning the Pilots of RMB Interest Rate Swap Transaction", a pilot scheme to facilitate financial institutions to hedge against market fluctuation through interest rate swaps.

The Shanghai Stock Exchange (SSE) was founded in 1990. Based on the information from SSE, as of the end of December 2012, there were 954 listed companies, with a total market capitalisation of Rmb15,870 billion (or US$2,523 billion). The development of the stock market has triggered demand for product innovation. Combined with the gradual relaxation of local regulations, structured products have become a growth engine in the financial industry.

Key events that triggered the development of structured products in China include the following.

1. In 2005, the Notice on the Issues of Business Scope of Derivatives Product Transaction by Domestic Commercial Banks was issued. The notice allows domestic commercial banks to engage in derivatives products linked to equities and commodities (Chunling 2009).

2. The Qualified Domestic Institutional Investor (QDII) scheme became effective in 2007. It enables commercial banks to pool funds in the domestic market and invest in the offshore market (China Securities Regulatory Commission 2007).

3. In 2009, the People's Bank of China and the State Administration of Foreign Exchange approved the National Association of Financial Market Institutional Investors to put into effect the Master Agreement on the Trading of Financial Derivatives on the Inter-bank Market. The agreement covers trading of interest rate derivatives, exchange rate derivatives, bond derivatives, credit derivatives and gold derivatives. It was later revised to include equity derivatives.

4. In 2012, the China Insurance Regulatory Commission introduced rules that relax restrictions on the investment of insurance proceeds. The range of eligible investment products was expanded.

5. In 2012, the Securities Association of China won the approval from the China Securities Regulatory Commission (CSRC) for a pilot scheme to engage in derivative business by seven securities companies ("Regulations on Over-The-Counter Trading for Securities Companies"). Seven securities companies are allowed to issue, to transfer and to trade OTC products on this platform.

In China, structured products are mainly offered through the wealth management product platform of commercial banks. The value of wealth management products offered by commercial banks reached Rmb2.5 trillion (or US$397 billion) as of December 2012. Foreign banks accounted for 4.2%. The number of wealth management products was 28,239. The products are mainly divided into four types: fixed return, minimum return guaranteed, principal-guaranteed floating return and non-principal guaranteed floating return. Despite such a short history, the types of options embedded in the products are quite diversified, ranging from vanilla options to range accrual, rainbow options (worst-of or best-of options), knock-in–knock-out options and Asian options (payouts are determined by the average price of the underlying instrument over the preset period).

Concerns about the growth of shadow banking, which off-balance-sheet wealth management products are part of, resulted in tightened regulation by the CSRC in 2013 Q1. Under the new rules, commercial banks have to fully disclose information on wealth management products. Risk warnings are required and misleading representation is prohibited. Despite more stringent regulations, the growth of high net worth individuals should continue to pave the way for China to be a major structured product hub in the region. At the end 2012, the number of Chinese high net worth individuals, individuals with at least Rmb10 million (or US$1.59 million) in investable assets, was 700,00, more than double the number at year-end 2008 (Bain & Company 2013).

CONCLUSION

Each Asian market has its own set of drivers – behavioural, economic or cultural – for structured product growth. The Lehman Brothers breakdown has drawn the markets closer. Investor protection, particularly related to "product suitability" and "disclosure", has become the cornerstone of regulations. Increased awareness of counterparty credit risk and product liquidity risk has also triggered a shift of the demand–supply equation from "extensive" to "selective". In general, "keep it short and simple" has become the norm in the industry.

The author gratefully acknowledges the assistance provided by Mr Wilson W. T. Law for data collection.

1 The Hong Kong Monetary Authority disallowed the use of the term "deposit" for structured investments in 2011. This also applied for DCD in Singapore, which was replaced by "dual currency investment" in 2006.

REFERENCES

Arumainayagam, C., 1997, "Hong Kong", in S. Allen and K. Matthews (eds), *Asian Equity Derivatives Handbook* pp. 115–32 (Jersey: Euromoney Publications).

Bain & Company, 2013, Chinese High Net Worth Individuals Shift Wealth Management Focus From Growing To Preserving Assets; Overseas Diversification On The Rise, Finds New China Private Wealth Report, Press Release, Bain & Company, Inc, May, 7.

Chen, P. W. K., M.-C. Chiang and E. H. Chow, 1998, "An Analysis of the Capital Guaranteed Trust and Its Innovation in Taiwan", in J. J. Choi and J. A. Doukas (eds), *Emerging Capital Markets: Financial and Investment Issues*, pp. 167–77 (Westpoint, CT: Quorum Books).

China Securities Regulatory Commission, 2007, Qualified Financial Institutional Investors Offshore Securities Investment Management Pilot Scheme, China Securities Regulatory Commission website, Central People's Government of the People's Republic of China website, June 21.

Chunling, X., 2009, "Legal Rules of China's Financial Derivatives Products Transactions", Sichuan Academy of Social Sciences, Institute of Finance and Trade Economics, Issue 7, Financial Development Research Shanghai Municipal Development & Reform Info Net, September 14.

Feng, Y., 2013, "2012 Wealth Management Products Issuance Reached a New High, Foreign Banks Expected to Achieve the Highest Return" Puyi Wealth Research, Plexun Bank, January 25, URL: http://bank.hexun.com/2013-01-25/150590922.html.

Financial Supervisory Commission, 2008, "Impacts of the Financial Difficulties of Three Companies Including Lehman Brothers Securities on Local Financial Institutions", Financial Supervisory Commission Republic of China, September 15.

Hong Kong Exchanges and Clearing Limited, 2006,"The Profile of Derivative Warrants Listed in Hong Kong", *Exchange*, October, pp. 51–60.

Hong Kong Exchanges and Clearing Limited, 2010, *HKEx Fact Book 2010*.

Hong Kong Monetary Authority, 2012, "Complaints Statistics Concerning Lehman-Related Investment Products (up to 27 Sep 2012)", September 27.

Jung-yoon, L., 2012, "Trade in Equity-Linked Warrants Collapsing." *Korea Joongang Daily*, April 20, URL: http://koreajoongangdaily.joinsmsn.com/news/article/article.aspx?aid=2951748.

Ko, H., and W. J. Moon, 2011, "How Koreans Deal with Foreign Exchange Rate Risk: A Behavioral Law and Economics Perspective on the KIKO Forward Contract", Working Paper.

Korea Exchange, 2011, *KRX Fact Book 2011*.

Laws and Regulations Database, 2013, "Directions for Banks Conducting Financial Derivatives Business", Banking Bureau, Financial Supervisory Commission, Republic of China (Taiwan), URL: http://www.lexology.com/library/detail.aspx?g=378699a3-163d-436d-85e0-5537fc4135b1

Legislative Council of The Hong Kong Special Administrative Region, 2012, "Report of the Subcommittee to Study Issues Arising from Lehman Brothers-related Minibonds and Structured Financial Products", June.

Mi-ju, K., 2012, "Elderly Investors Protected from Impulse Buys", *Korea Joongang Daily*, November 30, URL: http://koreajoongangdaily.joinsmsn.com/news/article/article.aspx?aid=2963207.

Monetary Authority of Singapore, 2009, "Investigation Report on the Sale and Marketing of Structured Notes linked to Lehman Brothers", July 7.

Monetary Authority of Singapore, 2012, "Explanatory Brief: Securities and Futures (Amendment) Bill 2012 and Financial Advisers (Amendment) Bill 2012", *Speeches and Monetary Policy Statements*, October 15.

Securities and Futures Commission of Hong Kong, 2006, "The Retail Structured Notes Market in Hong Kong amid a Rate Hike Cycle", *SFC Quarterly Bulletin August 2006*, September, Research Department, Supervision of Markets Division.

Securities and Futures Commission of Hong Kong, 2012, Survey on Sale of Non-exchange Traded Investment Products for the year ended 31 March 2012.

Securities and Futures Commission of Hong Kong, 2013, "Code on Unlisted Structured Investment Products", in *SFC Handbook for Unit Trusts and Mutual Funds, Investment-Linked Assurance Schemes and Unlisted Structured Investment Products*, Section IV, Second Edition, April.

Singapore Department of Statistics, 2012, *Population Trends 2012*.

Yulchon, 2011, "Appeals Court Finds KIKO Agreements Valid", *The Legal 500*, October.

6

Japan: Part 1

Hiroshi Wakutsu and Toru Sano
Enzo Co, Ltd

In this chapter and the next, we trace the history of structured products in Japan. In order to understand the complete picture, we first review major structured products and the prevailing circumstances such as the economic and regulatory environment in chronological order. In this chapter, we concentrate on the products used by institutional users, particularly by financial institutions. In the next chapter, we shall discuss how structured products were spread out to non-professional users, and ultimately to retail users.

The most distinctive characteristics of the Japanese economy after the 1980s were the emergence and collapse of the asset bubble between the late 1980s and early 1990s, and the protracted recession which followed. Throughout this economic slump, the Bank of Japan (BoJ) followed accommodative monetary policy except for a few short periods. As a result of the introduction of the zero interest rate policy by the BoJ in 1999, Japan and its currency entered an ultra-low interest rate environment nearly ten years earlier than the US and the eurozone countries. In this declining interest rate environment, Japanese investors had great difficulty achieving their investment targets. For example, life insurers had many contracts with guaranteed yield that were signed in the late 1980s, when interest rates were much higher. Their most important objective in this low interest rate environment was to meet these obligations. The use of structured products was considered to be one of the few possible solutions. This is why most structured products invented and traded in Japan are investment products that aimed to enhance yield, ie, pay a high current yield. This proved to be the hallmark of the structured products market in Japan.

THE BEGINNING OF THE HISTORY OF STRUCTURED PRODUCTS: THE EMERGENCE AND THE COLLAPSE OF THE BUBBLE

Background

The dawn of the structured products industry in Japan goes back to the 1980s. There were three distinctive features of the Japanese economy at this time.

The first feature was the extremely rapid appreciation of yen triggered by the Plaza Accord, which was announced on September 22, 1986 by the G5 countries (US, UK, Germany, France and Japan). It intended to depreciate the US dollar (USD) in an orderly fashion, in order to reduce the large American trade deficit and the trade surpluses of Germany and Japan. The USD to Japanese yen (JPY) exchange rate, which was at around 250 JPY/USD at the beginning of 1985, fell to the low 120s in 1988. The value of the yen against USD more than doubled in this short period of time.

The second feature was the first long lasting economic boom since the late 1960s. Despite the rapid yen appreciation, the "high-yen recession" came to an end rather quickly. As a response to the yen's rapid appreciation, the BoJ turned to easy monetary policy. The government also put together comprehensive stimulus economic packages in April and September 1986 and May 1987 which included large-scale real estate development projects. As a result, the economy turned around in the latter half of 1987. The booming economy afterwards was led by growth in domestic demand, which was quite rare in Japan after the 1970s.

The third feature was the combination of stable inflation and sharp increase in land and stock prices. Land prices in Tokyo started to rise from 1984 and, in 1987, prices for commercial property in Tokyo recorded a 74.9% climb. Figure 6.1 shows the sharp upward movement of the stock index. Since these surges in asset prices were unexplained from the fundamentals of the Japanese economy, it was subsequently recognised as an "asset price bubble" (Ishii 2011, p. 131).

Corporate behaviour behind the asset price bubble

Around this time, the activity called "Zaiteku" became popular with companies (Zaiteku is an abbreviation of *zaimu tekunorojii*, which means "financial technique"). Although it sounded as if it were a

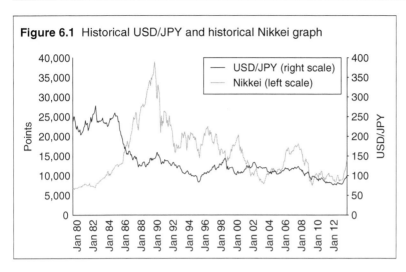

Figure 6.1 Historical USD/JPY and historical Nikkei graph

new technique, in reality it meant speculative investment management. With the expectation of a bull stock market, companies could raise funds at a very low cost through equity-linked financing such as convertible bonds and bond-with-warrant issues. A good portion of the proceeds were invested in trusts called "Tokkin funds" (these invest speculatively and were owned by Japanese corporates), from which they found their way into the Japanese stock market. This exacerbated the upward spiral of the bullish stock market, and prompted easier equity financing, and subsequent inflows of the raised funds. Such Zaiteku helped companies by providing stability through positive finance account balances in the "high-yen recession" period. However, after the economic recovery, Zaiteku itself became an objective.

The relaxation of regulations concerning the issuance of convertible bonds, warrants and commercial paper (CP) which took place in the 1980s helped lower the financial cost of companies. In most cases, CP was issued to earn an interest rate margin between the CP rate and rates of longer term deposits. The interest rate for long-term deposits remained relatively high as a result of severe competition among banks. The proceeds were used for speculative investment (Zaiteku) purposes rather than to fulfil the needs of the company's core businesses. Many large institutions took this Zaiteku opportunity aggressively and inflated both sides of their balance sheet. Funds flooded into the asset markets and caused a sharp rise in stock and land prices.

As blue-chip companies, who had been the banks' largest customers, increased their equity-linked financing instead of the traditional medium-term bank loans, banks had to tap a new customer base. Lending to non-traditional customers, especially to the real estate industry, non-bank lending companies and leasing companies increased among stiff competition between the banks. They even started actively proposing redevelopment plans to landowners with real estate collateral loans. This activity by banks accelerated the land price appreciation in the metropolitan area.

With a bullish stock market, the securities brokers profited greatly from the high turnover that was characteristic of the Tokkin funds. In these arrangements, a trustor (investor, ie, the company that owns the assets) can retain the right to give investment direction to the trustee, who ostensibly manages the fund. Generally, the trustor entered into a discretionary investment contract with an investment advisor company and let them give instructions on their behalf. At the end of the trust term, all the trust assets were converted into cash and redeemed. It had an accounting advantage for the trustor in that securities held in Tokkin could be bought and sold separately from the same securities that it already held in its own account, and the book value of such securities in its own book was not affected. This advantage was especially attractive for companies with large securities holdings. From around 1985, there were many cases in which securities companies gave investment instructions directly rather than via an investment advisory company. By doing so, securities companies could control large amounts of speculative funds, which helped their own trading and easily collected significant trade commission. As a result, for securities companies, the proportion of revenue from institutional customers became higher. To beat competition, there were many cases in which securities companies guaranteed a certain return on Tokkin. (It was called "Nigiri", which means "grasp".) It is said that the standard guaranteed yield was around 8%, but it went as high as 10% towards the end of the bubble. After the collapse of the bubble, the securities companies had to compensate losses occurred in these Tokkin. It not only caused enormous losses to them but also caused controversy nationwide as it demonstrated that they were treating their customers unfairly (Ishii 2011, pp. 332, 334–346).

The collapse of the asset bubble

With the clear intention of ending the asset bubble, the BoJ raised the official discount rate from 2.5% to 6.0% in the short period between May 1989 and August 1990. Meanwhile, the Nikkei Stock Average plunged from the beginning of 1990, after reaching its historical high of 38,915.87 at the end of 1989. Ten months later, in October 1990, it almost halved the value and was trading around 20,000 (Figure 6.1). In March 1990, in order to control land speculation, the Ministry of Finance (MoF) issued a circular notice to financial institutions that they should maintain the rate of increase of their real estate related loans to be not greater than that of their total loans. Following this notice, the number of real estate related loans extended by financial institutions was dramatically reduced, and land prices in the metropolitan area started to decline sharply. This was the collapse of the asset bubble. The 3% consumption tax that was introduced in 1989 also discouraged such investment (Komine and Okada 2011, p. 375).

As discussed, in the bubble era, many companies tried to earn margins by ballooning both sides of their balance sheet. On the asset side, they mostly invested in Japanese stocks, which caused a tremendous loss. However, many believed that it was a temporary shake-out and it was commonplace for many companies to postpone realising or recognising their losses by using various financial techniques including structured products. Their ballooned liabilities became excessive debts and for a long time burdened the finances of those companies that were already suffering as the profitability of their main businesses declined in the economic slowdown.

After the real estate bubble burst, banks' real estate loans stopped performing and tormented banks for years. This was a major cause of the banking crisis in the late 1990s, when several major banks failed and others were forced into mergers.

The Tokkin with Nigiri led securities companies to compensate losses to their customers. The Securities Exchange Act at the time only prohibited the advance promise of compensation; compensating after the fact was allowed. Following the nationwide controversy it caused, the law was amended to also prohibit *ex post* compensation. The termination of many Tokkin arrangements put further downward pressure on the stock market.

Product history

Structured products were only introduced to Japan once markets for interest rates and currency swaps had been established. Currency swaps were introduced to Japan immediately after the liberalisation of foreign transactions in 1980. Japanese companies that had outstanding debt denominated in Swiss francs or Deutschmarks (DEM) contracted long-dated foreign currency transactions, taking advantage of the weak Swiss franc and weak Deutschmark then. By doing so, they managed to lock in large sums of foreign exchange profit and achieved very low funding cost in JPY terms. This was the beginning of currency swaps in Japan. It took two more years before interest rate swaps started to be used commonly. Japanese banks issued USD denominated fixed-rate bonds in the euro market and converted them to sub-Libor floating rate debts by using USD interest rate swaps. (The whole package was called "swapped foreign bond" issuance.) In April 1984, the MoF removed the regulation that all foreign exchange forward transactions had to be backed by actual demand. Following this change, issuing "swapped foreign bonds" became popular among blue-chip companies. Soon after, we saw the first round of structured products in Japan; these took the form of structured notes, which have occupied a central position throughout the history of structured products in Japan. In June 1985, the MoF allowed new structures other than standard fixed-rate bonds, such as floating rate bond, zero-coupon bond, deep-discount bond, dual currency bond to be issued in the euroyen market. Since then, various structured notes have been developed reflecting market level, views on markets and specific demand at different times. The first major investors in this new asset class were life insurers. In order to understand why they became the biggest buyer we need to examine the economic, regulatory and accounting environment they were operating under.

The biggest investors – life insurance companies

Up to around 1980, life insurance companies in Japan enjoyed stable investment management and low funding costs. Most of their investment was done through loans to blue-chip companies with relatively high interest rates, while guaranteed yields on the insurance contracts, which determined their funding costs, were kept low. However, this cosy business environment had changed in the 1980s.

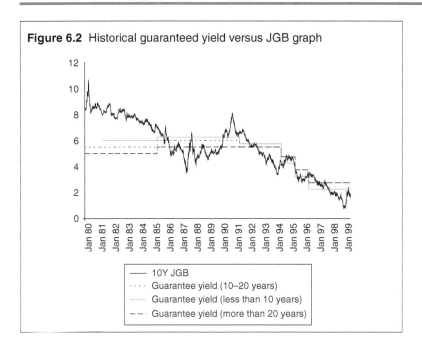

Figure 6.2 Historical guaranteed yield versus JGB graph

Legend:
— 10Y JGB
···· Guarantee yield (10–20 years)
— Guarantee yield (less than 10 years)
– – · Guarantee yield (more than 20 years)

First, on the asset side, the slowdown of the post-war high-speed economic growth and new funding methods that become available to blue-chip companies decreased these funding needs. Instead, life insurers had to increase their securities investment. As a result, they became exposed to more market risks, such as interest rates, stock prices and foreign exchange rates. On the liability side, their funding costs went up as they raised the guaranteed yield. The rate for personal insurance had been kept at 4% for long time but it was raised in 1980 to as high as 6.25% (Figure 6.2). Given that the yield of a 10-year Japanese government bond (JGB) was only about 5% at that time, it is clear that the rate was set at a level that was not sustainable. With this artificially high guaranteed yield, products such as payment-in-full endowment insurance policies became extremely popular. It worked just like an investment product – the policy purchaser pays an insurance fee in full at the beginning and the contract matures and repays investment proceeds in 10 years. It is not hard to imagine that it raised life insurers' funding costs significantly. The guaranteed yield is applied at the time of the signing of the new contract and kept unchanged until it is terminated. Even though the guaranteed yield was lowered from 1990 to match lower market rates, the new low guaranteed yield was applied only to new contracts, but could not be retrospectively applied to existing contracts. Therefore, contracts signed in the late 1980s restrained management of life insurers for a long time. The reasons that the guaranteed yield reached an unsustainable level were said to be that the life insurance market was maturing and they needed a promotion; that there was a public opinion that life insurers were making excess profit; and that the MoF applied pressure on them.

There was another thing that pushed the funding costs of life insurers even higher. The dividends to policyholders were kept artificially high in the 1980s. A stable dividend was considered to be a very important selling point. It was regulated that the normal dividends, which were paid to policyholders each year, had to be funded only from income such as interest or dividends of that year. This "income-only dividend rule" was kept till 1995, when the Insurance Business Act was amended. Until then, maximising income gain had been an extremely important objective for the investment management of life insurers. In bond investment, it made receiving high coupons very important. This may be considered to be the most important motivation for increasing foreign bond investments from the early 1980s when the interest rate differential between Japan and the US increased. The success in foreign bond investment due to the relatively stable currency market in the first half of the 1980s encouraged the life insurers (Uemura 2011, pp. 192–197).

At this time, the MoF limited life insurers' foreign bond investment. This limit was first set at 10% of total assets, but amended to 30% in August 1986. The self-imposed limit on monthly growth of foreign bond investments as a proportion of growth of total assets was lifted around this time as well. This is very interesting if you recall that the start of yen appreciating against USD was triggered by the Plaza Accord in September 1985, and this became a long-term trend. The appreciation of the yen inflicted large foreign exchange losses on life insurers. However, despite these adverse circumstances they increased their foreign (mostly USD denominated) bond investments in synchronisation with the easing of the limits. Most foreign bond investment for the purpose of income gain was made in US Treasury Bonds, which were very liquid up to 30-year maturities. At that time, with their enormous fund size and active trading, Japanese life insurers attracted attention as a major force in this market and were known as "the Seiho" (an abbreviation of "life insurance" in Japanese).

Why did they increase foreign bond investment? While they were suffering from large foreign currency loss, the rise in the stock market produced much larger unrealised gains to their portfolio. The foreign exchange losses could be easily offset by recognising the unrealised gain of their equity portfolio from time to time. They could recognise the high coupon they had received from high-yield foreign currency bond investment as income gain, while offsetting the corresponding foreign exchange losses with equity gains. To put it simply, they could convert capital gain of their equity portfolio to income gain. By doing so, they could achieve the most important investment task of boosting their income in order to pay the dividends (Kofuji 1989, pp. 136–137).

Outside the US Treasury, the "swapped foreign bond" (foreign currency bond issued by a Japanese entity) was also an important investment outlet. The main reason was that a bond issued by a Japanese entity was excluded from the foreign bond investment limit set by the MoF. As insurance companies who wanted to increase foreign currency bond investment while maintaining this limit competed with each other, the terms of such issuances were set in the issuers' favour. As a result, Japanese issuers could achieve funding much lower than Libor after they swapped the cashflow to floating rates. Such bonds were called "sushi bonds", which meant that no one but the Japanese would buy.

The beginning of structured assets

Various structured notes were issued from around 1985, targeting life insurers who required coupons higher than normal fixed-rate notes (8% was often considered to be the benchmark). The simplest form of providing such high coupon was to issue bonds that carried fixed coupon much higher than the market level at over par, and redeemed at par (these are called "high–high bonds").

The best known structure was the dual currency structure, which was issued frequently from 1986. It is the origin of many later foreign currency exposed embedded structures, such as the reverse dual currency structure and power reverse dual currency (PRDC) structure, which we shall discuss later.

With a bullish stock market, there were some equity structures as well. The eurodollar warrant note that started from around 1987 became extremely popular and enabled issuers to achieve negative funding costs. There were many issuances of equity-linked (Nikkei Stock Average linked) notes from around 1988. This opened the way for fixed-income divisions of firms to participate in the equity rally.

With the ability to tailor cashflow, various other structures were invented. Examples include long-term prime rate-linked, step-up, step-down and callable. Asset swaps and repackaged notes enabled investors to separate the effective cashflow from the issuers' credit.

There was an interesting development in the domestic market as well. A foreign exchange linked loan that major city banks started to offer from 1989 became very popular. The best known structure was an Australian dollar linked loan called a "Koala Loan", offered by Sanwa Bank. It is an example of one of the few structured products in Japan that aimed to reduce funding costs; most aimed for yield enhancement, ie, high current coupons.

After the collapse of the bubble, how to resolve the severe losses on their Nikkei index linked notes became a serious issue for life insurers. In many cases, the solution was for dealers to buy back the impaired bond at par (above its fair price), and sell a new bond (usually another leveraged Nikkei index linked note) which did not have par value, at par. The long-term bearish market was not yet expected, and investors considered that they could postpone recognising the losses until a rebound in the stock market resolved their problem.

Product particulars
(a) Dual currency structure

In this structure, a yen fixed coupon is enhanced by setting a high-yield currency (mostly USD in the early days, then the Australian dollar) as the redemption currency. As the present value of the redemption payment was smaller than that of low-yield currency (yen), more value could be allocated to coupon payments. It was designed to meet the demand of life insurers whose investment goal was to maximise income. After institutional investors moved away from principal-at-risk products, it became one of the popular structures among retail investors.

Structure description

Typical terms.

Issuer: Typically highly rated European financial institutions or government agencies.

Initial payment amount: ¥10,000,000,000.

JPY notional amount: ¥10,000,000,000.

USD notional amount: USD amount that is equivalent of JPY notional amount converted at predetermined USD/JPY rate; normally the spot rate at execution was used (= $10{,}000{,}000{,}000/FX_0$).

Coupon: fixed rate (eg, 8%) of JPY notional amount paid annually in JPY.

Maturity: Typically 10 years (retail target issues in later years were much shorter).

Redemption amount: JPY equivalent of USD notional amount at the time of redemption (or USD notional amount in USD).

There was a leveraged version called "heaven or hell". It set the redemption amount to be the JPY of twice the USD notional amount minus the JPY notional amount, at the time of redemption. It doubled the foreign exchange risk and achieved even higher JPY coupon than the normal dual currency structure by adding a foreign exchange forward (long USD/short JPY from the investor's point of view).

Form of transaction. Typically, they were euroyen bonds issued by a non-resident (of Japan), or domestic bonds (called Samurai issuance) issued by a non-resident. The first issuance of dual currency euroyen was in June 1985. The first dual currency Samurai bonds were issued by Bank of China and the Federal National Mortgage Association (Fannie Mae) in April 1986, which was only a month after Samurai issuance was allowed. The retail target issues in the 1990s were sold as Uridashi bonds (retail-target publicly offered bonds).

Investor's payout. The investor would incur a foreign exchange loss when JPY had appreciated at the time of redemption relative to the exchange rate at the time of inception. Conversely they would have gained if the JPY had depreciated. The break-even point should be when the exchange rate at redemption is equal to the forward rate predicated by the interest rate differential between the two currencies when the trade was first entered into.

Product characteristics

Major investors and their motivation. As discussed, the major buyers were life insurers. They did not mind taking risks in principal in exchange for a high coupon. It was beneficial from their investment planning point of view because this structure let them determine what JPY fixed coupon rate they would receive until maturity at the time of investment.

In the 1990s, dual currency notes with AUD became very popular among retail investors who sought for high yield. It was one of the longest selling structured products for the retail market together with reverse convertible structure, and paved the way for the spread of derivative embedded products.

Regulation, accounting background. The "income-only dividend rule" led life insurance companies to buy dual currency notes craving for high coupons. The MoF's regulation considered the dual currency structure to be a euroyen bond as it was redeemed and settled in JPY. It did not contribute to the precious foreign bond investment limit applied to life insurers even though it was effectively redeemed in a foreign currency from a risk point of view.

Structuring and distribution. Arrangers were predominantly Japanese securities companies. They took investors' investment objectives and negotiated the bond issuance with issuers. Issuers normally transacted a hedge swap to convert the liability to USD floating rate debt. The counterparty of the hedge swap was normally a European/US swap dealer with strong credit (as in many cases credit qualities of the arrangers were not good enough for the issuers to take).

The reasons why it worked. Due to the interest rate differential, high-yield currency is expected to depreciate against the low-yield currency. In general, investors were not as bullish on JPY as the forward rate implied. After the interest rate differential between USD and JPY narrowed, higher yielding currencies such as AUD and the New Zealand dollar (NZD) became popular.

Pricing and risk management issues. The typical maturity of this structure was 10 years. This was considered to be long dated at that time as the swap market was not liquid for these maturities in some currencies.

Outcome

After the burst of the bubble, the unrealised gain in the equity portfolio started to run out. Insurance companies exhausted their capacity to offset significant foreign exchange losses. Some took the loss as it was, while others postponed recognising the loss in their accounts by using repackaged notes while they waited for the yen to weaken. In order to achieve this, the arranger bought back the underwater dual currency bond and sold it to a special purpose vehicle (SPV) at par. The SPV then issued a new dual currency repackage bond with higher yield currency such as NZD and sold it to the original investor.

(b) Koala loan

The Koala loan was a package of an ordinary JPY denominated fixed-rate bank loan and a coupon swap offered by major city banks. It aimed to lower loan interest payments by adding foreign exchange exposure. The most popular currency used in this structure was AUD. It was revolutionary that a structure which involved swap contract was marketed broadly to banks' client base including middle size enterprises.

Structure description

Typical terms. *Loan part*

Lender: Japanese major city banks.

Borrower: a company.

Loan amount: ¥1,000,000,000.

Loan rate: JPY 5% of the loan amount (normal loan rate).

Maturity: Typically five years.

Coupon swap part

JPY notional amount: ¥1,000,000,000.

AUD notional amount: AUD amount that is equivalent of JPY notional amount converted at predetermined AUD/JPY rate (FX_0, normally, spot rate at execution was used. For example 100.00) ($=¥1,000,000,000/FX_0 =1,000,000,000/100 =AU\$10,000,000$).

Borrower pays: JPY 5% on JPY notional amount paid in JPY.

Borrower receives: AUD 6% on AUD notional amount paid in AUD.

Maturity: Matches the loan.

Borrower's payout

Let AUD/JPY rate on each payment date be FX_i. The net payment by the borrower on each payment date would be $1,000,000,000 \times (5\% + 5\% - 6\% \times (FX_i/FX_0))$. As the rate that the borrower receives is larger than it pays in the coupon swap, the net borrowing cost will be lower as long as the foreign exchange rate stays where it was at the inception (in our example, $5\% + 5\% - 6\% = 4\%$ when $FX_0 = FX_i$). However, the borrower will be worse off when JPY appreciates against AUD beyond a certain level (in our example, $5\%/6\% \times 100.00 = 83.33$). To leverage up the foreign exposure risk, the rates of coupon swap could be raised. For example, the JPY5% and AUD6% in our example could be JPY10% and AUD12% (ignoring any margin that the lender bank takes). By leveraging the coupon, borrowers can reduce borrowing costs further in the scenario of stable AUD/JPY (in our example, $5\% + 10\% - 12\% = 3\%$ when $FX_0 = FX_i$). In exchange, the borrowing cost would increase at the doubled pace once it hit below the break-even AUD/JPY rate (in our case below 83.33).

Product characteristics

Major users and their motivation. Users were loan borrower clients of major city banks including middle sized enterprises. Since there was no principal risk, it was considered to be a middle-risk middle-return product. At the beginning, it was marketed to companies with foreign currency payment, such as importers. The pitch was that this package could provide some offsetting benefit through lower coupon in a JPY weakening situation, in that their foreign currency payments become larger in JPY terms. However, the fact that it reduces borrowing costs as long as the AUS/JPY rate holds at the level of inception appealed to a much broader range of borrowers. It was aided by the broadly shared view that further JPY appreciation was unlikely, especially after JPY strengthened substantially.

Structuring and distribution. The lender banks tried to convert conventional loans to this structure, which was more profitable. At the

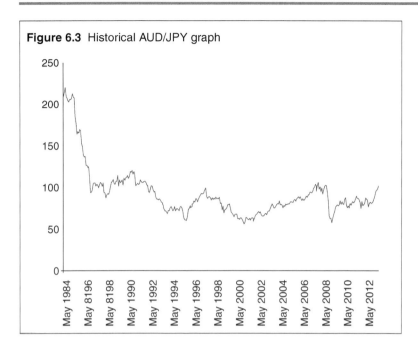

Figure 6.3 Historical AUD/JPY graph

time of execution, the banks executed a coupon swap with a swap dealer to hedge the exposure. Usually, an upfront fee payable to the lender was embedded in this hedge swap. The term of the coupon swap was set according to that of the hedge swap. The benefit to the lender bank was that they could recognise this upfront fee as revenue at the time of execution. From lender banks' point of view, it was easier to receive a larger upfront fee when the coupon swap was leveraged.

The reasons why it worked. The large interest rate differential made the structure work. For example, in 1990, the five-year rate was around 15% in AUD, while the equivalent rate in JPY was 5%. This difference narrowed in later years, but the structure continued with alternative currencies such as NZD.

The structure was held because of the view that JPY would not appreciate as much as the forward rate implied. In that sense, it took advantage of the similar gap between market-derived future and users' perception as the dual currency structure did.

The net payment formula that calculates difference between two values defined in two currencies is a predecessor of the PRDC structure, which we shall discuss later.

Pricing and risk management issues. Neither the Australian government bond market nor AUD swap market then were developed and liquid. The deal flow and resulting position was very large relative to the size of these markets, and as a result most dealers ended up with similar positions that could not be properly hedged.

Outcome

As Figure 6.3 shows, the AUD/JPY, which was trading above 100 in 1990 and 1991, decreased to the 70s in the middle of 1993 and to about 60 in 1995. Borrowers of Koala loans suffered from higher funding costs. The impact was very serious when the coupon was leveraged. There were many court battles regarding selling practice and accountability.

THE BEGINNING OF "THE LOST 20 YEARS"
Background

The economy continued to expand for a while even after the collapse of the asset bubble. However, as the negative wealth effect cooled down the consumption and capital investment, the Japanese economy entered a recession in 1991, which turned out to be the beginning of a long stagnation called "the lost 20 years".

As we discussed earlier, in the bubble years, companies whose risk tolerance level went up following the rise in their asset value inflated both sides of their balance sheet. After the bursting of the bubble, the asset side of the balance sheet shrank, and they were left with excessive debt. They needed to reduce debt and shed unproductive assets to improve the quality of their balance sheet. With the sharp deceleration of the economy, companies started to suffer from excess capacity and payroll, which with their excessive debts came to be called the "three excesses". Figure 6.4 shows that production capacity was tight at the end of the 1980s but turned in 1991 and stayed excessive for a long time thereafter. It also shows that the employment condition followed a similar route with a little delay. This phenomenon became a heavy drag on the economic recovery for a long time and the deterioration of corporate balance sheets increased non-performing loans (NPL) for banks. The banks' NPL problem eventually caused a financial crisis in the late 1990s.

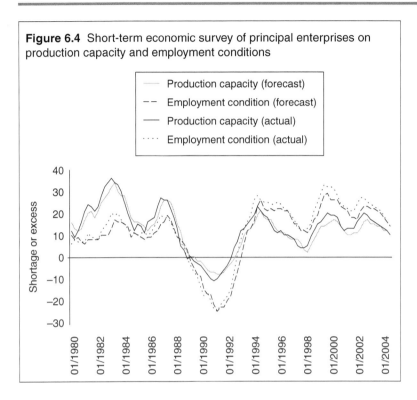

Figure 6.4 Short-term economic survey of principal enterprises on production capacity and employment conditions

In addition to this negative legacy of the bubble economy, the appreciation of yen from 1993 hurt the export-driven economy (especially in 1995, when it reached the then record of 79.75 (JPY/US$) (Figure 6.1)). From around 1993 the economy started to stagnate and then slid into deflation. This created high "real" interest rates. which increased the burden of outstanding debt for borrowers. The Great Hanshin-Awaji Earthquake that hit the Kobe area on January 17, 1995, added to everyone's woes.

The Japanese government implemented a series of very substantial economic stimulus packages from March 1992. They mostly consisted of large public investments and did not have as much impact on the overall economy as planned. Because the construction industry, which was the biggest beneficiary of the public works, suffered severely from the three excesses, adding demand to them did not produce much new capital investment or employment. Thus, public-works-dependent stimulus packages could not produce the economic ripple effect that was hoped for (Komine and Okada 2011, pp. 403–404).

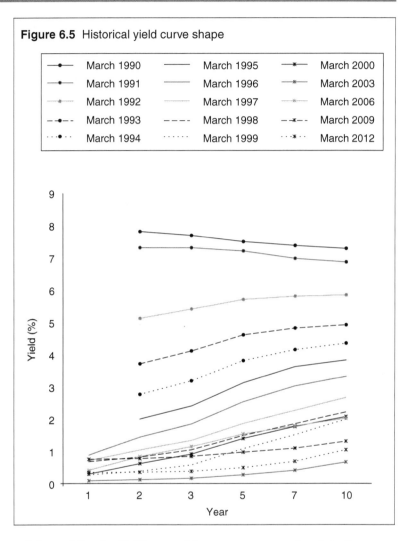

Figure 6.5 Historical yield curve shape

Meanwhile, the BoJ lowered interest rates to stimulate the economy. From July 1, 1991, when they cut the official discount rate by 0.5% to 5.5%, they lowered the official discount rate nine times. On the ninth occasion, they set the rate at 0.5% and encouraged the uncollateralised overnight call rate, which was the benchmark short-term rate, to be below the discount rate. Following these actions, yen interest rates declined significantly, to historic lows.

The biggest change in regulation was the introduction of the Bank for International Settlements regulatory framework, which took effect in March 1992. Banks in Japan, whose capital adequacy ratio was generally small, required recapitalisation and asset compression. It caused banks as investors to have a strong preference towards low-risk-weight assets, which favoured highly rated banks and supra-national agencies, such as the World Bank, as issuers of structured notes.

There were changes in regulation that had a large impact on structured note business. There was a restriction against euroyen bonds being brought to Japan unless they were "seasoned", ie, 90 days after their issue date. The MoF lifted this restriction in 1994 for sovereign issuers, in 1995 for non-resident issuers and in 1998 for all issuers. Euroyen bond issuers were required to receive approval from the MoF each time they issued. In 1995, this rule was eased so that they could receive a pre-approval that was effective for one year. These moves enabled tailor-made structured euroyen notes to be issued in a timely manner using flexible medium-term note programmes. In fact, in 1994, when they took first action for sovereigns, the number of non-resident euroyen issues more than tripled to 2,024 from the previous year's 638.

Product history

In the rate declining environment after 1993, achieving a required return became harder and harder for investors. Life insurance companies and pension funds faced great difficulties because lowering guaranteed yield for new insurance contracts tended to lag the market substantially, as policyholders were reluctant to accept worse terms. Life insurers were still struggling with the legacy of high guaranteed yield from contracts written before the bubble burst. The use of derivative embedded structured products was one of the few tools they had for generating high income.

In the early 1990s, various interest rate options such as swaption and caps and floors were developed. These options were incorporated into structured products. It started with simple European (= one time) callable bonds – typically a 10-year structure with issuer's option to call at the end of the fifth year. Then it moved on to multi-callable structures where the issuer has the option to call multiple times. The idea was to achieve a higher coupon by increasing the value of the option that the investor effectively sells. However, in the mid-1990s, the sluggish equity market and falling long-term interest rate made it even more difficult for investors to achieve certain returns. One solution was that various types of exotic options were developed and incorporated into structured assets. The development of these structured products was led by global dealers who imported the technologies from their global network.

The yen yield curve was inverted with BoJ's tight monetary policy at the beginning of the 1990s. The collapse of the bubble and post-bubble recession prompted the BoJ to ease. The BoJ's action pushed the short end of the curve, which led the curve to normalise (upward sloping). As time went on, the BoJ eased further as the deflationary situation became apparent, and the curve flattened and went lower (Figure 6.5).

As the curve changed its shape and level like this, structures that take certain risks on the yield curve drew investors' attention. The most popular structures were inverse floaters, which gain when floating rates go down, and constant maturity swap (CMS) spread structures, where payments are dependent on the difference between two points on the yield curve. These structures became quite common among investors and variations of them were sold broadly even in the mid-2000s.

The inverse floater started as a bullet five-year structure in the early 1990s, and the callable structure was first seen around 1995. The biggest buyers were local financial institutions, but it was popular with cash-rich corporations as well. It was their preferred structure as first, it was simple enough, second, it carried high initial coupons and third, it matched their bullish view on the bond markets. It was also a popular structure to be used in structured loans in the 2000s by local banks. Reflecting the generally bullish movement in the interest rate market from the early 1990s for two decades, investment in this structure generally ended with a success, except for a short-lived bearish period. Investors tended to reinvest in the same structure when bonds or loans expired. As a result, this structure became common for a long time.

The reverse dual currency structure was very popular especially among life insurers. It was called "reverse" dual currency because it reversed the currency combination of the dual currency structure from JPY coupon and foreign currency principal to foreign currency coupon and yen principal. It first appeared in the early 1990s and quickly became popular. It paid higher coupon than regular yen fixed-rate bonds, and did not have foreign currency exposure for redemption payment, which appealed to those life insurers who suffered from substantial foreign exchange loss from their foreign bond portfolio. It started with 10-year structures using USD or AUD as coupon payment currency. Later on, with lower JPY rates, various twists were added to the basic structure. Examples include extended maturities to 20 or 30 years, callable structure, chooser structure. By far the most popular development was the PRDC structure which first came out in 1998 and was sold explosively for 10 years. We will discuss PRDC in detail later.

Product particulars

(a) CMS spread structure

This structure first appeared around 1992. Similar to the inverse floater, in general this structure suited bullish market trends and it remained popular for decades. Initially, it was used as a tool to take a relatively short-term bet on yield curve shape in swap form. When it first came out, the coupons were linked to short-term swap rates and money market rates, for example, the 3Y swap rate–3M Libor. As time advanced, euroyen note issues with various combinations were seen. In the 1990s, the most popular structure was probably 10Y–2Y swaps. Liquidity in very long-dated swaps improved after the MoF started to issue 30-year maturity JGBs in 1999. The yield curve flattened with easy monetary policy and the maturities chosen were extended as well. After 2000, major power companies issued domestic public offer notes with 20Y–2Y structure and the investor base of this structure expanded massively.

Structure description
Typical terms.

Issuer: Typical issuers of euroyen notes were supra-agencies, sovereigns, highly rated European financial institutions or government agencies. For public issues, issuers were typically power companies.

Initial payment amount: ¥10,000,000,000.

JPY notional amount: ¥10,000,000,000.

Coupon: 10-year swap rate – 2 year swap rate + 1.0% (minimum 0%) of JPY notional amount paid semi-annually.

Maturity: Typically 10 years (20 years in later years).

Redemption amount: JPY notional amount.

Form of transaction. It started with the euroyen note. After 1999, blue-chip companies such as major trading companies and banks issued publicly offered bonds in the domestic market and expanded their investor base. The loan form became popular in the 2000s as well. It followed the path that the inverse floater took.

Investor's payout. Initial coupon was higher than a straight fixed-rate bond of the same maturity. Under normal circumstances, forward spread of two indexes is calculated to narrow as it goes far forward, and expected coupon of this structure goes down below the fixed rate. An investor is better off if the then prevailing spreads do not narrow as quickly as the forward rate suggests. A callable or knock-out structure was introduced from around 1998, which allowed further coupon pickup.

Product characteristics

Major investors and their motivation. The investor profile and their motivation was very similar to the inverse floater. The high initial coupon was very appealing. It was a rare structure that benefited from bear-steepening, at least from an income point of view. It is appealing to bond investors as normally their portfolio loses when the longer end of the curve is sold. Having said that, if the whole curve sells off in parallel, then investors lose. For those institutions who did not take foreign exchange risk but still sought to enhance yield, together with the inverse floater, this was one of very few choices.

Regulation, accounting background. After mark-to-market (MTM) accounting was introduced, banks preferred structures that could be categorised as "available-for-sale securities". The fluctuation of the market value of these securities was shown on the balance sheet but did not hit the banks' income statements. This structure, similar to the inverse floater, was considered to be suitable as it had little credit risk and no principal risk. Some investors even chose to categorise this structure into "hold-to-maturity" securities which was not subject to MTM at all.

Structuring and distribution. As this structure is more complex than the inverse floater, only global dealers could offer this structure initially. Until their technology caught up, and the regulation clearly allowed this in 1998, Japanese firms had to get foreign firms to write hedge swaps with issuers.

The reasons why it worked.   With a positively sloping yield curve, the forward short-term rates quickly increase and the forward curve flattens. However, according to historical spread analysis at the time, it was readily believed that spread would not go down as much as the forward rate suggested.

Pricing and risk management issues.   At the beginning, the pricing method of CMSs was not standardised, especially the question of whether or not to price in convexity, which caused differences in pricing among dealers.

Because the coupon is floored at zero, this structure involved pricing of an option on spread of two CMS rates in addition to pricing of CMS. The pricing of the spread option was heavily affected by correlation between yield curve points. Assigning an appropriate correlation was a challenge, and managing the correlation exposure on the book was another headache for dealers.

Liquidity of long-dated swaps was another issue. For example, when 20-year swap rate became liquid and people preferred to use it as a reference index on 10-year-maturity bond, dealers needed 30-year curve point to price and hedge the structure which may not be liquid at all. This was why the 20-year CMS structure was broadly spread only after 30-year swap became somewhat liquid following the launch of 30-year JGB.

Outcome

Similar to the inverse floater, this was a structure in which investments were generally successful, even though the MTM value may had been volatile at times. Occasionally, there were some investors who could not bear the unrealised loss and were forced to get out, but most investors held them until they were called or redeemed, even after the Lehman crisis.

(b) Reverse dual currency structure

In this version foreign exchange risk is reduced, compared with dual currency structures, by not taking foreign exchange risk in principal but taking it in coupon instead. Although coupon pickup was not as much as the dual currency bonds, it was enough to make this structure extremely popular. The concept of taking foreign exchange risk only in the coupon became the base concept for almost all foreign currency risk embedded structures developed since then.

Structure description
Typical terms.

Issuer: Typically, supra-agency, sovereign, highly rated European financial institutions or government agencies.

Initial payment amount: ¥10,000,000,000.

JPY notional amount: ¥10,000,000,000.

USD notional amount: USD amount that is equivalent of JPY notional amount converted at predetermined USD/JPY rate (FX_0, normally, spot rate at execution was used)(=10,000,000,000/FX_0).

Coupon: Fixed 5% of USD notional amount.

Maturity: Typically 10 years (extended as time advanced).

Redemption amount: JYP notional amount.

Form of transaction
Euroyen notes, loan by life insurers, domestic bonds in later years.

Investor's payout
The investor would incur a foreign exchange loss when JPY was appreciated at each coupon payment relative to the inception, and a gain when it depreciated. In real terms, the break-even point should be the forward exchange rate derived from the interest rate of the two currencies, where low-yield currency (JPY) should appreciate against high-yield currency (USD).

Product characteristics

Major investors and their motivation. These were life insurers and pension funds, who required high coupon and did not mind taking foreign exchange risk. In later stages the product was sold massively in the retail market.

Regulation, accounting background. For the same reason as the dual currency structure, it suited demand for high coupon from life insurers. Using this structure for loans was advantageous as loans without principal risk were not required to be marked-to-market.

Structuring and distribution. From the point of view of risk management, it was simple enough for any financial institutions with existence in swap market. However, it was after December 1998 that Japanese securities companies manufactured the whole package including hedge swaps as the regulation was unclear before then. Loans by life insurers to foreign borrowers were mostly arranged by foreign firms as they have much better issuer coverage outside Japan.

The reasons why it worked. It achieved high stated coupon without taking foreign currency risk in principal. The yield level of JPY was so low that yield pickup from the coupon still made a difference. When the long-dated swap market became more liquid, investors opted for longer term structures, as that increased the coupon pickup.

INVENTION OF THE POWER REVERSE DUAL CURRENCY STRUCTURE
Background

As mentioned, the reverse dual currency structure evolved into the PRDC structure, which was by far the most popular product in the history of structured products in Japan. PRDC was invented in around 1998. Before discussing the structure itself, we should first learn about the period following the last section.

In early 1997 the economy started to show signs of recovery, thanks to the easy monetary policy adopted by the BoJ and a surge in consumer spending in anticipation of a consumption tax hike from 3% to 5%. However, the drop in consumer spending after the hike in consumption tax, termination of income tax cut and increase in the social security burden for fiscal reconstruction and the Asian financial crisis from July 1997 all affected the economy negatively and gave rise to economic stagnation. And then the financial crisis occurred.

The NPL problem of banks was getting worse as the fall in property prices had been continuing since 1991. In November 1997, Yamaichi Securities, which was one of the four largest securities firms in the country, and Hokkaido Takushoku Bank, one of the 13 city banks, fell into bankruptcy. In November 1998, the Long-Term Credit Bank of Japan and Nippon Credit Bank, which were two of the three long-term credit banks, went under. The accounting fraud that was

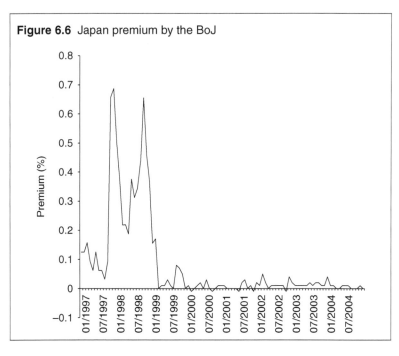

Figure 6.6 Japan premium by the BoJ

revealed after these bankruptcies raised questions about Japanese banks' financial soundness and evoked a sense of distrust in the Japanese financial accounting system. Japanese financial institutions had to pay an extra cost called the "Japan premium" when they raised funds in foreign markets. The Japan premium went as high as 1% at its peak in late 1998 (Figure 6.6). The short-term money market became dysfunctional and banks that were insecure about their ability to support funding reduced bank loans. Figure 6.7 shows that the banks' lending attitude became very tight in 1998. This credit crunch caused a sharp slowdown in the economy. In order to overcome the situation, the government injected ¥7.5 trillion to the 15 major banks in March 1999, while the BoJ started a zero interest rate policy in February 1999. Following these countermeasures, the confidence in the financial system returned and the Japan premium disappeared (Nakamura *et al* 2011, pp. 15–17).

Through this financial crisis, it was recognised that mergers and corporate restructuring were necessary for the banks' survival, and expansion was necessary to compete with major global banks. The banking industry went through consolidation and three major financial conglomerates were formed (Mizuho Financial Group,

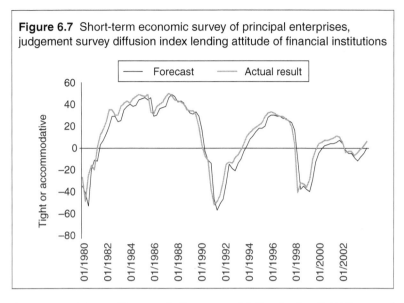

Figure 6.7 Short-term economic survey of principal enterprises, judgement survey diffusion index lending attitude of financial institutions

Sumitomo Mitsui Financial Group and Mitsubishi UFJ Financial Group). On the other hand, in the life insurance industry, several medium-sized companies who could not bear high guaranteed yield and NPL went bankrupt between 1997 and 2001. However, as other larger companies could survive both issues by realising unrealised profit of their equity portfolio, large scale industry reform did not take place.

After this period, the Japanese economy started to recover, led by a surge in external demand boosted by the dot-com bubble in the US. It recorded a real growth of 3.3% in the 12 months from 1999 Q3 to 2000 Q2. Following this result, the BoJ terminated its zero interest rate policy in August 2000.

On the regulation side, in November 1996, Prime Minister Hashimoto started the Japanese version of the Big Bang financial system reforms with the aim of recovering Tokyo's position as a major financial market like London or New York. Its principles were "free, fair and global". This financial system reform set out to prove that free market principles of transparency, reliability and international openness work. Various systems were introduced or amended for this purpose; they included diversification of mutual funds, complete clearance of securities derivatives, complete liberalisation of commissions and fees in stock brokerage, and the establishment of the Financial Services Agency (FSA). Among many changes in 1998, the

Securities and Exchange Act was revised to officially allow financial institutions to offer various OTC derivatives such as equity derivatives, fund derivatives, credit derivatives and weather derivatives to their clients. With this clarity around lawfulness of these businesses, Japanese institutions started offering full-scale OTC derivatives to their clients and started to manage risk associated with client deals internally.

First generation of long-dated foreign exchange products
The product evolution and market dynamics

Before we start.　In the mid-1990s institutional investors in Japan were still encumbered with high-yield liabilities and wanted to reduce their exposure to the stock market. This alone generally, or in other countries, would not drive investors to take foreign exchange risk which has nothing to do with asset liability management. However even before the deregulation of foreign exchange trading, the USD/JPY exchange rate had been a key parameter for investors given the high proportion of Japanese blue-chip corporates that were exporters and the exchange rate having a significant influence over their performance. Foreign exchange rates are closely followed in the national press and by the public.

The rebound process from the then all-time low (post World War II) on USD/JPY from July 1995 left the market with a sense of security which set a lower boundary to USD/JPY, such that ¥100 to the US dollar would be supported and if not the historical low (80) would be. This view was vindicated for a decade, which is quite significant. Another freely traded currency pair that had held a target level that became reflected in long-dated investments was the Swiss franc against the Deutschmark, though the two economies were arguably a lot closer to each other.

So it is probably not surprising that, by the mid-1990s, products linked to foreign exchange rates, such as reverse dual currency structures, were offered in Japan to a broad range of investors, including retail.

The evolution process

In the beginning, the distributors were domestic securities firms; the swap counterparties were the foreign banks who were able to enter into swap agreements with the issuers, who were mainly supranational agencies or European sovereign agencies, which were the international banks with high ratings or derivatives divisions of insurance companies. The domestic securities firms initially did not have the capacity to price.

Another key characteristic of these product groups was that, with some exceptions, transactions took place privately, meaning that they were not observable by anyone apart from the investor, issuer, distributor and the swap counterparty. Therefore it was difficult to put together the full picture; even though some vendors tried aggregating transactions, it was not impossible for dealers to make key transactions invisible to them if investors should request that this be done.

As discussed earlier, institutional investors had realised that investing long term in foreign currency risk should not risk principal. This does not mean that they were not actively trading the foreign exchange market but rather that they would not generally buy-and-hold foreign currency denominated assets without currency hedges. So, we were left with a reverse dual structure, a bond or a loan that pays coupons in a foreign currency.

Unlike dual currency notes, reverse dual currency notes generally had maturity longer than 10 years. This was not surprising since the whole point of investing in this structure is to generate a pickup in coupons and the compounding effect of the interest rate differential would give you higher coupons even if the two yield curves were completely flat and there was no benefit in investing in longer dates if the coupons were in the same currency as the notional. For example, if there was a 3% interest differential in the notional currency and the coupon currency and both yield curves were flat, the 10-year structure would provide the investor with about 16–17% pickup, and 20-year structure 33–35%, assuming interest rates in single digits. The pickup mentioned here is against the coupon payable in notional currency, which is another interesting point. As interest rates in Japan fell further the required yield enhancement increased and just paying coupons in another currency was not generating enough yield.

As described earlier, the issuer will swap back the cashflows of the bond into their preferred funding cashflows, usually in USD and paying Libor plus or minus a spread. Therefore the swap counterparty needs to be able to price these swaps and hedge them in the market.

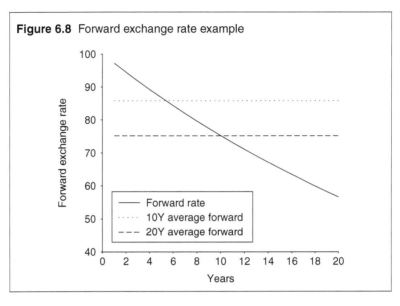

Figure 6.8 Forward exchange rate example

By the mid-1990s the JPY swap market had good liquidity up to 10 years and 20 years and was tradeable. We would not be exaggerating to say that the trading of the 30-year JPY swap rates was induced by such structured business.

Also by the mid-1990s the JPY rates were by far the lowest among the G7 rates which were tradeable. This meant that against any currency, forward exchange rates reflected large appreciation, which turned out to be the case, but investors did not anticipate it. The combination of the FX forwards and the general view on the exchange rates provided investors and dealers, distributors and swap houses with an excellent opportunity if they were willing to take the risk.

Selling options – Choosers (reverse dual) structure

Initially investors looked to sell options that would allow the issuer to pay coupons in two to three currencies such as USD, AUD and DEM. The premium generated by selling these options would be used to increase the coupon of the notes. Again, the swap counterparty would be required to price these options. However, generally speaking the liquidity of the FX option market was limited to maturities of up to 12 months. The simple version of options pricing requires the underlying price, maturity, discount curve and volatility of the underlying. Since it was not impossible to trade cross-currency swaps out to 30 years, banks were able to determine the price of

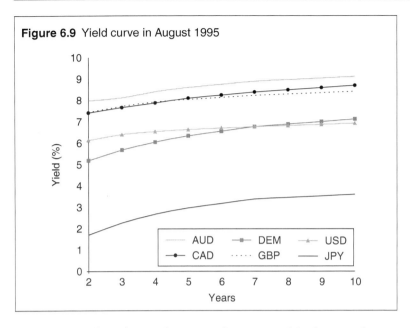

Figure 6.9 Yield curve in August 1995

the long-dated FX forward price with a reasonable degree of accuracy. However, determining the volatility required a more theoretical approach. Obviously banks had to price these illiquid products at a price that could be justified. However, the actual risk itself did not accumulate at a great pace due to the fact that if the coupon was 5%, the notional of the options would be 5% of the bond notional. The pace of the decline in long-dated JPY rates also accelerated and this product group did not have a very long lifespan.

Powered reverse dual currency notes

PRDCs are a structured note where the coupons are a call option on a foreign currency against the yen. The coupon formula, usually described as $(X\% - Y\%) > 0$, where $X\%$ is in foreign currency and $Y\%$ is in JPY, looks somewhat complicated. However, all it says is that the coupon will increase if the foreign currency appreciates against JPY and if JPY should appreciate, then at some point the coupon will be 0%. The combination of the FX forwards implying a continuous JPY appreciation and the general view that the JPY would not appreciate beyond ¥100 against the USD provided an excellent opportunity, since you could come up with a coupon formula which looks like it will pay a coupon, but in fact the FX forwards are implying the likelihood of any coupon being paid was low.

Theoretically, the Choosers (reverse dual) structure could also produce a 0% coupon, which would require one of the currencies to have no value, which is an extreme and implausible outcome. It clearly depends on the coupon formula but, generally speaking, power reverse duals would generate larger margins for the swap counterparty and the distributor compared with Choosers. This could be another reason why Choosers did not last very long. Also it would be fair to say that the investors who had a view on currency pairs outside of USD/JPY were limited, which made Choosers a harder sell.

The introduction of the coupon formula, which was broadly accepted within the industry, led to some variations such as Capped PRDCs – not necessarily a major hit but popular with some institutions. We will examine the structure later on but a Capped PRDC pays a coupon which is a call spread on the foreign currency.

Although the callable PRDC was relatively popular prior to the new millennium, we would like to cover the structure in more detail before discussing the callable structures.

Product particulars

First, we should define some common terms. Since the amount of the coupon can only be calculated once the notional and the coupon are determined, we need an FX rate to convert the JPY notional into a foreign currency amount that will be used to calculate the foreign currency coupon amount – we shall call this the notional FX. The notional FX will be determined prior to executing the transaction and will not change throughout the life of the notes.

(a) Choosers (reverse dual).

Issuer: AAA rated agency.

Notional amount: ¥10,000,000,000.

Issue date: 3 weeks from trade date.

Maturity: 30 years from issue date.

Redemption: 100% of JPY notional.

Coupon: The minimum of the following amounts.

- USD notional amount × 5%.
- DEM notional amount × 5%.

Table 6.1 Chooser coupon look-up table

Coupon rate (%)	USD	AUD	DEM
3.000	72.00	48.00	42.00
3.250	78.00	52.00	45.50
3.500	84.00	56.00	49.00
3.750	90.00	60.00	52.50
4.000	96.00	64.00	56.00
4.250	102.00	68.00	59.50
4.500	108.00	72.00	63.00
4.750	114.00	76.00	66.50
5.000	120.00	80.00	70.00
5.250	126.00	84.00	73.50
5.500	132.00	88.00	77.00
5.750	138.00	92.00	80.50
6.000	144.00	96.00	84.00
6.250	150.00	100.00	87.50
6.500	156.00	104.00	91.00
6.750	162.00	108.00	94.50
7.000	168.00	112.00	98.00

Investor receives minimum of the three coupons corresponding to their JPY cross rate in the table.

- AUD notional amount $\times$ 5%.
- USD notional amount: ¥10,000,000,000 divided by USD notional FX.
- AUD notional amount: ¥10,000,000,000 divided by AUD notional FX.
- DEM notional amount: ¥10,000,000,000 divided by EUR notional FX.
- USD notional FX = 120.00.
- AUD notional FX = 80.00.
- DEM notional FX = 70.00.

Coupon payment date: March 20 annually.

Notification: The issuer will notify the note holders of the currency of the coupon 30 days prior to the coupon payment date.

Depending on the investor, the foreign currency coupons would be converted back into JPY and in some cases the choice of currency and the JPY amount would be determined prior to the previous coupon payment. This is to cater for investors who did not have a foreign currency account, or to allow investors to be able to calculate exactly how much accrual income they are generating for that year.

Apart from the fact that this was probably the first structure with long-dated FX options embedded into it and there were some large high profile transactions which became somewhat public and surprised the community, there is not much to be said.

(b) PRDC

Issuer: AAA rated agency.

Notional amount: ¥10,000,000,000.

Issue date: three weeks from trade date.

Maturity: 30 years from issue date.

Redemption: 100% of JPY notional.

Coupon: USD Notional amount $\times$ 12% $\times$ FX_i minus JPY notional amount $\times$ 7%, where the coupon will not be less than 0.

USD notional amount: ¥10,000,000,000 divided by USD notional FX.

USD notional FX: 120.00.

FX_i: USD/JPY rate observed on screen XYZ 30 days prior to the coupon payment date.

Coupon payment date: March 20 annually.

Since the investors can only receive cashflows from the notes, the coupon formula needs to net the two cashflows. This is where FX_i comes in. The fixing of FX_i can be done by referring to a screen, which is updated by a market information vendor, or be determined by the calculation agent of the notes, who is usually the swap counterparty.

Another point to note is what the formula pays depending on the level of FX_i. If USD/JPY is at 120 on the fixing day of FX_i, then the coupon paid will be 5% and if USD/JPY at 100 the coupon is 3.0%. The point where the coupon becomes 0% is USD/JPY at 70.

Clearly this is what investors look at when deciding on the coupon formula. Investors generally do not focus on the upside but look at what the return is even when their undesirable scenarios materialise. A capped PRDC would be a more conservative structure than the "plain" PRDC.

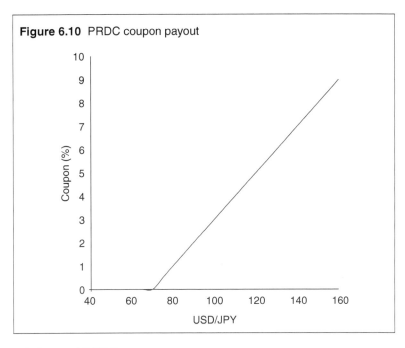

Figure 6.10 PRDC coupon payout

(c) Capped PRDC

Issuer: AA rated agency.

Notional amount: ¥10,000,000,000.

Issue date: three weeks from trade date.

Maturity: 30 years from issue date.

Redemption: 100% of JPY notional.

Coupon: USD notional amount × 10% × FX_i minus JPY notional amount × 3%, where the coupon will not be greater than 4.5% of JPY notional amount or less than 0%.

USD notional amount: ¥10,000,000,000 divided by USD notional FX.

USD notional FX   120.00.

FX_i: USD/JPY rate observed on screen XYZ 30 days prior to the coupon payment date.

Coupon payment date: March 20 annually.

The investor investing in such a structure would have a strong view that USD/JPY will not trade under 90 and they are willing to give up the upside of their coupons but in exchange will receive 4.5%

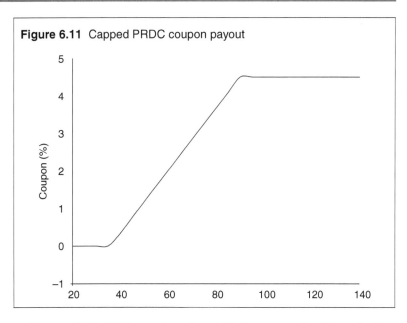

Figure 6.11 Capped PRDC coupon payout

as long as USD/JPY remains above 90. In terms of pricing derivatives, the investor giving up the upside beyond 90 will translate
into the investor selling USD/JPY 90 strike calls to the issuer, who
will then sell them to the swap counterparty. So net the coupons
the investor receives could be described as call spreads on USD/JPY
where the investor is long 36 strikes and short 90 strikes.

$$FX_i = 90$$

$$4.5\% \times 10{,}000{,}000{,}000$$

$$= 10\% \times 83{,}333{,}333.33 \times 90 - 3\% \times 10{,}000{,}000{,}000$$

Solving for FX_i when the coupon is 0%

$$0\% \times 100{,}000{,}000$$

$$= 10\% \times 83{,}333{,}333.33 \times X - 3\% \times 10{,}000{,}000{,}000$$

$$X = \frac{300{,}000{,}000}{8{,}333{,}333.33}$$

$$= 36$$

Another point to note is that unlike the "plain" PRDC, for which
the swap counterparty was just selling call options to the issuer
through the swap, although there is a strike mismatch, the swap
counterparty was able to buy some FX options by adding the cap.

As the PRDC products became popular, banks were left with a short position in USD/JPY volatility, and ideas about how to recover such a position, or structures with less pronounced risk profiles, were needed.

Second generation of PRDC
The callable PRDC

Why callable?   Like any other callable structure sold in the world, the callable PRDC emerged not from investor interest or requirement per se but rather to offer further yield enhancement, ie, higher coupons. The reason why we consider callable, and beyond, to be second generation is due to the complexity in pricing and managing these products, which are beyond the scope of Black and Scholes models. Each bank would have its own model, usually based on a multi-factor tree model. There would often be significant differences in prices arising from both the difference in their models and their risk appetite.

It may not be obvious why, since the JPY yield curve was steep, the forward interest rates were pricing-in raising rates, and as FX forwards were pricing-in JPY appreciation (so expected coupons of the notes were declining), these call options should not be significant and merit a greater intrinsic value. However, at the time the USD/JPY exchange rate was quite volatile and that had a positive impact on the value of exchange rate options. Also the issuers did not heavily penalise the fact that their liability could be terminated prior to maturity, which helped the callable structures to show a pickup relative to the non-callable structure.

From the swap counterparty's point of view, the callable version did not leave them with too much FX volatility to buy back since they were purchasing FX options through the call option/early redemption feature.

Update on client segment

Initially, the main client sectors investing in reverse duals or Choosers were large institutional investors, such as insurance companies and pension funds, investors with fixed liabilities and even some regional banks. Partly since, given the marketing effort and cumbersome pricing process, discussing such structures with an anticipation of small investment was not justified. As interest rates remained low and operations were getting smoother, we started to see other client segments, mainly PRDCs, starting to look into this product group. The expansion of the client segments had an effect on new products since some of these investors did not necessarily require principal protection at maturity; in other words they were willing to risk principal in exchange for a higher initial coupon and did not worry about the valuation of their investments. These institutions could be cash-rich corporates, religious organisations, foundations or schools. The second generation products were able to pay a higher coupon and still enabled both distributors and swap counterparties to be rewarded to such an extent that the workload was justified, as the call options were generating additional value. Also, as 30-year maturity became a requirement, institutional investors turned down these structures, saying that they could not form a view on foreign exchange or the issuer credit 30 years ahead.

The introduction of new accounting standards with regards to derivatives and securities holdings to listed companies and financial institutions by the year 2000 also put some, though not all, institutional investors off the product group as the transaction cost was relatively high. By the end of the 1990s the markets had experienced some significant FX moves (such as the appreciation of JPY against USD from 147 to 120 in the summer of 1998), which negatively affected the valuation of their holdings of PRDC. In the new millennium, the size of transactions became smaller, though there were some large tickets, and we saw an increase in the number of tickets placed with accounts of investors who did not care too much about the valuation of their investments.

Principal risk

As mentioned, one new significant variation of the callable structures was a structure in which the investor would take principal risk in the same currency as in the coupons. This structure, mostly denominated in USD or AUD, would redeem JPY if the notes were called. If the notes were not called and held till maturity, the principal would be paid back in foreign currency and the notes were able to be priced using the usual model for pricing principal protected callable structures, by fiddling the cashflows. Another feature of the principal risky structure was that usually the swap counterparty would initially look to be long, net buying, foreign exchange options through the call option.

Product particulars

(a) Callable PRDC

Example terms: Callable PRDC.

Issuer: agencies or financial institutions rated AA to AAA.

Notional amount: ¥1,000,000,000.

Issue date: three weeks from trade date.

Maturity: 30 years from issue date.

Redemption: 100% of JPY notional.

Coupon: USD notional amount $\times$ 12% $\times$ FX$_i$ minus JPY notional amount $\times$ 8%, where the coupon will not be less than 0.

USD notional amount: ¥1,000,000,000 divided by USD notional FX.

USD notional FX: 120.00.

FX$_i$:   USD/JPY rate observed on screen XYZ 30 days prior to the coupon payment date.

Coupon payment date: March 20 annually.

Early redemption: The issuer has the right to redeem the notes at 100% on every coupon payment date with 10 business days' prior notice.

There was a variation in which the coupons were a capped yet callable PRDC issued in the Samurai format. This was unusual: given the cost and workload, the dealer's preference would be a euro medium-term note format.

(b) Callable PRDC with principal risk

Example terms: Callable PRDC with principal risk.

Issuer: agencies or financial institutions rated AA to AAA.

Notional amount: ¥1,000,000,000.

Issue date: three weeks from trade date.

Maturity: 30 years from issue date.

Redemption: 100% of USD redemption notional.

Coupon: USD notional amount $\times$ 12% $\times$ FX$_i$ minus JPY notional amount $\times$ 4%, where the coupon will not be less than 0.

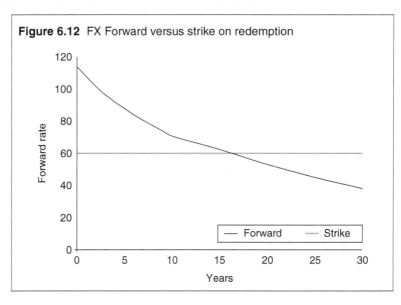

Figure 6.12 FX Forward versus strike on redemption

USD notional amount: ¥1,000,000,000 divided by USD notional FX.

USD notional FX: 100.00.

USD redemption notional: ¥1,000,000,000 divided by USD redemption notional FX.

USD redemption notional FX: 60.00.

FX$_i$: USD/JPY rate observed on screen XYZ 30 days prior to the coupon payment date.

Coupon payment date: March 20 annually.

Early redemption: The issuer has the right to redeem the notes on every coupon payment date with 10 business days' prior notice.

The USD redemption notional FX was usually set at lower levels than the USD notional FX. As you may guess, the values of the call options were higher than the PRDC without redemption risk, obviously depending on how the coupons and the redemption formula were set, but there is effectively an FX option embedded with the size of the notional. Also the call options were less likely to be exercised given that these call options were 30-year Bermudan options. (Bermudan signifies a midway point between American and European options. American options can be exercised at any time during the life of the option; European options can only be exercised on the maturity date. Bermudan options can be exercised periodically during the life of the option (usually on annual/coupon dates).) In order to exercise, the option holder would have to give up the future option value. This uncertainty of the timing of the call option to be exercised was not something that the distributors appreciated since if the option was exercised, they would be able to re-approach the client with a new transaction. This is one of the reasons why there were some structures where the early redemption was determined by the level of FX rate instead of just the option of the issuer, which is effectively the swap counterparties option.

With the target redemption concept developed overseas, there was a variation of PRDCs called FX targeted accrual redemption notes for which the coupon formula was similar but highly leveraged and most of the time taking principal risk targeting the similar client base.

Risk management

Although the liquidity of long-dated FX options had improved to a certain extent, risk management remained a challenge. This is due to many swap counterparties having the same risk profile and needing to enter into similar hedge transactions together. As the outstanding balance increased, the problems managing the risks became more pronounced. Let us take the Callable PRDC with principal risk as an example. If USD depreciates against JPY, then the swap counterparty is less likely to exercise the call option than before the movement in foreign exchange, because the JPY amount the swap counterparty needs to pay in order to cancel this swap is worth more than the remaining cashflow of the swap, ie, the coupons which are USD call/JPY put FX options and the redemption. So the swap has a longer expected maturity, which means that, in order to remain risk neutral, the swap counterparty or, say, the trader who is managing the risk, needs to receive USD swaps (buy USD bonds) and buy FX options in order to offset the impact of the market movement to their position. In addition there is less value in the call option so the swap counterparty needs to buy back some options there as well.

Rebalancing interest rates and FX option risk became the more challenging aspects of risk management as the outstanding balance of PRDC increased, up to the period of extremely volatile and illiquid market triggered by the default of Lehman Brothers. It is not clear how much of an impact there was on the USD swap market given its scale and the variety of its participants. It was, however, certainly having a material impact on the AUD swap market and the traders making markets in AUD interest swaps came to understand what was happening and were able to anticipate the trades that their colleagues, who were responsible for hedging the structured products, needed to do. You can easily imagine that information being magnified as traders moved shops or to hedge funds.

There were newcomers to the derivatives business in Japan, too. Foreign banks that were not even recognised as market makers of JPY interest rate swaps were entering the market since it was deemed to be lucrative and, in a way, easy. Although the veterans might have had the experience and technology, they did not have the power to stop some of the newcomers from aggressively quoting prices, overlooking the lessons learnt by the market. For a reasonably rated bank, all that was required to enter the market was pricing capability and credit lines with the issuer since the end client base would be accessible by talking to the domestic distributors who had branches all over Japan. Generally speaking, most of the newcomers did not last too long, and some even exited the market before the Lehman crisis.

CONCLUSION

The development of structured products in Japan was driven by yield enhancement effort. It had been a continuous battle against an ever-lowering interest rate environment. It started from simple cash-flow manipulation, but soon evolved to various option-embedded products, which extended their maturity as liquidity improved. The products diversified to include many underlying assets such as interest rate, equity, foreign exchange and credit from a relatively early stage. Initially, and for many years, the major users of them were large financial institutions such as life insurers, major banks and pension funds, but they were gradually accepted by less sophisticated investors such as local banks or even by retailers that needed some yield from their investment. On the other hand, in the late 1990s when the soundness of the financial sector became the national interest, large banks and insurers started to move away from riskier structures.

Among many underlying assets, foreign exchange risk has always captured the attention of investors and there have been a series of popular products such as dual currency, reverse dual and PRDC. The invention of the PRDC was the highlight of the history of structured products in Japan prior to the millennium. It was such a powerful and popular product that it attracted not only Japanese dealers and global dealers but also many foreign newcomers to the market.

In the next chapter, we shall discuss how the MTM accounting rule affected traditional users and how the market expanded to a broader user base.

REFERENCES

Ishii, S., 2011, "The Plaza Accord Domestic-Demand Expansion Policies and the Bubble (Focusing Between 1985 and 1989)", in T. Komine (ed), *The Record of the Japanese Economy: From the Second Oil Crisis to Collapse of the Bubble (1970s–1996)*, pp. 129–370 (Economic and Social Research Institute, Saiki Printing Co, Ltd, Ohita).

Kofuji, Y., 1989, "Foreign bond investments and stock sales by life insurance companies", *Bunken Journal* 89, pp. 103–143.

Komine, T., and K. Okada, 2011, "The collapse of the bubble and measures against non-performing loans (focusing between 1990 and 1996)", in T. Komine (ed), *The Record of the Japanese Economy: From the Second Oil Crisis to Collapse of the Bubble (1970s–1996)*, pp. 371–559 (Economic and Social Research Institute, Saiki Printing Co, Ltd, Ohita).

Nakamura, M., M. Nagae and K. Suzuki, 2011, "Financial crisis and deflation (focusing between 1997 and 2001)", in T. Komine (ed), *The Record of the Japanese Economy: Financial Crisis, Deflation and Recovery (1997–2006)*, pp. 1–181 (Economic and Social Research Institute, Saiki Printing Co, Ltd, Ohita).

Uemura, N., 2011, "Life Insurance Companies' Management Difficulties", in K. Ikeo (ed), *Non-Performing Loans and the Financial Crisis*, pp. 185–214 (Tokyo: Keio University Press).

7

Japan: Part 2

Hiroshi Wakutsu and Toru Sano

Enzo Co, Ltd

In this chapter, we cover how the user base of structured products has broadened since the start of the new millennium.

The biggest change has been the introduction of mark-to-market (MTM) accounting. This changed the institutional investors' behaviour towards risky structured assets. It clearly became difficult to own assets with overly fluctuating values, both throughout the holding period and at inception. In structures with large and illiquid risk, such as long-dated foreign exchange and its volatility, margins that dealers require tend to be large and in many cases it was as much as over 10% of the notional amount. This means the MTM value for the asset starts from below 90 for the investment of 100. This was not acceptable for investors who had to recognise the difference as an unrealised loss. Even if an investor chooses to hold the asset in a non-marked-to-market account, they are still required to understand their risks and properly manage them, which could be a burden to them. The FSA enforced higher standards on banks' understanding of market risks in their investment portfolio.

The interest rate continued to be extremely low and meeting yield targets was a challenge for every investor. Many large financial institutions went for floating rate credit products such as credit-linked notes or the notorious collateralised debt obligations (CDOs), which were somehow allowed favourable accounting treatment. Many institutional investors continued to invest in structured assets but only to low-risk principal-protected structures. Many institutions that were less concerned with MTM value started to use structured notes. More and more structured products were introduced into the retail market.

Some products that we discussed in the previous chapter were first introduced to institutional investors and then became popular in the retail market. In the second half of this chapter, we shall take a comprehensive look at the progression of the retail market and its distributors.

INTRODUCTION OF MARK-TO-MARKET ACCOUNTING AND EXPANSION OF USER BASE

Background

The dot-com bubble in the US collapsed by the end of 2000 and the US stock market started to fall from the beginning of 2001, as did the Nikkei Stock Average. In March 2001, the Japanese government officially admitted that the country was in a mild deflation, noting that the consumer price index (CPI) had been negative for more than two years. As a countermeasure to this deflationary situation, the Bank of Japan (BoJ) took a first step to introduce quantitative easing in March 2001. The overnight rate, which was at 0.01% under the zero interest rate policy, went down to 0.001%, bringing the longer end of the interest rate curve down. From 2002 to 2007, the economy recovered mildly, driven by export demand (called "unrecognisable recovery"). In November 2005, the CPI recorded a positive result; however the GDP deflator continued to be negative and the overall deflationary environment did not change. The quantitative easing was continued until March 2006. Meanwhile, the Japanese yen was incredibly stable in this period, maintaining a USD/JPY rate of 100–130.

"There can be no economic growth without structural reform (no reform, no recovery)" was the catchphrase of the Koizumi regime, which took office in 2001. They promoted an end to the non-performing loan (NPL) issue as one of their top priorities. On October 20, 2002, they implemented the Financial Revitalisation Program, which aimed at reducing the ratio of NPL held by major banks (8.4% at the end of March 2003) by about half in two years. They tightened asset assessment, applied uniform standards on asset assessment, disclosed the difference between banks' self-assessment and inspection by the FSA; injected public funds into under-capitalised banks and rigorously reviewed banks' business rehabilitation schemes. At the end of March 2005, the NPL ratio of major banks was reduced to 2.9% as targeted, and the drawn-out NPL issue was brought to an end.

Almost all major banks received public funds and required earnings recovery according to their business rehabilitation scheme. The super-low interest rate in a deflationary environment made investment more difficult than ever for all yen-based investors. Around this time, banks and securities firms started marketing structured products to their cash-rich clients, such as small and medium enterprises (SMEs), schools and foundations, as a new source of revenue. The audience of structured products became much broader than traditional professional users such as life insurers, major financial institutions and some large corporations.

Introduction of MTM accounting

It was recognised that the proportion of derivative transactions or structured assets, the market value of which can be volatile, had gradually increased in the balance sheets of companies. At that time, while risk management of these assets was performed using market prices, acquisition costs were used for accounting purposes. Therefore, unrealised profit or gain began to have a greater impact on corporate management. It was also necessary to modify the Japanese accounting system in line with international standards in order to allay the suspicions about the accounting disclosure that had arisen in the financial crisis in the late 1990s. With that, MTM accounting was introduced for trading securities from the period beginning April 1, 2000. One year later, MTM accounting was applied to available-for-sale securities, although P&L was not recognised until the actual sale. Bonds held to maturity were not subject to MTM accounting. The clarity in accounting treatment of some of the derivative products encouraged proactive use of derivatives for cost reduction. At the same time, it triggered the unravelling of cross-shareholdings, which put downwards pressure on the stock market for some years (Baba 2006, pp. 70–77).

Introduction of the Finance Instrument and Exchange Act

As we discussed, the super-low interest rate environment encouraged wider distribution of derivative embedded products due to both investor demand for higher yield and distributor demand for revenue. Thus, there was increased need to enforce the updated rules for investor protection. To serve this purpose (and more) the Finance Industry and Exchange Act became effective from September 2007.

It aimed to enhance users' protection and convenience by

1. establishing a cross-sectional regulatory framework for a wide range of financial instruments and services, and

2. introducing different rules depending on the characteristics of financial instruments and attributes of investors.

The new law categorised investors as either professional investors or general investors and set a different level of duty for distributors to perform at the time of solicitation prior to a sale of financial products. When a client is classified to a general investor, it imposes a relatively heavy burden of responsibility regarding disclosure of risk liability in written marketing materials. Some high-risk complex products were no longer considered suitable for some customers who lacked sufficient experience and loss tolerance. Appropriate risk disclosure at the time of solicitation of complex derivative embedded investment products became a point of dispute in lawsuits when large losses were incurred by investors in later years (Kodachi 2007, pp. 32–33, 35).

Investor type and product particulars

In order to secure certain investment revenue under the super-low interest rate environment, institutional investors had to take some additional risk. The simplest solution was to extend the maturity of the investment. As a result of investors' demand, the longer end of the yield curve flattened to the extent that it recorded the then historical low rate of 0.43% in 10-year Japanese government bonds (JGB) in June 2003. (Although the yield went up to nearly 2% immediately after recording the historical low, it stabilised in a range centred around 1.5% for years thereafter. The sudden hike was called "VaR shock" it was caused by sell orders from banks who exceeded their VaR limit after a small initial sell-off.)

Investment also went to highly rated corporate bonds to take credit risk, resulting in a squeeze of credit spreads. In 2000, the spread over JGB for Aa-rated bonds was around 0.30% or lower. Eventually, credit spread for lower credit was pushed down as well (after 2002, spread for single A-rated bonds were below 0.2%). During this time, credit-linked notes (CLNs) and credit-linked loans (CLLs) that took advantage of credit default swaps' (CDSs) wider spread than corporate bonds attracted investors who were demanding higher

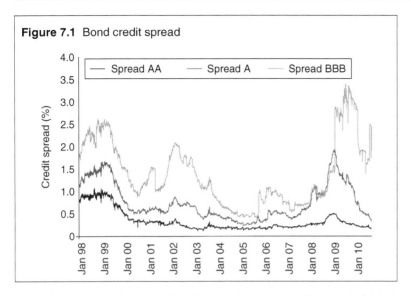

Figure 7.1 Bond credit spread

spread. Investors from the banking industry who demanded high credit quality and wide spread went heavily for synthetic CDO from 2000 (except for the period of global credit crunch in 2002 triggered by the failure of WorldCom). However, the party ended with the sub-prime and Lehman crises.

In this era, structured products were distributed to a much wider investor base from the limited audience of large financial institutions. In the following, we review some of the new major user groups in this era, typical products that they used and their motivation.

Local financial institutions

In Japan, there are over 100 regional banks and hundreds of smaller banking institutions called credit unions. As they are all regulated by the same regulator under the same accounting standards and capital adequacy requirements, they tend to take a similar full-line service model. In a full-line service model, smaller institutions need to post higher returns on investments, because there is a certain reverse economy of scale. In addition, smaller institutions' funding costs are usually higher as their credit quality in generally lower. Furthermore, from 2000, when offsetting profit was sought to write-off NPLs, fund management at local banks came under serious pressure.

Until 2003, the interest rate curve continued to flatten. In this period, the securities investment divisions of many small institutions invested in CMS spread notes (such as 20-year CMS–2-year

CMS) and power reverse dual currency (PRDC) notes with 25–30 years to maturity and successfully posted high revenue. In around 2005, the loan division also started to invest in similar products, using a structured loan format. In structured loans of this sort, borrowers were typically major corporations with high credit quality, or the Tokyo branches of foreign banks. The borrowers entered into hedge swaps with arrangers and achieved cheaper funding than usual. It served multiple purposes for loan divisions of local banks who wanted to build relationships with high-grade corporations, increase outstanding loan amounts and achieve high coupon simultaneously. These investments generally went well as a substantial portion were redeemed early.

After the VaR shock, larger regional banks, whose investment targets were generally lower than smaller credit unions, started to prefer investment without duration risk. They went to other risks such as equity-linked notes, CLNs or CDOs. As most local banks avoided foreign currency denominated investment, yen denominated synthetic CDOs were more popular than USD denominated cash CLOs. Towards the end of the boom of CDOs (which ended in 2007–8), highly leveraged structures such as CDOs of CDOs or CDOs of asset-backed securities (ABSs) were placed to those who wanted even higher returns.

After the Lehman crisis, these local banks had to recognise substantial losses in their structured investment portfolio. It led to a temporary relief of capital regulation for banks subject to domestic standards – they did not have to subtract unrealised loss of securities portfolio from their capital amount.

Listed companies

In this period, many listed companies continued their efforts to downsize their balance sheets and improve their quality. They unravelled cross-shareholding after the introduction of MTM accounting, bought back shares and retired, cut liabilities and reduced fixed costs. Some of them reduced borrowing costs by using swaps to convert their fixed rate borrowing to floating rate.

With these efforts, helped by a mild economic recovery, corporate revenue was in an upwards trend and retained earnings were increasing. There were many cases where these cash-rich companies invested excess cash into the interest rate and foreign exchange structured notes that we have discussed, or into CDOs. Some of them (mostly power companies) used debt assumption schemes using CDOs to remove their external debt from their balance sheet.

(a) Cost reduction by converting existing fixed rate coupon liability to floating rate

Many companies used swaps to reduce the borrowing cost of their existing external debt. Among them, simple fixed to floating swaps became common. Some of them used structured coupons for extra savings in their borrowing cost.

Structure description

Typical terms.

Notional amount: ¥10,000,000,000 (matches outstanding amount of an existing bond issuance).

Maturity: Four years (matches an existing bond issuance).

Borrower receives: JPY 3.5% (matches coupon of an existing bond issuance) on the notional amount.

Borrower pays: USD 6M London interbank offered rate (Libor) + 0.48% on the notional amount paid in JPY. The rate is capped at 3.5% as long as the USD 6M Libor is set below 7%.

User payout. Users' net cost of borrowing is capped at original cost unless USD Libor goes beyond 7%. In the early 2000s when Libor was around 2%, it looked pretty attractive.

Product characteristics

Regulation, accounting background. The hedge accounting needed to be applied to the whole package in order for it to work. As long as the hedge accounting was applied, the swap (together with the original external debt) was not marked-to-market and did not create noise in the income statement.

Structuring and distribution. The concept of reducing cost was usually marketed by arranger or lead manager of the existing debt. Foreign dealers with advanced derivative structuring capability also approached them with competitive structure.

The reasons why it worked.   The steepness of the USD yield curve then made the example attractive to users. The forward USD Libor went up much more rapidly than users expected as the forward period extended.

Debt assumption

Debt assumption is one of a number of defeasance structures. An entity with an external debt sets up a non-cancellable trust which contains a "risk-free" asset that is only used to repay the interest and principal of such a debt. By doing this, it can be assumed that there will be no extra liability caused by such a debt for the original debtor, and such a debt can be taken off from their balance sheet. The interesting question is the definition of the risk-free asset. According to the "Practical guidelines for Accounting Standards for Financial Instruments" set by The Japan Institute of Certified Public Accountants, a risk-free asset was to be "financial assets with high credit rating such that principal and interest payment is highly probable, such as JGB, government agency bond or bonds that are rated AA or better by more than one rating agency". Some companies took advantage of this and used highly rated CDOs as the trusted asset. As CDOs were then paying much higher spread than regular corporate bonds of similar credit rating, CDOs were much more cost-efficient assets for debt assumption. This idea was marketed to those corporations by global dealers with CDO structuring capability.

After the sub-prime and Lehman crises, there were cases where the entrusted CDOs were downgraded below AA and could no longer be considered risk free. In such cases, the downgraded CDOs had to be replaced by other high quality assets. In the midst of the global financial turmoil, the CDO market crashed and it became very difficult to find a bid to buy back even from a professional dealer. It caused a huge loss to those companies who used CDOs for debt assumption.

Unlisted companies (SMEs)

As discussed previously, in the Financial Revitalisation Program, implemented in October 2002, major banks were required to halve their NPLs and recover earnings simultaneously. They heavily marketed the cost reduction scheme using foreign exchange derivatives to a broad customer base, especially to SMEs who were new to these products. Securities companies and foreign firms followed, but banks had the advantage of better knowledge of the client's financial status, as they were their major lenders. They also had better access to collateral, which was necessary for contracting derivative contracts with these weak credit counterparties.

There were many SMEs struggling in an environment in which domestic demand was generally shrinking with deflation and a declining population. They had difficulty in expanding abroad to exploit new demand. Therefore, for their survival, the reduction of their import and borrowing costs was an important management challenge. These foreign exchange derivative products were marketed as a hedge for yen weakening or immediate borrowing cost reduction, and this was very appealing to SMEs.

There were cases where major banks had abused their superior bargaining position against SMEs, for whom they are a major lender, for the purpose of maximising their fee income. In such cases, banks made importers enter contracts that were excessive relative to their USD purchase demand from their importing business, and the whole package became a speculation on foreign exchange.

The upfront fee revenue from the sale of the derivative contracts contributed to improvement in the revenue of major banks. But the mass-marketing of the leveraged complex structure to unsophisticated customers left mis-selling issues and brought about many lawsuits, especially after the financial crisis in 2008, when a sharp rise in the yen triggered large losses to those customers (Hedge Transaction Permeation Association 2010, pp. 6–7).

(b) Cost reduction swap by taking leveraged foreign exchange risk
Structure description
Typical terms.

Maturity: 10 years.

User receives:

- US$10 million in USD if monthly FX rate $\geqslant$ 95.00.
- US$30 million in USD if monthly FX rate < 95.00.

User pays:

- US$10 million $\times$ USD purchase rate in JPY if monthly FX rate $\geqslant$ 95.00.

- US$30 million, USD purchase rate in JPY if monthly FX rate < 95.00.

Payment date: last business day of each month.

Monthly FX rate: USD/JPY spot rate five days prior to each payment date.

USD purchase rate: 95.00 (that is set to be ¥20 less than the spot rate of the contract date).

Knock-out clause: if USD/JPY spot rate on knock-out monitoring date exceeds trigger FX rate, the contract will be terminated at next payment date.

Knock-out monitoring date: 10 days prior to each anniversary.

Trigger FX rate: 115.00 (usually spot rate of the contract date) at the first anniversary. Thereafter, increases by ¥2 each year.

User's payout.   Users could buy USD cheaper than the spot rate. However, they needed to buy triple the amount when USD is cheaper than the rate at which they agreed to purchase.

Product characteristics

Major users and their motivation.   The main users were importers who needed to buy USD for their main business and aimed to reduce the purchase cost of USD. In the above example, they can buy USD ¥20 cheaper than the spot rate at the inception.

Regulation, accounting background.   In 2006, the revised accounting operational guidelines rejected the application of hedge accounting to foreign exchange forward contracts over one year. Until this revision, long-dated foreign exchange contracts had been quite popular, even among listed companies. After this revision, the main users shifted to unlisted companies who were neither tightly restricted to the guidelines nor obliged to disclose the MTM fluctuation to the general public.

The reasons why it worked.   As the USD/JPY was in a trading range for a lengthy period, users did not expect rapid yen appreciation. Therefore, being able to purchase USD at a substantially cheaper rate looked very attractive, compared with the downside risk they needed to take in exchange.

Table 7.1 Universities that suffered from unrealised loss in their investment portfolios

Name of university	Unrealised loss as of March 2011	Change from previous year	Unrealised loss from securities investment	Unrealised loss from OTC derivatives
Keio University	(19,674)	(1,570)	(18,068)	(1,606)
Nanzan University	(18,666)	(733)	(8,938)	(9,728)
Shibaura Institute of Technology	(4,444)	711	(4,262)	(182)
Tokyo International University	(3,950)	(2,482)	(1,171)	(2,779)
Senshu University	(3,481)	(688)	(3,323)	(158)
Rissho University	(1,565)	945	(1,189)	(376)
Mukogawa Women's University	(1,282)	(582)	(1,151)	(131)
Kinki University	(898)	(517)	56	(954)
Tokyo University of Science	(765)	508	(621)	(144)

Source: Source: Weekly Toyo Keizai 2011, pp. 106–107. All figures are in ¥ million. Losses are given in parentheses.

Schools, religious organisations and foundations

The investment unfriendly environment hit cash-rich schools and religious organisations as well. In those organisations, budgets assumed certain (rather high) investment returns from their funds. Even when returns from funds with traditional investment strategies were not sufficient to cover the budget, it was not easy for them to restructure budgets or reduce the funds for expenditure. As a way out of the quagmire, to achieve their high target yield, they were pulled into high-risk–high-return investments using various structured products such as PRDC notes with principal risk or CDOs.

The Lehman crisis and market turmoil damaged the financial situations of these schools and religious organisations. Even though their accounting statements were still based on historical cost, the annotated valuation loss grew large. The high-risk–high-return character of their investments caused large valuation losses relative to the size of their funds (Table 7.1). For example, Keio University disclosed that they were sitting on a ¥53.5 billion valuation loss at the end of March 2009. Their total fund size then was about ¥130 billion. In 2008, Komazawa University realised a ¥15.4 billion loss in its derivative portfolio by closing it out. Nanzan University also closed out its derivative portfolio and realised ¥22.9 billion loss by 2012. These losses became a tremendous burden to higher-education management especially in the environment of continuing ultra-low rates and a declining youthful population in the country. An executive director at Keio University commented in 2011 that structured notes were not suitable for investment by schools and they were planning to reduce their holding of structured notes to zero as soon as market condition allowed (Weekly Toyo Keizai 2011, p. 105).

(a) Swap for investment purpose with leveraged foreign currency risk
Structure description
Typical terms.

Maturity: five years.

User receives: US$10 million in USD × monthly FX rate, paid in JPY.

User pays: US$10 million × USD purchase rate, paid in JPY.

Payment date: last business day of each month.

Monthly FX rate: USD/JPY spot rate five days prior to each payment date.

USD purchase rate: initially 95.00 (that is set to be ¥20 less than spot rate of the contract date). Once any of the monthly FX rates is set below 103.00, the USD purchase rate is set using the following formula

new USD purchase rate

$$= \text{previous USD purchase rate} + (103.00 - \text{monthly FX rate})$$
$$(7.1)$$

However, the USD purchase rate is not greater than 150.00 and not smaller than 95.00.

Knock-out clause: if any monthly FX rate exceeds the trigger FX rate, the contract will be terminated at the next payment date.

Trigger FX rate: 122.00 (spot rate of the contract date + 7).

Assumed spot rate at execution: 115.00.

Form of transaction.   This is a swap contract between a user and an arranger. In many cases, the bank requires collateral from the counterparty based on the MTM value of the swap. The swap form is considered more cash efficient than bond investment even if the bank has to post collateral.

Investor's payout.   This is a structure called a "snowball" (Figure 7.2). The user makes a high return as long as the USD/JPY rate stays around where it was at execution (in this example, around 115). However, once it falls (yen strengthens) below 103, the return quickly disappears and turns to loss. With the formula that refers to previous payout, the increase in loss accelerates – like a snowball – as long as the USD/JPY stays below 103. On the other hand, profit increases when yen weakens, but the whole structure is terminated relatively quickly (in this example, it is cancelled when the yen weakens by ¥7).

Product characteristics

Major investors and their motivation.   Schools and religious organisations with very high target yield were seen to be the main users of these highly leveraged structures. They started from normal unleveraged structures, but became increasingly leveraged as time passed.

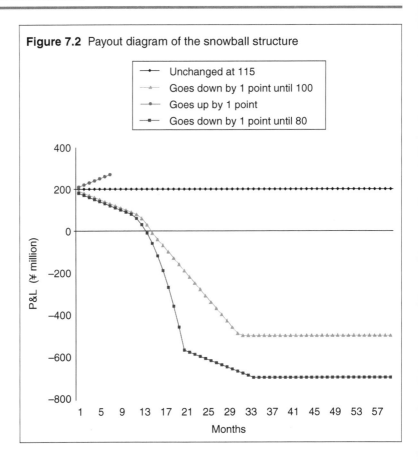

Figure 7.2 Payout diagram of the snowball structure

Regulation, accounting background. The accounting rule for these organisations was still based on historical cost basis, and these positions were not required to be marked-to-market. The disclosure requirement was also limited.

Structuring and distribution. Usually, highly leveraged products bring higher profitability to dealers. All the firms, including foreign houses with structuring capacity, were very keen to enter this market sector.

The reasons why it worked. Once again, the value came from the gap between the view that stable JPY continues and the theoretical forward that implies steep appreciation of JPY.

Pricing and risk management issues. Pricing and managing path-dependent options were tricky and calculation heavy.

Local authorities

The super-low interest rate environment also affected the investment behaviour of local authorities. Many of them started to take very long duration risk and foreign exchange risk, mostly by purchasing PRDC notes. In local authorities, staff at investment divisions were normally rotated to other divisions after two or three years and it was therefore unlikely that they would become experts. As a result, they tended to invest in products that were recommended to them by securities companies with which they had close relationships. They also had habit of following the crowd. In this case, the crowd was purchasing PRDCs. Investment was helped by the fact that local authorities were not bound by MTM accounting rules, and hence they were not overly concerned by the fluctuation in the values of their holdings, and they were used to taking long-dated exposures as they regularly dealt with long-term projects in their mainstream operation. According to a survey by the Ministry of Internal Affairs and Communications as of May 2009, there were 24 local authorities investing a total ¥43 billion in structured notes, led by Kobe City, which invested ¥16.5 billion.

Local authorities started to use structured products for their liability management as well. Local authorities with high credit quality aimed to achieve cheap funding through structured bond issuance or structured loan borrowing. The frequently used structures were CMS spread and foreign exchange linked. In principle, the risks taken by local authorities were similar to popular investment structures such as CMS spread notes or PRDCs. Usually, counterparties of local authorities in these structures were local banks that were based in the region of such local authorities. They had to lend to those local authorities for relationship reasons anyway. By lending through these structured loans and hedging the structured cashflow through hedge swaps, they could achieve higher net returns. Local banks' lending usually took a loan format as this did not have the burden of marking-to-market for investors. According to a survey by the Japanese Ministry of Internal Affairs and Communications as of February 2009, there were 15 local authorities that used structured borrowing to a total value of ¥424 billion (Weekly Diamond 2009, pp. 79–80).

(a) Structured note/loan structure for local authorities (USD/JPY trigger structure)
Structure description
Typical terms.

Borrower: local authority.

Lender: local bank in the same region as the borrower.

Initial payment amount: ¥10,000,000,000.

JPY notional amount: ¥10,000,000,000.

Redemption amount: JPY notional amount.

Maturity: 10 years.

Coupon: if USD/JPY $\geqslant$ 90.00 then fixed 1.00%, otherwise fixed 6.00%, of JPY notional amount paid in JPY, paid semi-annually.

Borrower's payout
Similarly to investment in PRDCs, the borrower benefited from initial favourable coupon and took bets on forward rates. The bet was that USD/JPY rate would not fall as much as the theoretical forward rates implied.

Product characteristics

Major borrowers and their motivation. Local authorities' motivation was to reduce borrowing costs, even though their borrowing costs were already pretty low, reflecting the very low interest rate environment. In 2008 The Japan Local Government Bond Association issued a report entitled "Diversification of local authorities' borrowing by using structured borrowing", which was very supportive. It reported that 17 agencies had outstanding structured borrowing as of July 2007.

Regulation, accounting background. There was no specific regulation for structured borrowing. There were no unified rules on reporting to local assemblies or to community residents, and it was at the discretion of each local authority.

Structuring and distribution. It was arranged mostly by a foreign firm with a few followers. The position that the dealer takes was very similar to the popular PRDC notes described above. Accumulation of similar positions was a major risk management issue.

Outcome

The indexes used for the trigger did not have much relevance to local authority business. After the yen was rapidly appreciated below 90 in 2008, high interest payments were triggered and boosted the borrowing cost. Many of those agencies had to give some excuses to local assemblies, such as that the total borrowing cost would be still cheaper than straight fixed rate borrowing.

THE LEHMAN CRISIS AND THEREAFTER
Background

The world economy was disturbed by the sub-prime mortgage crisis from the second half of 2007 and following the Lehman crisis in September 2008. The Japanese economy, which was under an export-driven slow recovery, was also affected. A historically sharp slowdown was caused by losses in exports and subsequent inventory adjustment. The government implemented economic stimulus policies several times. However, they were not as effective as hoped. The confusion caused by the change in administration in September 2009, from the long-ruling Liberal Democratic Party (LDP) to the first-time government of the Democratic Party of Japan, did not help either.

The BoJ, which had terminated its quantitative easing policy in 2006, turned around and lowered its policy rate twice in 2008. In October 2010, they implemented what they called comprehensive monetary easing (CME). CME was composed of three measures:

1. zero interest rate policy;
2. clarification that the zero interest rate policy would be maintained until the BoJ judged that medium-to-long-term price stability was in sight;
3. establishment of an asset purchase programme to lower the risk premium in various financial assets.

Through this period, the JPY interest rate did not show any extreme movement, while the corporate bond market lost liquidity for BBB or lower credit. The Nikkei Stock Average dropped from 12,214 at the close of September 12, 2008 to 6,994.90 on October 28, 2008 – which was a 26-year low – and remained sluggish thereafter. In the foreign exchange market, JPY started to appreciate from the summer of 2007. After the crisis, the currency was bought as a safe asset, and it entered the 70s, which was a historic high level after the outset of the Greek debt crisis in the summer of 2010. The reverse trend of weaker yen and strong stock market did not materialise until late 2012 when the LDP party returned to power and started to implement its reflationary expansionary policy called "Abenomics".

On March 11, 2011, the Great East Japan Earthquake hit the Tohoku area. A tsunami struck the coast and more than 180,000 lives were lost. The direct loss caused was estimated to be somewhere between ¥16 trillion and ¥25 trillion, which is the largest amount in world history. The tsunami also struck a nuclear power plant in Fukushima, resulting in a serious nuclear accident which caused radioactive pollution and an electric power shortage. The economy shrank immediately but recovered with reconstruction demand in the second half of 2011. However, this recovery did not last after the second quarter of 2012, as the strong yen prevented export demand from growing. The exporters were said to be suffering from "sextuple difficulty": the historically strong yen, high corporate tax, delay in a free trade agreement with trading partner countries, inflexible labour regulation, stricter environmental regulation and uncertain electricity supply.

Even though the direct impact of the sub-prime mortgage crisis was not as serious as it was in the US or in Europe, many investors had to recognise valuation loss or loss on sale. The lower stock market and much wider credit spread indeed caused loss (Figure 7.1). For investors in structured products, a much bigger problem was caused by the appreciation of the yen to a historic high. As discussed in the previous sections, in almost all long-dated foreign exchange related products, it was designed that the end users would enjoy high coupon or low cost as long as yen did not appreciate as much as the theoretical forward rate suggested.

The market movement and the impact on each party

Needless to say, the market movement after September 15, 2008, went against all participants in the PRDC space. The investors were suffering from the appreciation of JPY against USD and the Australian dollar (AUD). These investors were not supposed to worry about their MTM too much but the Japanese investors could be said to overreact to such chaotic events and environments of uncertainty; investors generally decided that anything that was not Japanese was risky and realised what was happening to their investments when they asked for a bid on these notes. The distributors, who had realised the situation a bit earlier, were concerned because the JPY exchange rates, which had held for 10 years, had collapsed and the philosophy of the business had been lost. The swap counterparties had been badly bruised, as they tried to remain risk neutral, and were revising their risk management strategy. Not many were in the position to add risk to their inventory, if they were to do so the client would have to pay a hefty price. At this point, certain issuers had some dependence on the Japanese structured notes market, and were also in trouble because the PRDC market was not the only capital market that was not allowing them to put in place their funding programme and to the extent that some issuers stopped buying back their own debt, which just worsened the price for these securities since there was no one else who was in a position to buy these illiquid notes. Also, the banks were facing higher long-term funding costs, which made their paper cheaper. The muddle lasted for a while and the focus for swap counterparties was risk reduction. At the same time the likes of AIG were exiting the business, which meant that they had to sell their portfolios of derivatives.

Swap counterparty positions related to JPY derivatives on products such as fixed rate callable or callable reverse floaters were pretty much called and the balance was delicate. The relatively troublesome risk was the group of CMS spread products, which tend not to be callable. PRDCs were the main issue.

Client interest

The problem in the first place was that investors in Japan were not being rewarded for taking risk, which was the breeding ground for PRDCs. Post Lehman, clients who had ammunition for investment were presented with an excellent opportunity to invest in credit products such as Japanese bank capital, subordinated-debt, issued overseas in USD. Although some investors might have lost money on foreign exchange, at the time the Japanese financial sector looked compelling compared with other developed countries. The track record of the Japanese government also encouraged the Japanese to invest in these products. Another product group that continued to gather interest was plain emerging-market-currency-denominated debt, such as the Brazilian real, which was popular prior to the crisis but continued to see interest. Some short-dated AUD-related structures remained popular as not only were there AUD investments which needed to be rolled as investors did not want to take a big hit on the FX loss, but also it was the only G10 currency that yielded anything overnight. New interests on PRDCs in USD or AUD did not re-emerge until the LDP was elected into the government in late 2012, and the foreign exchange market was making a turnaround.

THE HISTORY OF RETAIL PRODUCTS
Background

The strength of structured products clearly shows in the way it has morphed in order to fit the needs of investors through various changes over time in, for example, the market environment, accounting systems, tax systems and regulations.

This change is not an exception for structured products targeted towards retail customers. However, to understand the situation in more detail, we must concentrate on the distributors who sold the products to these retailers. Japanese domestic financial products' structures have been influenced ever since the restrictions to the sale of securities over-the-counter (OTC) at banks were eliminated. As a result of this dissolved restriction, retail customers' capital investments in hedge funds and structured products have increased through such products as mutual funds and in individual variable annuity life insurance contracts.

Another factor that led to the expansion of domestic brokerage business and helped widen the range of structured products sold to retail consumers was the collapse of the bubble. Numerous banks and security firms were forced to reorganise their structure, which led to many security firms joining banking groups. Other large banks such as Shinsei Bank and Aozora bank, as well as other big local banks, began to create subsidiary security firms to further strengthen their companies.

Subsequent to the Financial Instruments and Exchange Law in 2007, distributors have been obligated to give "amateur investors" a thorough explanation of structured products upon purchasing; we suspect that the authorities understood the underlying intention of the distributors before the change in law.

There are two ways in which distributors sell unlisted products such as (certain) structured products to retail customers:

1. to file information on the product with the authorities before selling to a wide unspecific group of investors;

2. to sell the product to a limited group of investors without filing the structured products' information with the authorities.

This choice varies for each distributor's business policy, as well as with total sales and, depending on what choice they make, certain restrictions may be imposed. Both choices are bound by certain related rules and do not disadvantage the investor in any way. Furthermore, the same rules apply in situations such as selling securities to institutional investors, but in most cases, the latter choice is taken.

On the other hand, retail customers invest with all sorts of different intentions. For example, in the late 1980s, life insurers invested in euro bonds issued by Japanese corporates based on the specific tax system and restrictions given at the time. This kind of thinking does not always apply when distributing to retail customers. Some investors look for products with high interest rates, while some seek tax related advantages. Others may look for a product with the assumption that they will receive an income in the future.

As the market environment, accounting system, tax system and regulations change over time, investors' demands and distributors' intentions differ and structured products delivered to retail investors have changed based on the factors listed above. There may be products that have sold a large number within a short period of time, while some products may be unstable on a monetary basis regardless of whether or not it has been sold on the market for over 10 years.

Chronological development

The following events explain how structured products have morphed themselves over time, in order to meet the needs of diverse retail customers.

Plaza Accord (1986) – "wide (bank debenture bond)" yield 8% (1990)

Around this time, life insurers started to handle products such as dual currency bonds and Nikkei Average Link bonds, while in retail such structured products were yet to be considered.

The main products that were favoured by retail customers at the time were listed products (stocks) and products that were up for public subscription and secondary distribution (public offering (PO)/initial public offering (IPO), warrants, convertible bonds, domestic mutual funds). Despite the many products that became listed on the market (1985, Japanese Government Bond futures; 1987, Osaka 50 Stock futures; 1988, Nikkei 225 futures; 1989, Nikkei 225 options) it was rare for a regular retail investor to choose them.

Most risk-favourable investors were pitching their money on margin trades with leverages. These are very similar to CFDs.

Thus, stock spot transactions, margin transactions and mutual funds became the main products for retail targeting sales at security firms and, indeed, managed to yield high earnings with the help of fixed commission rates.

However, with the repeated official discount rate hikes after 1989, investors who did not want to take risks proactively bought long-term bank debentures (called "wide"). In the following year, the introduction of the first "wide" – a long-term bank debenture that had an interest rate of over 8% – caused crowds of people to wait outside the issuing banks' branches before they opened, leading to a so-called "wide" phenomenon. Furthermore, due to the regulated high interest rates, postal savings accounts that offered high interest on fixed deposits boomed, causing many people to shift their money from regular banks.

With the accumulated shift in money to bank debentures and postal deposits, proposals for principal protected structured products that could meet the needs of these investors when their money was to be redeemed in the year 2000, were not well received by retail distributors or investors due to the characteristics of the fund at that time.

The collapse of the bubble (1990) – Revised Securities and Exchange Act (1998)

In the last trading session of 1989, the Nikkei 225 Average scored an all-time high of 38,915.87 that was to be followed by a 63.5% drop

(¥14,194.40) by August 17, 1992. Most private investors failed to keep up with the extreme volatility in the stock market.

From the 1986 Plaza Accord onwards, retail sales that based their marketing strategies on the "waterfront" scenario failed to correspond to the big fall in the stock market during the 1990s. Security firms could only recommend investors to "go long" based on the decline in price and failed to construct a successful "short" business model.

The results were inevitable, and caused investors who were doing margin trades with limited funds to cut their losses after a number of margin calls. Even for those with enough funding to take physical shares, delivery ended up with further unrealised losses as the stock prices continued to decline. Some investors who took a long-term investment approach hoping for the stocks to rise after multiple purchases as contrarians were considered lucky if they ended up with latent gain.

It was evident that the biggest reason retail investors became the main buyers at such an unfavourable time in the stock market was due to the lack of experience by both the investors and sales covering retail clients of securities firms, who failed to guess that the Nikkei averages' lower quotation to fall beyond the low price would drop down to 50% of the peak price times 80% minus 20% range = peak price × 32% (Japan's old market saying).

It is true that the Nikkei 225 average did not fall under 12,453.08 until 2003, when it reached 7,603.76, despite such harsh events that hit the market (the bankruptcy of insurance companies (eg, Kyoei Life, Chiyoda Life, Taisei F&M)), the bursting of the IT bubble and the protracted decision to inject public capital into Resona Bank.

However, during these 10 years or so, the Japanese stock market's main index – the Nikkei 225 average – stayed within the box range of 14,000–20,000. Nonetheless, it was rare for private investors who bought stocks after the bubble burst to enjoy unrealised profits in their portfolio.

Retail investors had realised that they should not buy Japanese stocks around July 1991 when the discount rate finally fell, from 6.0% to 5.5%, after four consecutive rate hikes. This time around, the price of land had dropped sharply. Most wealthy retail investments were backed by real-estate assets. Asset formation by launching businesses and/or IPOs was accelerated in the second half of the 1990s after the installation of Advanced Information and Communications Network Society headquarters by the Murayama cabinet in August 1994; for example, Rakuten was founded in February 1997. From this point on, retail distributors eagerly sold utility bonds instead of equities. The policy change to selling bonds instead of equities was well received by investors who had not shown interest in traditional investment trust funds. Bonds' placement fees had contributed the revenue of retail houses. For the sales people, bonds were something they could promote with a positive feeling. The bubble buster, the BoJ, lowered the discount rate repeatedly and the rate reached 0.5% in September 1995. Institutional investors were aggressively trading in the secondary markets, while retail investors preferred new issues. However, the absolute coupon level had come down so much that straight bond issuance ceased to attract the retail investors. From this time on, the structured bond business became one of the pillars of securities house business. In the early 1980s insurance companies had invested in the structured bonds issued by non-residents in the euro market. By the early 1990s the situation had not changed much. Existing rules had not adopted the legal provisions on euro issued bonds to be distributed to retail in Japan. Hence, in the early rise of the structured notes issuers had to carefully pick investors with the capacity to understand the legal environment, and retail distributors had to be educated to comply with the law.

At the time, investors required bonds with higher coupon rates due to the decline in interest rates that was affecting the fixed-income market. To meet these needs, security firms launched structured products, starting with callable bonds. Once the yield curve started flattening and the coupon rates of these callable bonds started declining, products such as callable bonds with reverse floater type interest rates and dual currency bonds with the same type of structure helped raise the coupon level.

It did not take long for investors to walk away from these dual currency bonds that came with exchange risks upon redemption. Thus, JPY settled FX-linked notes that based the redemption price on a formula by plugging in the FX rate at issuance and the FX rate at the redemption. At that time, the calculated FX rate was set at a level with higher value to yen than the current spot rate, and helped to reduce the risk of yen appreciation. Yet, the benchmarked FX rate was set above the forward rate but below the spot rate, by which the present values of the differentials were used to higher coupon and to charge sales commission for distribution companies. In addition, there was no need to switch the currencies upon settlement, ultimately eliminating the cost of exchange commissions, which thus became more acceptable for investors.

Yet, despite attempts to contrive the marketability of dual currency bonds, after experiencing losses upon redemption many investors started to look towards products with no exchange risks. As a result, reverse dual currency bonds were produced.

In the beginning, there was a 0% spread over five-year interest rates between the AUD and JPY, which made five-year reverse dual bonds with terms acceptable to most investors, ie, 8% coupon. However once the spread between AUD and JPY started to shrink, the only way to secure the interest rates of those in favour was to extend the tenor to maintain the same level of coupon. As a result, bond tenors were stretched to 7 or 10 years and numerous reverse dual currency bonds were sold at that time.

During this period, many retailers gained experience in selling products to large investors who made investments in the order of millions of US dollars. At security firms, structured notes distribution was expanded to investors who would make investments in multiples of US$100,000. The next move for security firms was to extend their targets towards mass retail via public offerings.

Before distribution houses offered securities – in this case, structured notes – through the public offering method, the issuers were required to file a Securities Registration Statement with the regulatory authority. As mentioned earlier, most of the structured bonds were issued by European governments, financial institutions, international organisations and overseas subsidiaries of Japanese companies.

In reality, the financial executives of issuing companies never took part in writing the registration statements. Instead, a Japanese lawyer was appointed to write the statement with the help of designated (by the issuers) arrangers who provided the contents of details about risk analysis and terms of the issuance. Arrangers had also been known to be the swap agents who helped the issuer to finalise issuing costs for the structured product between the swap dealers. The parent company of the arranger (normally a Japanese security firm) was known to have a lot of control over the issue terms for the structured products, and was thought to affect the terms of the deals.

The arrangers also faced competition from underwriters in the Euro Bond league table, and were constantly struggling to meet the needs of issuers who wanted to issue bonds with low coupon while distributors, on behalf of the salability to retail investors, wished to have high coupon.

Assuming the issue cost borne per issuer is a given expense, the cost of securities registration statement and distribution fees paid to securities houses indirectly worsens the terms of the deals. Securities houses – arrangers – make good spreads in between the swap providers and the issuers. A part of the swap spread is used to compensate the terms of the deal. The deterioration of the terms lowers investment appetite, and ends up decreasing the deal size. The decrease in the deal size increases the fixed issue cost in proportion. If the arranger tried to inflate profits on the distribution side by assuming smaller transactions, the deal size would get even lower since the terms would be even worse. On the other hand, arrangers cannot ask issuers to pay higher finance costs as they would not be able to secure the mandate. Thus the arranger's standing in the league table would drop significantly.

The decrease in the size of sales caused the lawyers' fees to increase relatively, and directly affected the earnings of security firms. Even if the firm were to foresee the problem and take action by reorganising the issuing costs, the decrease in sales could not be stopped. On the other hand, if the firm were to raise the issuing costs, their position as a mandated distributor could be taken away and the whole project would not work.

This situation led security firms to carry out bigger projects – massive retail target deals – and improve their product marketability, by meeting the needs of investors through selling products with embedded exotic options, to mend the conflicts of interest between the issuer, the investor and the firm.

As the market environment changed and products evolved over time, the mass media started focusing on clients that had suffered huge valuation losses/redemption losses. The change in society required firms to give investors a thorough explanation about product risks. The change forced the implementation of required regulations, the establishment of distribution business model for securities firms and an increase in the number of investors equipped with product knowledge. All these things have contributed to a strong foundation for retail structured products.

At the time, Nomura securities led the structured products market since they were ahead of the competitors in the retail target bond marketing at first. But in no time the other big firms had caught up with Nomura.

In order to further enhance the sales capability of structured notes, security firms encouraged more private placements with large investors, improvement of the marketing capability of retail structured products and strengthening the back office to look after structured products. Apart from a small number of second tier houses and all the first tier houses, distributors could not meet those requirements and therefore the retail target structured product market ended up being monopolised by those top-tier retail houses. Initially the size of the reverse dual bonds was around ¥1 billion; it grew to beyond ¥100 billion soon after.

As the project scales became larger and larger, the earnings made by structured products increased. The distribution of structured products business provided an important boost for the houses that had been struggling from the downfall of the stock market and the decrease of commission revenue earned from mutual funds distribution.

Yet, around the time when the structured products business was establishing itself, the spread between domestic and foreign currency interest rates started to rise. In order to maintain the prevailing rates, reverse dual bonds' tenors had to be longer than 10 years. Basically, retail investors tend to disfavour long-term investment, while securities companies strategise to obtain maximum returns from finite client assets. To fulfil both sides' desires, shortening the tenor had to be coordinated.

Schemes with as early redemption as possible were favoured, reverse dual currency bonds with FX triggered early redemption structures and callable bonds with rate triggers were introduced. In a short period of time, those early redemption structures started to have multiple observation periods to increase the probability of early redemption. Retail investors were attracted to early redemption features that potentially allowed them to recover their invested capital sooner. The structured product market in retail space then grew rapidly.

Early redemption structures were further developed, ie, observation dates were every coupon date or every business day before maturity. Retail investors had increasingly focused on current yield per deal but did not consider improvement on the return per term based on long-term investment.

On the other hand, products such as multi-callable type structured products that were tested for early redemption by the issuer were continually being developed. Swap providers would be given full authority to judge whether the bond should be redeemed. However, the reason for the early redemption was not really clear to the retail investors. Eventually, it became difficult for retail investors to estimate when the product would be redeemed, and many failed to understand the reasons why that choice had been made. Gradually, investors lost interest in the product.

After finding out that bonds with high current yield and short terms were fairly acceptable to investors, the next product development theme moved towards diversifying currencies. The underlying currencies were expanded from USD to GBP, AUD, New Zealand dollars (NZD), Mexican pesos (MXN), etc. By choosing higher yield, more exotic and less liquid currencies in order to achieve higher coupon on the bonds, dealers had to bear more responsibility on sales promotion.

As a rate-linked product, coupons linked to CMS rates (eg, 10y swap rate–2y swap rate + 1.0%) were introduced. The CMS spread structure is a structure that investors take a bet on steepness of the yen yield curve which we have discussed in detail in Chapter 6. It was the first structure with relatively complex formula that was offered to retail. Not that many retail investors bought the product due to its complexity; however, the distributors were criticised for not giving a thorough explanation upon selling. Compared with dual currency bonds and equity-linked notes (which we will talk about later), CMS-linked bonds did not have redemption risk. Nonetheless, the CMS-linked bond project reconfirmed the difficulties of structured bond business.

During the process of diversifying underlying assets and product features, the risks that investors were taking became more unique and specialised, and the increased complexity of products created the responsibility for security firms to explain them more carefully. Hence, the secondary distribution business done through the marketing model in which sales approach a large number of investors was never the easiest route. However, the ratio of structured products sold through private placement began to increase once again. At this stage, many of the sales people working at the branches of large security firms had gained a wide range of product knowledge. On the other hand, the number of investors who understood the market environment and the products in conjunction with the embedded risks was gradually increasing.

Furthermore, the number of structured product issuers was increasing, allowing arrangers to choose an issuer that indicated favourable conditions to investors. Security firms would no longer have to depend on major secondary distribution proposals but, instead, meet the needs of investors by matching them with the appropriate product depending on the market environment. Security firms that could foresee what any occasion might demand ultimately increased their earnings.

On the other hand, the market was attempting something new. Subsequent to the public funding that Resona Bank received in 1997, the Japanese stock market recovered and structured products that were linked to Nikkei Average futures were beginning to be accepted by investors.

These structured products were designed to monetise the premium by shorting the knock-out (KO) put options and to add them on to the relevant interest rate, causing the current yield to be more attractive than straight bonds. The products involved high volatility underlyings compared to interest rates, and exchange rates that short-dated structured products, ie, less than one year, attracted certain investors.

Structured products linked to single stocks were relatively higher in volatility than the Nikkei Average futures. It took a while until these could be sold domestically to retail customers after the revision of the Securities and Exchange Act in December 1998, which defined them as "over-the-counter derivatives".

At around the same time, principal-protected Nikkei-linked notes were introduced to the market. These notes were designed to buy call options with their discount premium, assuming the note was a zero-coupon one. If there were excess amounts of the discount premium left after buying the same notional worth of call options as the face value of the note, it would be treated as coupon. Thus the Nikkei-linked note was no longer a zero-coupon note but a Nikkei-linked note with a fixed coupon. This product was designed to attract those who expected the Nikkei Average to go up, but were not 100% comfortable being bullish, allowing them to enjoy the upside capital gains while principal was 100% protected. Soon after the introduction of this product, the rates dropped further to the extent that the call options with a notional worth the same as the face value of the note. Under these circumstances, bond structures were shaped to be able to purchase options by lengthening the bond tenors, choosing further out-of-the-money strike prices, and lowering the discount premiums – as the amount for the option premium represents less than the face value of the note – were tested out. As the result of trial and error, investors moved away from these types of products since they invited undesired long-term investments and complicated the relationship between the redemption amount and the volatility of the Nikkei Average at redemption. Having said that, emerging capital gains with structured products were further developed later to become funds using constant proportional portfolio insurance (CPPI) and the products wrapped within variable annuities.

Japanese mega-banks have been restructured since the start of the 1990s. From 1994, securities subsidiaries of mega-banks launched the sale of structured products. In 1995, the bail-out of the Jusen housing loan companies was decided. In 1997, Nissan Life, Sanyo Securities and Takushoku Bank filed for bankruptcy, and Yamaichi Securities opted for voluntary closure. In 1998, 21 large banks received injections of public capital. After all these events, the Nikkei Average had rebounded from 12,787.90 in October 1998 to 20,833.21 in April 2000. This was more than 60% appreciation in one-and-a-half years. Internet-based securities houses and day traders using Internet securities services had arisen by this time. Second tier securities houses and securities subsidiaries of mega-banks had all started to promote structured products.

In December 1998, the government lifted the ban on OTC sales of investment trust funds at banks. Banks started to promote structured products more than traditional investment trust funds, whose results were heavily influenced by the performance of fund managers; it was considered to have better reception by banks' traditional customers since structured products' redemptions were pre-patterned results depending on the relevant market conditions. This amendment made to the Securities Exchange Law defined the majority of financial derivatives trading as a part of financial institutions' operations. Before the amendment, domestic players were reluctant to participate in the OTC derivatives businesses since they were considered to violate articles 185 and 186 of the Penal Code. Thus, this revision provided a spark for the structured product businesses to further expand. At the same time, a charter amendment at securities exchanges had taken place with the abolition of the obligation that stock orders go through the exchanges. This amendment helped make the stock settlement much easier, particularly for those exchangeable bonds and reverse convertible notes that contributed to the development of equity structured products.

Hence, in 2000, the importance of structured products had grown exponentially since the collapse of the bubble in 1990.

Introduction of reverse convertible notes via secondary offerings in 1999 and post IT bubble and Sony shock in 2003

In 1999, Nikko Securities and Travelers group (Citigroup) jointly established Nikko Salomon Smith Barney securities in Tokyo. Daiwa Securities and Sumitomo Mitsui Banking Corporation jointly created Daiwa SMBC Securities. Nomura announced its decision to stay independent. In 2000, Mizuho Securities was created, by merging two securities companies under Mizuho Financial Group's umbrella. In 2002, Tokyo Mitsubishi Bank created Mitsubishi Securities by merging three securities houses under Mitsubishi's umbrella with Kokusai Securities sold by Nomura Securities. Even at the second tier level, Tokai Maruman Securities, which had succeeded Sanyo Securities and Yamaichi Securities businesses, merged with Tokyo Securities and became Tokai Tokyo Securities. Securities houses were dying to capitalise themselves, while banks wanted to take up securities businesses. Both intentions had accelerated restructuring.

In 1999, reverse convertible notes (RCNs) were introduced in Japan for the first time. RCNs, like other coupon bonds issued by European sovereign and financial institutions, redeem in stocks depending on the stock price at the maturity. As conditions of the bond terms, the reference stock, the reference stock price, the number of shares to be settled (usually expressed as face value amount/

reference stock price) and reference date before the redemption (usually 10 business days prior to the redemption date) were defined. When the closing stock price of the reference stocks on the reference date was less than the reference stock price, the settlement would take place in shares, otherwise it would be redeemed in cash.

The RCN structure is a very simple one. When the bond terms were set, investors sold put options with the strike price being the reference stock's reference price, and received the put option premium. This premium amount was to be added onto the plain vanilla coupon of the bond to make up a yield enhanced structured bond. Ordinarily, reference stock prices were set at around 80–95% of the share price of the reference stocks at the determination date of the bond conditions. Hence, investors bought the shares at a lower price than the share price of the issuance even if the bond was redeemed in the reference shares. As will become clear, RCNs involve target buying in the reference shares.

Although RCNs were orthodox products prior to the amendment made to the Securities Exchange law, the product could not be promoted to the retail investors in Japan. As mentioned earlier, the previous status of the law defined derivative trades based on interest rates and index futures as the underlying; however, it did not define the derivative trades underlying as cash equities. Therefore, domestic houses could not find the legal basis to legitimise such trades as one of the operations performed by financial institutions. Furthermore, if the trades took place on domestic turf they could be seen as gambling, and the person who executed the trades could potentially be penalised. Even if the trades were understood to be legal, they were highly likely, given the physical settlement, to be recognised as trades under the tax law. Also the physical settlement could potentially be seen as the violation of the Exchange stipulation of making all the trades through the exchanges.

Bearing in mind the above situation, domestic securities houses limited sales of the products to their overseas securities subsidiaries to sell to non-residents in the euro market. The regulatory authorities were aware that it could be inferred that they had consolidated the opinions of the securities industry in order to develop the relevant legal systems. In any event, RCNs were highly saleable products that domestic securities houses proactively played out in the retail market after the amendment made in December 1998.

RCNs attracted three types of investors. The first were those bullish in the share price of the reference stocks. These investors understood the product as a high-yield product and invested. The second were those not bullish but not expecting a huge drop in the share price. To these investors, sales highlighted the effectiveness of the target-buying method, and they responded positively. The third group took advantage of the Nikkei Average starting to bottom out around the 13,000 level, thinking that even if they ended up with the physical shares at settlement they could expect to outperform the original bond investment by holding the shares.

There was another reason why securities houses were willing to promote RCNs, and that was because of the high degree of freedom in choosing single stocks as the reference stock. Each single stock had different characteristics from the index or the market as a whole that allowed distributors to build suitable strategies to promote the products. Hence the offerings were not greatly influenced by equity market trends. In addition, there were always stocks with volatility higher than index volatility. There was a great degree of freedom of design, regardless of the market situation.

The retail investors in Japan got interested in recovering their investments in the short term. The volatility of the equity market was higher than that of the debt market. And there were many single stocks with volatilities higher than the index volatility. Taking liquidity into consideration, there were roughly 100 names constantly available to be structured as the underlying of RCN. This large universe of availability actually eliminated the competition among the securities houses since the probability of multiple houses choosing the same underlying, as well as the same issue date, the same strike price, the same tenor, etc, was very low. Consequently, if a house managed to offer a condition that fulfilled investors' absolute demand level it did not need to improve the condition. Consequently the RCN market has boomed in a short period of time.

Initially, in December 1998, RCNs were sold via private placements; however, demand for RCNs was so much higher than expected that they started to be sold in public. Top tier distributors' placement power was so immense that RCNs were sometimes sold beyond their reference stock's daily trading amount. As a result, securities houses needed to take the reference stock's liquidity into consideration.

Therefore, RCNs using the Nikkei Index as their reference asset were developed, which, using the Nikkei Index helped to expand the universe of investors. Nikkei Index markets, both futures and cash, had such a greater liquidity than singles stocks that large public offerings became possible. Since there were no ETFs on Nikkei Index, the redemptions had to be settled in cash. This product feature alerted investors to the fact that the redemptions could be less than par amounts of the bonds and the notes required further improvement. This effort led to the introduction of Nikkei-linked knock-in (KI) RCNs. Basically, this product was designed to replace short vanilla puts with short knock-in type synthetic long forwards. These synthetic long forwards were simply a combination of short KI put options and long KI call options. When these options were embedded in bonds, in the eyes of retail investors, the product feature was dramatically improved.

(a) Knock-in/knock-out NKY-linked note
Typical terms.

Issue date: March 3, 199*x*.

Maturity date: September 3, 199*x*.

Coupon: 8%.

Reference: Nikkei Average Index price.

Observation period: issue date to 10 days prior to the maturity date.

Knock-in level: reference price $\times$ 60% on the pricing date.

Redemption amount: 10 business days prior to the maturity date.

Redemption price: the reference market's closing price on the redemption amount.

Strike price: the reference price $\times$ 90% on the pricing date.

Redemption amount:

- **Case 1:** if the reference market price had never traded below the knock-in price during the observation period.
  Redemption amount = 100%.

- **Case 2:** if the reference market price had traded below the knock-in price even once during the observation period.
  Redemption amount = redemption price/strike price.

Major buyers and their motivation.   Retail investors are the major buyers. In order to enjoy income gains, they take risks in a familiar underlying. At the same time, knock-out options are applied to invite potential early redemption and knock-in options are attached to decrease the risk of redemption below par. For those who think future Nikkei prices will be at or above knock-in price level, this is an attractive product.

Regulation, accounting background.   The separate withholding tax on interest received is only 10%, which is attractive in comparison to the highest bracket tax, 50%.

Structuring and distribution.   Arrangers are mainly Japanese securities companies. Issuers are typically highly rated overseas government agencies and financial institutions. Issuers enter into equity swaps when bonds are issued and fund on USD base with a floating rate. Swap providers are mainly US and European investment banks.

The reasons why it worked.   The Nikkei Average Index futures' market had high liquidity. Also, the volatility of the Nikkei Index was higher than rate markets, foreign exchange markets and other asset classes that had the Nikkei as an underlying could produce relatively higher coupon.

As we can see, the holders of the above notes were to receive the par at redemption if the Nikkei does not fall more than 40% during the observation period and the bond does not get knocked in. At the same time, the investors can enjoy a high return of 8% per annum. The sales talk would be "do you think the Nikkei will fall by 40%? If the Nikkei does not fall more than 40% the bond will redeem at par".

Even if the options were knocked in, since the strike price of the options was set at 90% of the reference price, unless the reference market price were above 90% the bond would not be less than the par amount. Furthermore, if the reference market price on the judgement date was exactly the same as the closing of the pricing date the bond could even redeem over par, ie, 111% = 100/90. If the reference market price on the judgement date was below 20% of the pricing date it was designed to get away with the redemption amount of 88.9% = 80/90, which was less than the decline, −20%, of the Nikkei Index. This series of Nikkei-linked KI notes was so well received by

Table 7.2 Comparison between fund-wrapped structured notes and regular structured notes

	Knock-in funds	Equity-linked bonds with KI feature	Comparison
Underlying asset	Nikkei Stock Average price		Indifferent
Term	Option term; strike price; knock-in level; redemption test dates are set to be the same		Indifferent
Sales commission	3% to distribution company	Distributors make a spread when bonds are structured	If distributors make 3% in both cases there is no difference
Trust fee	1% per annum to trustee bank, investment trust management company, and distributor	NA	Funds are more expensive
Product selection	The management company examines the issuer's credit and the suitability, and it acts practically as the bond arranger	Securities company, the distributor, selects issuer and negotiate various terms	If the capability of the management company and the securities house are the same in the arranger role they are indifferent
Mark-to-market	Management company does the MTM on a daily basis; the mark is shared with the trust bank, and the trust bank announces the information on the following day	Distributor informs the investors on a monthly basis	Funds absolutely MTM more frequent

Table 7.2 Continued

	Knock-in funds	Equity-linked bonds with KI feature	Comparison
Sale before maturity	Impossible	Impossible	Indifferent
Minimum unit	US$100	Between US$5,000 and US$10,000	Funds allow you to invest in a small amount
Target investors	Investors not familiar with structured products	Investors familiar with structured products and cost-conscious	Funds are more for beginner investors in structured products
Distribution	Banks	Securities houses	Banks are legally prohibited from distributing bonds
Structuring and responsibility	The management company is separate and independent of the distribution company; the distributor does not bear management responsibility	Structuring is done by the distributor; the distributor does not bear the management responsibility	In the case of funds, the distributors do not participate in structuring; in both cases, the distributor does not bear the management responsibility

the retail investors that top tier distributors had sold ¥20–50 billion every month. Before this product, structured notes usually meant rate-linked or foreign-exchange-linked products. The Nikkei-linked KI note was the product that expanded equity-linked structured products.

The market for Nikkei-linked KI notes rapidly expanded because of their ability to provide fine adjustments. For instance, for those investors concerned that the Nikkei could drop more than 40%, the product could be delivered at a 50% KI level while shaving the coupon a bit. When investors were more bullish than the prior example, the note could be designed with a 70% KI level and higher coupon. For those investors who required both a lower KI level and higher coupon, the note could be designed with higher volatility reference stocks as its underlying.

The flexibility of the product forced the securities houses to improve internal communication between their sales department and their structuring group and the communication between sales and investors to capture the real needs of investors in order to generate high demand at the time. In the mean time, structured products sold via private placements had increased to billions of yen per month per distributor due to both sales teams and investors gaining experience and knowledge about the products.

There was a new venture – and that was banks' OTC sale of investment trust funds. In 2000, trust banks were not capable of evaluating equity swaps and credit management of their counterparties. Thus, KI trust funds did not execute OTC swaps but bought structured notes.

How were these fund-wrapped structured bonds better than regular structured notes? A comparison of fund-wrapped structured notes and regular structured notes is given in Table 7.2.

According to Table 7.2, in the case of KI funds, it is clear that trust fees were borne by the investors; however, asset management companies took responsibility for the management, ie, selection of the structured notes, daily MTM of the notes and their publication. Chuo Mitsui Trust and Banking started such KI fund promotion ahead of their competitors. The sale of KI funds was thought to be a new business model allowing trust banks to compete against commercial banks. Since the funds could be distributed with a smaller unit amount and they had increased the transparency, the total sale amount quickly increased and soon reached hundreds of billions of yen.

Products had evolved to match investors' needs. KI forwards were replaced by KI puts. This literally meant taking out long KI calls, which saves the KI call premium cost. Hence the coupon level improved a little bit. Other attempts were made not to knock-in easily by the configuration of the judgement dates. However, when the probability of KI falls, the option premium that the coupon receives will decrease accordingly. It is a trade-off, and distributors need to grasp accurately what investors want in terms of risk versus return. The distributor's capability directly influenced their revenue.

KI equity-linked notes with KO features were developed in 2002. The structure can handle both indexes and single stocks as the underlying. The KO feature on the KI options was there to encourage early redemption and the KI feature would be removed as soon as KO conditions were met. As we all know, retail investors in Japan favour early recovery of their invested principal. Thus, KI equity-linked notes with a KO feature became a suitable refinement. In case of the KI, an RCN with KO feature described in the term sheet would behave as follows.

When the underlying stock XXX surges by 10% after the pricing date, it fixes the early and par redemption amounts at the next coupon payment date. The investor in this product receives 7% per annum coupon regardless of early redemption.

Investors had to face more issues before the market matured. From the bursting of the IT bubble to the decline of the Nikkei to 7,000 and the Lehman shock, we had experienced market illiquidity.

(b) ENMAN bond
Typical terms.

Issue date: March 3, 199x.

Maturity date: March 3, 200x.

Coupon:

- **Case 1:** if the closing price of Nikkei Index five business days prior to the coupon payment date was above coupon judgement price, coupon = 4% (per annum).

- **Case 2:** otherwise, coupon = 0.5%.

Coupon payment date: The corresponding dates in March, in September and on the maturity date after the issue date.

Coupon judgement price: Nikkei Average Index price × 90% on the pricing date.

Early redemption judgement price: Nikkei Average Index price × 120% on the pricing date.

Early redemption: If the closing price of Nikkei Average Index five days prior to coupon payment dates, excluding the maturity date, were above the early redemption judgement price, then the bond would be redeemed on the immediate next coupon payment date at 100%.

The ENMAN bond was invented in 2002 after the IT bubble when the equity market was trending downwards. The structure was designed not to incur redemption loss and ENMAN bonds were easily accepted from investors. Even if the coupon was determined to be 0.5%, the bond could potentially pay 4% if the Nikkei market recovered after six months or a year. The fact that one single bad market event would only affect the bond's performance temporarily – with the rest of coupon determined by the reference market conditions of the following period – was viewed favourably by the market participants. ENMAN bonds continued to be popular until 2005, when the Nikkei Average reached 15,000. The volatility of the Nikkei had dropped and the lower long-term rate had resulted in lower coupon. In order to compensate the coupon, the tenors of bonds started to be lengthened to 20 years. Even with the early redemption feature, the retail market had lost its interest in ENMAN bonds. After the Sony shock in 2007, Nikkei started to decline from the 17,500 level, and before the Lehman shock ENMAN issues could not attract investors. In order for this product to revive, we probably need to wait for the Nikkei Average to trend upwards from 15,000.

Impact of the Lehman shock

The drawbacks of sophisticated structured products came to light during the Lehman crisis. Hedge-fund-linked products and credit-linked products failed to provide liquidity, and some of those products could not even post mark-to-market values. Those who invested in these products had no way of knowing the value of their investments.

Table 7.3 Product acceptance changed after Lehman shock

Product	Prior to Lehman shock	Post Lehman shock
PRDC	Re-boomed due to the spread between domestic and international rates widening	Dramatically reduced because the spread narrowed
Equity-linked funds with knock-in feature attached	Some banks sold them periodically, and they had grown to be one of their revenue pillars	Diminished because most of the outstanding funds had knocked in and legislation on product solicitation was introduced
Hedge-fund-linked fund	Market had expanded and the sale size had started to be US$500 million to US$1 billion per offer because hedge fund managers used managed accounts and due to the increase in the number of guarantee companies	Market had shrunk because many funds failed to provide liquidity and failed to display the price
Hedge-fund-linked fund (CPPI)	Some hedge funds and the Hedge Fund Index were used and offered in the form of CPPI; principal protection and provision of liquidity had attracted investors	Most positions were at OTM level so investors could not expect excess returns; CPPI's viability was questioned and the market had shrunk
Straight foreign bonds	Emerging currency denominated straight debts were very popular due to their relatively high rates	Sharp appreciation in JPY had created some unrealised losses in the JPY base, but the liquidity was never lost; the market reboomed after Lehman shock
Credit-linked bonds/CDOs	The structure looked somewhat simpler than other structured notes, so some investors picked them up; they are also high rate notes	The market shrank when investors understood the complicated structure used in CLNs and CDOs

Equity-linked bonds and PRDC markets shrank for a while, but for different reasons. The relevant market conditions did not facilitate attractive terms for those products. Interest differential between non-JPY currencies and JPY remained tight which was not ideal for PRDCs. Dealers had no appetite for adding risk either. However, equity-linked bond markets have recovered completely in a year or so driven by demand from investors. Acceptance of structured products changed after the Lehman shock (Table 7.3).

Retail investors look for investments that are easy to understand. In the early 1990s, fixed-income retail investors had invested in dual currency bonds and later reverse dual currency bonds. In the same period, equity-linked product retail investors had invested in convertible bonds, asset swapped convertible bonds and bonds with warrants. The rise of equity structured products in the retail space slowly started to grow in 1995. This time around those convertible bonds and warrant markets had quickly shrunk due to the lack of supply by Japanese corporates. Nikkei-linked products were structured to replace those traditional equity-linked products; however, retail investors did not jump on these new equity-linked structured products.

In December 1998, the Securities and Exchange Act was revised to lift the ban on OTC derivatives trading by securities houses. This expanded the availability of structured products for retail in Japan. Namely, PRDC bonds, reverse convertible notes and Nikkei-linked bonds were invented and sold in massive numbers into the retail system until the Lehman shock in 2008. However, from 1999 to 2003 equity products did not boom so rapidly. Equity-linked products, along with other structured products (eg, hedge-fund-linked CPPI, variable annuity products), started to be purchased after the state capital injection into Resona Bank took place.

CONCLUSION

In the early 1990s, structured products were either FX linked or rate linked, and they were issued to target institutional investors. For the retail structured product markets to boom, the participation of securities houses was indispensable. This was made possible with the revision of the Securities and Exchange Act in late 1998.

The equity-linked product market started to grow after 1999, and growth was further accelerated after 2003, triggered by the state capital injection into Resona Bank. At that point the equity market up-trended. Retail investors had long loved PRDC – until the foreign domestic rate spread decreased, around the time the Lehman crisis hit the market.

The Lehman crisis made investors aware of what is important in their investments: stable liquidity and frequent mark-to-market on their products. A lot of newly invented structured products failed to fulfil these requirements. Accounting, law, and market conditions have affected structures and their salability. Since the late 1980s, the revision of the Securities and Exchange Act, mark-to-market accounting applications, injection of state capital into Resona Bank, and the Sony and Lehman shocks have dictated the fate of structured products in both retail and institutional markets.

REFERENCES

Baba, N., 2006, "Financial Market Functioning and Monetary Policy: Japan's Experience", *Monetary and Economic Studies* 24, Institute for Monetary and Economic Studies, Bank of Japan, Tokyo, pp. 67–104.

Hedge Transaction Permeation Association, 2010, "Proposal on accounting and tax treatment of hedge transactions", January, Japan Commodity Futures Industry Association, Tokyo, pp. 1–21.

Kodachi, K., 2007, "The Regulatory Impact of the Financial Instruments and Exchange Act to Banks", *Nomura Capital Markets Quarterly*, Spring, pp. 31–44.

Weekly Diamond, 2009, "The Trap of Foreign Exchange Structured Products", Oct 17, Diamond, Inc, Tokyo, pp. 74–84.

Weekly Toyo Keizai, 2011, "Financial Strength Ranking of 635 Private Schools 2011", October 10, Tokyo Keizai Inc, Tokyo, pp. 104–107.

8

A History of the US Structured Products Industry

Scott Mitchell and Daniel Roose
JP Morgan

This chapter will discuss the history and evolution of the structured products industry in the US, with a primary focus on meaningful developments in the market for retail oriented structured products. Overall, the growth of the structured products market in the US has to a large extent mirrored the growth in the financial services industry generally from the mid-1990s to the middle of 2013. Over this period structured investments have moved from an alternative investment initially available to a small subset of ultra-high-net-worth private bank clients and a handful of retail clients of large wirehouse distributors, to a widely available investment vehicle held by many large and small retail investors alike. The increase in the availability of structured products since around the mid-1990s is also evidenced by the significant expansion in providers and available wrappers/distribution types. In addition there has been a dramatic increase in payouts available, as well as in the variety of available underlying assets.

Much like the macro-market environment, the growth in structured products has been characterised by several distinct periods of boom and bust. Specifically, the market grew strongly from its inception in the mid-1990s until the financial crisis starting in 2008, with significant retraction in the second half of 2008 that carried into the first half of 2009. Remarkably, and for reasons we shall delve into more deeply later in this chapter, the market recovered more quickly (and with some new, hard-to-predict characteristics) than almost anyone had envisioned in late 2008 and has been experiencing another round of expansion and innovation, starting in roughly mid-2009 and continuing to the time of writing in late 2013.

INDUSTRY INCEPTION AND EARLY YEARS (1995–2004)

The first structured products (specifically, cross-asset linked embedded derivative securities primarily intended for retail market distribution) in the US market are generally viewed to have arisen in the mid-1990s. During the mid-1990s the product set was predominantly oriented towards various types of institutional investors who were statutorily or otherwise prohibited from transacting in over-the-counter (OTC) derivatives but sought a comparable degree of customised and/or specific exposure. Often these investors were mutual fund managers, many with a fixed-income/yield mandate seeking equity performance to supplement prevailing investment grade corporate bond yields. This was especially true of the dramatic rise in the US equity markets over the latter half of the 1990s, with many institutional investors beginning to expand into early structured notes purchases to add enhanced yield opportunities to bond portfolios.

While much of the early market issuance was institutionally focused, there were areas of emphasis on retail product issuance. In particular, varieties of principal-protected products (taking advantage of the high interest rate environment at the time to structure attractive products) were offered to US retail clients, especially through well-established retail brokerage channels such as Merrill Lynch. From the mid-1990s, up until the Securities and Exchange Commission's (SEC) Plain English Prospectus Mandate, issued in 1998, many of the securities offered were disclosed via dense and multi-featured prospectus-style documentation. While some offerings in this period were made available publicly to US retail clients, the SEC's requirement in 1998 that prospectus offerings be written clearly and in "plain English" made the offering documentation more transparent, decipherable and of interest to a wider array of retail clients and their brokers and investment advisers. The required content and suggested organisation contained in this guidance formed the basic outline that most structured product offering material in the US market continues to follow, albeit with some important modifications made around the mid-2000s.

Another key US market development in the mid-1990s that paved the way for much of the retail distribution activity over the next decade and a half (especially for SEC registered products) is generally referred to as the "Morgan Stanley reading room". In 1996, at the request of Morgan Stanley and their external counsel at Davis Polk & Wardwell, the SEC issued a no-action letter, which provided guidance on disclosure for registered offerings and products exchangeable for securities of an unaffiliated entity. The SEC agreed that, within certain parameters, a structured product issuer could rely on publicly available disclosure by the issuer of an underlying reference stock, rather than requiring typical underwriter-level diligence and liability. This shift in disclosure agreements heralded a dramatic increase in single stock linked structured products issuance that was to emerge over the next 10 years.

The US market for retail structured products began picking up speed and depth towards the end of the 1990s and into the 2000s, with a number of new entrants but still limited generally to large issuing institutions (primarily the large US and foreign banks) and internal sales focused on their own captive distribution channels. It is possible to observe some general characteristics of the prevalent distribution models at this point; namely that issuing entities with large internal retail brokerage networks (such as Merrill Lynch from early on, and Morgan Stanley especially after the acquisition of Dean Witter) focused on more traditional retail products and channels, as well as SEC registered offerings. Other institutions without an available retail brokerage channel focused more on their private client/wealth management distribution arms, and tended to emphasise private placements sold to high-net-worth clients rather than registered public distributions. Many of the efforts in these early years cantered around key product providers – attempts to brand their own product suite, and to differentiate their product offerings from those of their competitors. This trend continued despite the fact that many of these products were essentially quite similar in payout characteristics. This push dissipated significantly as the industry matured over the course of the 2000s. Finally, in the early 2000s, foreign issuers such as Soc-Gen and ABN AMRO began to issue notes that were distributed by independent third party "aggregators" such as Countrywide, LaSalle and Incapital to the independent broker-dealer community.

Despite the stock market downturn and recession of 2001 (following the bursting of the Internet tech bubble) interest in structured products continued to grow across the US market. As described above, different issuers focused on accessing and expanding this market from different angles. The overall trend was clear in moving away from relatively infrequent large-scale offerings aimed at institutional buyers, towards higher volume, tranche-based structured product issuances targeted increasingly to the full range of retail clients. During this time the industry began developing some of the characteristics that we still see in key product payouts and an emphasis on growing volumes of these standard products offered repeatedly month after month, often aligning with the typical monthly brokerage offering cycle. This pattern accelerated and grew as the industry entered its growth years in the mid-2000s and approached a state of relative maturity in the years immediately preceding the crash of 2008.

GROWTH ERA AND INDUSTRY MATURITY (2004–8 H1)

The years 2004–6 marked a key turning point for the structured products industry in the US. Between 2004 and 2006, many new product issuers as well as US distributors began building out their issuing and distribution capabilities. By the end of 2006 almost every significant financial service/investment provider in the US was involved in the manufacture and/or distribution of structured products. Additionally, this period also witnessed an increased emphasis on external, or third party, distribution with many issuing banks that had previously been focused on their own internal distribution channels building out coverage teams and capabilities to focus on selling that issuer's structured products into a wide variety of external distribution channels. Finally, this era saw not only significant growth in the volume of structured products traded in the US but also an explosion in their variety and, to some extent, their complexity. This remains the case even though the US market has not, generally speaking, become as variable or as diverse as other large global markets, most particularly that of EMEA.

The following example illustrates anecdotally the increase in volumes during this period. One of the authors of this chapter started as the junior member of the structured products sales team at a Canadian Bank's US subsidiary in late 2003. At that time, summarising the monthly issuance across the entire market was a three-to-four-hour task, with no more than 50 deals per month across the entire market. Today, the top issuers in the market typically issue well over

100 individual offerings per month. A number of independent media companies now publish summaries (for a fee of course!) that cover more deals for a given day than the monthly summaries the author prepared in 2003.

Client channels

The external distribution channels that characterise the US market and that have served as focal points for structured products distribution were largely well established by 2005–6, and provide context to the overall US marketplace and its most significant participants. Additionally, these various client segments tend to have differing investor bases and appetites for particular products, depending on their individual sophistication and portfolio requirements.

The first of these networks is made up of the various private banks and private wealth management channels, many attached to large US banks but also including other smaller wealth managers. These clients typically range from high-net-worth to ultra-high-net-worth individuals or family office type organisations of professional level sophistication. Generally, these clients tend to invest in tax-efficient (ie, usually seeking long-term capital gains treatment) principal-at-risk products that offer some form of leverage or yield enhancement on the upside, and partial protection on the downside. The trade-off, of course, is typically a cap or maximum return that limits investor returns on the upside. As a result, these products typically outperform a direct investment in a bearish or moderately bullish scenario, but underperform in very bullish scenarios.

Similar to private bank/wealth management entities are affiliated broker-dealers, also known as known as "wirehouses", which tend to have a more diverse clientele but are also typically attached to a large parent bank (examples at the time of writing are Morgan Stanley Smith Barney and Bank of America Merrill Lynch). These organisations and their clients tend to be more diverse in their investment focus, with an interest in tax-efficient principal-at-risk structures, similar to private bank clients. However, these are also often intermixed with other products, including principal-protected investments in either note or certificate-of-deposit (CD) form. These principal-protected investments (which are linked to varying asset classes but most frequently equity or interest rates) are often held in retirement or other tax deferred accounts to mitigate the prevailing income tax treatments imposed on these instruments by the US Internal Revenue Service.

Additionally, a distribution segment that became a much larger piece of the US market, especially in the years from 2004 to 2006, is a group generally referred to as unaffiliated or independent broker-dealers. This term is probably the broadest designation and can be used to describe broker-dealer entities without a parent bank, ranging in size from national networks, such as LPL Financial and Raymond James, to much smaller regionally focused broker-dealers. Generally, these entities consist of individual brokers who liaise with individual end investors to discuss and execute the purchase of a particular structured product. Similar to the affiliated networks discussed above, the products purchased in this distribution channel range widely from various types of principal-at-risk structures (discussed in more detail below) to a range of principal-protected products yielding both growth and income opportunities. Because structured products (notes and CDs) settle via the Depositary Trust Clearing Corporation (DTC) like conventional bonds, and most independent dealers do not have in-house product capabilities, there are very few barriers to entry to this segment of the market.[1] As the market has evolved, most issuers have built their businesses to focus on the largest 30–40 independent dealers, and partner with aggregators to promote their products to the smaller dealers (there are more than 600 independent broker-dealers across the US in total).

The final distribution segment of the US market is composed of registered investment advisers (or RIAs). RIAs are regulated asset managers (under the Investment Advisors Act of 1940) with investment authority and often discretion over customer accounts. Most RIAs outsource the custody of client accounts to firms like Charles Schwab, Fidelity or Pershing. The key distinction in this client segment is the drive away from a transactional brokerage model where a broker is paid a per-trade commission to compensation based on a percentage of assets under management (AUM). This compensation structure is mandated by the Investment Advisors Act of 1940 and incentivises the investment advisor to grow their AUM (and related percentage payout) versus maximising commission payments. RIAs can vary in size from several million dollars under management to some of the larger firms with multiple-billion-dollar portfolios;

these larger RIAs can rival institutional asset managers in terms of expertise and sophistication and tend to focus on a combination of strategic portfolio allocations and tactical, market-driven buying opportunities. Like the independent broker-dealers, there are few barriers to entry to cover RIAs. Because of their relative sophistication, most issuers create specific products and marketing efforts to target this segment.

Distribution wrappers and market impact

There have historically been three main groups of distribution wrappers in the US market, and we shall discuss each of these in turn as well as significant developments corresponding to any of them and how that affected the overall development of the US market in the years 2004–8.

As context, the US Securities Act of 1933 requires that any publicly available offering of securities in the US be registered with the US Securities and Exchange Commission (SEC). Additionally, the US Securities Act of 1933 provides for a number of exemptions from this public registration requirement, which drove various market developments both prior to and during this period. After the Plain English prospectus requirement issued by the SEC in 1998, and up until the streamlined offering documentation approach allowed under the SEC's Securities Offering Reforms of 2005, every offering of publicly available registered structured notes in the US had to be conducted under a lengthy prospectus supplement tailored to that specific offering and payout. Consequently, the time to market as well as the overhead cost to transact small to mid-size registered notes structured products offerings was extremely high, with the end result that very little of the volume of structured products issued in the US prior to 2005 was done in registered note format.

Prior to 2005, for this reason, much of the structured product issuance done in the US market was in private placement or certificate-of-deposit format. Each of these issuance wrappers suffered from their own separate limitations and, taken collectively with the SEC's registration requirements, represented a significant headwind to the development of the US structured products market in the early part of the 2000s. The exceptions to this general statement were notes issued by the US branches of foreign banks under an additional Securities Act exemption known as 3(a)(2), allowing bank-guaranteed securities to be sold publicly without requiring SEC registration. Through the 3(a)(2) exemptions, foreign banks with US branches were able to issue and publicly offer structured notes in small denominations that did not require registration with the SEC (US banks were able to take advantage of this as well but due to status as US entities were required to offer with a minimum investment of US$100,000, generally preclusive for wide retail distribution). Many large French banks were prolific issuers of 3(a)(2) notes, which in the early 2000s were the product wrapper of choice for these foreign banks to distribute through third party aggregators as well as through the independent broker-dealer channel. This wrapper effectively allowed them to access a wide variety of US retail clients.

Two other exemptions from SEC registration that were frequently used for non-institutional buyers of structured products (and that remain most widely used today) were Regulation D and Regulation S offerings. The exemption afforded under Regulation D was widely used for US high-net-worth investors but limited sales to not more than 35 retail investors. Alternatively, it allowed sales only to "accredited investors" (net worth of over US$1 million and steady income of at least US$200,000 for individuals). Additionally, sales to accredited investors required the execution of a cumbersome purchaser's certificate and had severe restriction on secondary market transfers (many of these issues remain today for Reg D offerings, making them still sub-optimal for widespread distribution). Regulation S provided for sales of unregistered securities to non-US persons only, which while useful offshore (even when marketed out of US issuing entities) statutorily precluded sales to any US persons.

The other available avenue for the distribution of structured products was, and remains today, bank-issued CDs. In addition to requiring an available bank issuer, CDs are by nature 100% principal protected, which limits the varieties of payouts available and possible tax treatments. While there were a number of fairly active issuers of structured products in CD format in the early 2000s, the principal protection requirement proved a non-starter for the multiple different payout scenarios sought by clients, especially those high and ultra-high-net-worth private banking clients who were the earliest high-volume purchasers of structured products.

All of this began to change on December 1, 2005 when the SEC modified their registration requirements and allowed certain issuers (known as WKSIs, or well-known seasoned issuers, and which included all large US and foreign investment banks) to automatically establish a "registered shelf" of securities, from which they could "take down" or issue individual tranches on a piecemeal basis. While this ability to establish a shelf had existed previously, and was how many issuers were handling issuance of registered notes already, the automatic registration aspect and, more importantly, the relaxation of strict requirements for offering prospectuses were a significant development. Specifically, issuers were now entitled to file a much broader range of offering documentation (known as a "free writing prospectus") rather than being limited to only the prescribed prospectus-style documentation. Moreover, the SEC codified the precept of access equals delivery, paving the way for issuers across the market to rely on a "documentation pyramid" with relatively short and simple deal-specific term sheet documents and hyperlinks to the full suite of underlying base disclosures. Perhaps even more importantly, electronic delivery and the concept of "access equals delivery" allowed issuers to further reduce costs because paper documents were generally no longer required. Many structured products issuers recognised this as a clear opportunity to multiply volumes of their structured products issuances that were publicly available and in particular to expand the variety of payouts, including those with principal at risk, that were widely distributable. Not surprisingly, in the early months of 2006, volumes and the variety of structured product issuance across the US market began to rise dramatically. In 2005 volumes were 5.3 billion, growing almost 400% to 21 billion by 2006.

Key US products

As the issuance of structured products expanded and diversified into 2006 the US market began to develop characteristics that were similar to other global markets but also different in several important respects. In particular, US tax laws had a notable impact on the varieties of different products preferred by different investor classes. As background, the product categories discussed below are the main varieties of structured products that have traded most frequently in the US market and remain the most relevant payout families (although in some cases modified).

The first broad category of products is known as principal-protected notes or the various market-linked certificates of deposit (all of which are required to be fully principal protected). While both of these products are referred to generally as PPNs, it is important to note that a bank-issued certificate of deposit typically includes Federal Deposit Insurance Corporation (FDIC) insurance up to applicable limits, while the "principal protection" in notes is entirely subject to the credit of the issuer. While protection is popular among many investors, in the US variance on ordinary income level taxation make these products generally most suitable for retirement or other tax deferred accounts. That said, principal-protected notes and certificates of deposit have been, and remain, one of the broadest and most prevalent categories of structured products in the US market. Generally these are structured by combining a bond component (generally described as a zero-coupon) with various option combinations that can offer, among other things, upside participation/leveraged upside participation, periodic contingent coupon payments or be subject to a maximum return.

One of the most popular principal-at-risk structures is a capped note with leveraged upside (typically structured as the client long a call spread, sometimes leveraged) with some or no protection, or buffer, on the downside. The downside is generally structured as the client being short some variety of a put, either at- or in-the-money (corresponding to the buffer/protection amount) or in some cases a knock-in put. This product is generally designed for investors who are moderately bullish on an underlying asset but seek to reduce some of their volatility exposure via buffered downside protection. This product is particularly popular due to its potential to outperform in all but one (significant upside) market scenario. Additionally, clients can tailor their exposure by customising the amount of leverage on the call spread, the capped return level (based the on strike of the short out-of-the-money call) as well as the degree of protection available through different varieties of put options. Finally, for many US investors, especially those of relatively high net worth, the possibility of receiving long-term capital gains on the performance of the structure (if the term is longer than one year) is a significant added attraction.

Probably the most widely offered product in the US retail structured products market, particularly prior to the financial crisis, is commonly referred to as the reverse exchangeable or reverse convertible. These products are designed for investors who are

- moderately bullish on an underlying asset but believe it will be range-bound in the short term;
- seeking a coupon rate that is higher than the yield from owning that underlying outright; and
- comfortable taking on the downside risk of the underlying.

Reverse exchangeables pay a fixed coupon and provide protection for the initial investment contingent on the underlying not declining below a stated initial level on any day during the term of the note. If the underlying does decline below the stated initial level, the investor is exposed to the entire downside performance of the underlying at maturity, and will typically receive physical shares rather than cash at the issuer's option. To create this structure from an options perspective, an investor is selling a put (usually with a knock-in barrier), thereby generating a yield that will vary based on the volatility of the underlying as well as the amount of buffered protection (which is in turn related to the type and strike of the put option the client is effectively selling). This is a product that gained in popularity over the mid-2000s and that became the best example of a highly commoditised offering allowing individual retail investors to tailor a product for their own portfolio and investment view. Much of the significant volume of reverse exchangeables traded in the 2007–8 period were individual clients tailoring these products for their own views and accounts. By 2008 most issuers would offer clients customised individual offerings for as low as US$500,000 in total notional. At the time of writing many issuers continued to offer even lower minimums, or even no minimums at all.

Similar to reverse exchangeable products but encompassing a wider variety of payout iterations is a product known generally as an autocall. Designed for investors who are neutral to moderately bullish on an underlying asset, or in many cases several underlying assets in worst-of or basket formulations, the autocall provided enhanced yield for investors willing to sell downside market risk. This structure is typically automatically called in accordance with a predefined schedule if the underlying traded within or above a specified range. One of the advantages of the autocall versus the traditional reverse exchangeable was that by structuring the first call and payment at maturity to be longer than one year, returns were taxed as long-term capital gains. Reverse exchangeables, on the other hand, with their monthly coupons, were not as tax efficient for high-net-worth investors. Other common features of various types of autocalls can include, but are not limited to, snowballing coupons that increase over time and are paid only if the autocall is triggered, and individually monitored coupon barriers which can put the individual coupons at risk. Finally, the automatic call feature can be replaced with a call that is at the issuer's discretion. Most autocallable products are principal-at-risk structures where the investor stands to lose some or all of their initial investment. In addition, these products usually include a buffer that offers some degree of protection, although depending on the type of buffer included the downside risk scenario can vary dramatically by product.

A further popular variety of principal-at-risk product is typically referred to as a market plus. The market plus is designed for investors who seek exposure to the appreciation of the underlying asset, sometimes with a contingent coupon or cap to return, and contingent protection to downside market moves. The structure generally pays out

   (i) appreciation plus principal at maturity if the underlying asset has appreciated from inception,

  (ii) principal only if the underlying has depreciated without the protection knocking out, or

 (iii) full downside participation if the protection has knocked out.

Unlike structures with static downside protection (for example, the typical capped leverage upside note described above), this structure has contingent protection, which means that depending on the monitoring period (continuous, daily, European) the downside protection amount can knock out at specific times based on the observation schedule of the buffer component.

One final broad-based variety of structured products that became increasingly relevant in the US market, especially in those main growth years of 2005–8, was the variety which was linked to various interest rates. Rate-linked structured products encompass a number of specific payout profiles, most of which are oriented towards generating yield by allowing clients to express directional views on rates. Most rate-linked structured products offer full principal protection at maturity and can be offered via registered notes or certificates of deposit. The products typically offer several different basic varieties of upside yield, linked to various rate indexes such as the London interbank offered rate (Libor), constant maturity swaps (CMS) or the consumer price index (CPI), and generally provide increased yield as these indexes rise. Other themes include expressing a view on the steepness of the yield curve, speculating on the evolution of broad-based rates based indexes as well as adding certain contingencies to coupon payments (for instance, an underlying threshold). Although, as mentioned, these rate-linked products are almost entirely principal protected due to the fact that they tend to trade with longer tenors (in many cases up to 15 years or more), duration and interest rate sensitivity are the primary risk factors.

Industry maturity

As the US market rounded out 2006 and headed into 2007 we witnessed the maturity of the structured products industry in that country. While some new entrants and distributors continued to emerge, the key participants and products were largely in place by late 2006. This period saw increases in "wholesaling" beyond the existing aggregators as well as the rise of open architecture among the larger private banks and wirehouse distribution channels. "Open architecture" refers to the practices of various investment banks to begin seeking issued product from all other structured product issuers, rather than limiting purchases to issuances from their own institution.

As issuers built up their external distribution teams starting in 2005 and into 2006, the question of how to most effectively access retail markets across the US confronted each of them. Several solutions arose to address this common problem, with some issuers investing directly in the hiring of additional salespeople and the development of teams with responsibility for national product coverage and distribution. Other issuers opted to partner with already existing internal or external wholesaling teams to discuss structured products along with more traditional retail investments such as mutual funds. Finally, the other alternative (which most banks continued to employ to some extent) was to continue to partner with third party aggregators. Until that point most aggregator firms had focused on breadth of distribution (covering as many dealers as possible) but most of those firms also began to build out whole-saling teams as well. In fact, by early 2008, if you were an RIA or an individual financial advisor, chances are you had at least one wholesaler knocking on your door offering to educate you about structured products. Regardless of which approach or combination of approaches was employed, the end result for the US investor was the dramatic growth in volume and variety of structured products available for immediate purchase and/or individual customisation.

This period also witnessed the rise of the open architecture model among and between the primary structured products issuers and their previously captive internal distribution networks. With the Securities Offering Reforms of 2005 and the increasing standard-isation of product offerings among issuers, pressure mounted on internal sales channels (both the private bank variety and affili-ated broker-dealer wirehouses) to begin allowing offerings by other product issuers into their client accounts. Driven in part by fidu-ciary responsibilities to seek the best price as well as the need for credit diversification in client accounts, this development reshaped the landscape of the market from 2006–8. While the pace of imple-mentation varied by specific channel, similar to the experience of retail investors across the US by the end of 2007, a private wealth client now had a wide menu of products and payouts across different issuers from which to select.

In addition to the diversification in product providers over 2006 and 2007, there was a notable rise in the variety of product payouts and underlying asset classes (and hybrid combinations of each) as well. Issuers began moving into relatively more exotic payout pro-files including "asset allocation" trades (where the underlying bas-ket was dynamically reallocated based on the current performance of a number of predefined possible compositions), different varieties of worst-of downside exposure notes and varying types of coupon-paying autocalls. These offerings were no longer linked exclusively, or even primarily, to equities. Most issuers made commodity, cur-rency and certainly interest-rate-linked products a meaningful por-tion of their product suite. Moreover, hybrid exposure to two or more asset classes into a single underlying reference basket became fairly commonplace. Fundamentally, as the market developed over the year preceding the crash of 2008, the combination of fairly high inter-est rates and relatively low volatility combined to make it possible for structured product issuers to offer new, innovative and in many cases quite attractive products and terms, both in principal-at-risk and principal-protected format. Over this period non-equity market issuance grew from less than 30 deals in 2005 to approximately 700 deals by 2007.[2]

The growth in the volume and the variety of structured products in these years was increasingly accompanied by the issuer's efforts (as well as those of their internal or external distribution partners) to streamline their issuance platforms for maximum efficiency and minimum cost. In many cases, banks with a parent or in some cases even subsidiaries with an active presence in overseas markets had a head start in the technology required for such platforms. Other issuers began the investments more or less from scratch, with varying degrees of success. Regardless, as the industry reached a stage of relative maturity in 2007 and early 2008, it became clear to most participants that the ability to do many customised deals efficiently and inexpensively was a significant competitive advantage (and for those issuers without a captive in-house distribution network, often viewed as an outright necessity).

Paramount among the needs for platform streamlining was a way to simplify, automate and reduce the overhead costs of per-deal legal documentation. The SEC reforms of 2005 paved the way for a simplified prospectus-offering-document style in the registered notes space (and which by extension opened the possibility in the certificate of deposit and the private placement contexts). The next step for issuers was determining how to assemble those simplified term-sheet-offering documents quickly and inexpensively. Many issuers turned away from a reliance on expensive and slow manual drafting by external legal counsel and began investing in internal documentation/drafting teams as well as technology solutions allowing for automated document generation. Painting a comprehensive picture of all of these efforts across the industry is difficult to do, but suffice it to say that these efforts were underway at each principal structured products issuer in the US as we reached the mid-point of 2008.

While issuers were united (although far from working in concert) in their recognition of the value of a streamlined issuance programme, there was little cohesion elsewhere across the industry at this stage. Beginning in 2006–7 there were some early efforts to establish industry working groups, most notably the Structured

Products Association, but at this stage most issuers were more oriented towards developing their own businesses than consolidating efforts and ideas across the space. Additionally, aside from some high level guidance issued by the SEC in early 2008 clarifying their expectations around the naming conventions for certain structured products, there was little of the regulatory pressure that can often serve as a catalyst for cross-industry dialogue and cooperation. By the summer of 2008, generally speaking, while the US market had reached a peak of issuance volume and innovation that was not to be reached again for several years, most of the key members of the industry were just turning their attention away from a solely growth oriented focus to develop some of the characteristics of a more mature marketplace.

INDUSTRY SHAKE-UP (2008–9)

As the spring of 2008 turned into the summer and the financial landscape across the US and beyond turned increasingly rocky, issuance volumes of structured products across the risk spectrum remained remarkably strong. However, with the nearly catastrophic events beginning in September 2008 and carrying through much of that autumn, like virtually every other financial/investment product at the time, new issuance of structured products – once one of the faster growing investment areas in the US – effectively ceased altogether. Over 2008 Q3 and especially into 2008 Q4 new issuance of structured products plummeted to a trickle (from a high of 737 deals for 4.0 billion notional in July to 324 products for 1.6 billion by December). In fact, the structured products industry (again, mirroring other financial assets more broadly) witnessed a massive push to de-risk, which in the case of structured products also meant selling back an investment in the secondary market.

September 2008–March 2009: the plunge

While market issuance had begun to slow in the summer of 2008, the declared bankruptcy of Lehman Brothers Holdings Inc on September 15, 2008 caused a wholesale cross-asset market tailspin that extended to the structured products industry. Lehman was one of the largest issuers of structured products in the US up until 2008, and investors in Lehman issuance found themselves looking at a return on their investments of cents on the dollar. Moreover, the credit concerns affecting every other US bank (with many of the very oldest, largest and most prestigious Wall Street firms teetering on the brink of insolvency) made the purchase of any financial sector related debt obligations, especially those which were structured and market linked, highly unpopular. Combined with the massive volatility and overall collapse in asset values, both across the equity markets and beyond, there was almost no interest in newly issued structured products.

Meanwhile, holders of structured products rushed to sell those investments at virtually any market price. While most banks continued to make a market in their own products, third party purchasers became scarce and some issuers even stopped buying back their own structured notes given their liquidity concerns in that autumn of 2008. Additionally, any prices that were honoured for structured products buybacks were generally deeply discounted from the initial purchase price, largely as a result of the equity market sell-off and the explosion of secondary market related credit spreads experienced by most issuing entities.

At the same time that issuers were buying back considerable volumes of outstanding structured products, the mark-to-market values of their offsetting hedge positions dropped dramatically. These drops were commensurate with the rundown in the underlying asset prices experienced across virtually every market segment starting in autumn 2008 and carrying through the first quarter of 2009. Furthermore, the vast issuance of "worst of" exposure products (where an investor assumes exposure to the worst performing of a series of assets for a considerably above-market yield) in the years predating the financial crisis meant that most issuers experienced sharp losses hedging the correlation exposure on their trading books. Since worst-of products were less prevalent in the US than Latin America and Europe, the US market was not as affected as others although for issuers steep losses overseas were also felt in the US. As a result of the losses on those positions and also the sharp decrease in new issues, most issuers questioned the long-term profitability of their structured products businesses; significant lay-offs ensued across the industry.

While the broader market began a slow rebound in the second half of March 2009, it took many months for any semblance of normality to return to the market overall, including the structured products market – and even then it was clear that things had changed. The fall-out from the bankruptcy of Lehman Brothers was particularly acute, and remains an ongoing matter, with various purchasers of Lehman structured products seeking to recoup losses from distributors of these products, chiefly based on claims of unclear disclosure and misrepresentations around the credit risk of instruments presented as principal protected.

Signs of rebirth: 2009 H2

While the overall US equity market was slowly climbing its way up from its nadir in March of that year, the structured products market showed some early signs of recovery and regrowth towards the middle of 2009 as well. However, not surprisingly after the experience of the preceding 12 months, general investment appetites and product risk tolerance had changed dramatically. Both purchasers and providers proved reluctant to begin offering the types of worst-of yield products linked to equity market stocks or indexes that had dropped so precipitously during the crash, a reluctance that was to prove remarkably enduring. The defining characteristic of the market tendencies that began to re-emerge in the latter half of 2009 was, again not surprisingly, an emphasis on principal protection and safety above all.

Most particularly, after the Lehman bankruptcy and the near-death experience of many other Wall Street banks in September and October 2008, US retail investors not only wanted principal-protected products but sought the additional protection of the FDIC insurance available through certificate-of-deposits. This immediately recut the landscape, as only certain pre-crisis issuers had the ability to offer bank-issued certificates of deposit (keep in mind some of these institutions had only recently become banks, and since that time had been fairly well occupied with concerns other than building structured CD issuance programmes). The product providers who could deliver product via the certificate of deposit wrapper most quickly in 2009 quickly found themselves with a relative competitive advantage in that changed landscape with an investor population seeking safety above all.

Unfortunately, unlike the earliest years of the structured products market, when high interest rates and relatively low volatility made it possible to structure products with very attractive upside payouts, the same near-zero interest rates and dramatically higher volatility of the period immediately after the crisis made offering an attractive principal-protected investment a considerable challenge. That said, the near-zero interest rates prevailing across the market made any yield alternatives (albeit even low ones) attractive. Given all this, product providers began considering ways to stimulate investor demand again for market-linked products with principal protection.

Yield generators and proprietary algorithms

During this period, two of the most widely used approaches to achieve this goal were

1. yield-generating stock basket products and
2. a new breed of proprietary algorithmic investment strategies created by product providers specifically for delivery in principal protected form.

The "yield generator" product is essentially a coupon-paying structure that can pay a periodic coupon based on the average of the performance of a series of underlying stocks with individual caps and floors. The product had considerable success in Europe and Canada pre-crisis, so in some ways it is surprising that it did not come to the US until this stage. The product proved a remarkably popular alternative to traditional certificates of deposit, which again at this stage were generally offering yields in the region of several dozen basis points annually, whereby a client could sacrifice the *de minimis* yield of a traditional fixed rate certificate of deposit for the opportunity to dramatically outperform in a rising equity environment (sometimes to the tune of 10% or 12% annually). By the middle and certainly the end of 2009, this product was available and purchased heavily in most retail distribution channels, with product offerings available from every structured product issuer with the ability to offer market-linked certificates of deposit.

The other product innovation during this period that was more diverse and probably more important for the longer-term development and prospects of the US structured products market was the proprietary algorithmic strategy. While in many cases development of these indexes predated the crisis of 2008, in the US market it was only post-2008 that many product providers began incorporating their own proprietary algorithmic index strategies into widely distributed retail structured notes and CDs. From the outset the proprietary strategies covered a wide range of asset class exposure and investment hypotheses. In the US the indexes that were incorporated into the first structured products of this nature in early-to-mid-2009 had a volatility control mechanism. Most of these early strategies contained a rebalancing mechanism that was activated systematically by various timing or market considerations and that reconstituted the underlying components to achieve maximum return for a given level of risk, or volatility.

This product family grew fast and quickly came to include representatives from all of the major asset classes and investment strategies. The most notable feature in the products first available in the US market in early to mid-2009 was the opportunity for diversified, dynamic market exposure (generally without a cap on the upside) while retaining the benefit of principal protection and in most cases FDIC insurance in the event of another market downturn. This was to prove a surprisingly persistent and important component of the US structured products market as the move from 2009 into 2010 witnessed a remarkable (and nearly impossible to predict one year prior) rebound for the industry as a whole.

2010–13

Although the US market for structured products recovered more quickly than almost any observer would have predicted at the end of 2008 or the beginning of 2009, the landscape remained fundamentally altered from the experience of the crisis and some of the new themes originating in the early part of 2009 continued for some time. Specifically, the rising relevance of market-linked certificates-of-deposit as enduringly popular products for retail purchasers remains a definitive characteristic. Initially this popularity came directly at the expense of interest in some of the other, previously popular, principal-at-risk structures (especially those with more exotic and worst-of exposure). However, as the memory of the crisis continued to fade from 2010 on there has been a demonstrable shift back to principal at risk in exchange for preferable upside terms. Finally, the rise of the proprietary algorithmic strategy delivered via the full suite of investment wrappers has only grown in importance for the US market and has expanded significantly in volume and variety from its originally narrow focus in early 2009.

In addition to narrowing the universe of issuers (through consolidation in some places and disappearance in others) the experience of the crisis left much less of an appetite on the part of both providers and purchasers for certain types of products. Market issuance overall dropped dramatically from 2008 to 2009, although by mid-2010 market issuance was approaching some of the highest levels seen in the pre-crisis era with the US market averaging well over 750 issuance and US$4 billion a month by 2010 Q2. Additionally, compared with the pre-crisis era a higher proportion of market issuance remained in principal-protected format well into 2013, another clear repercussion of the losses experienced by many investors and providers alike in the 2008–9 period. The shift towards principal protection evidenced by the rise of certificate-of-deposit issuance in 2009 only began to reverse in 2012 and into 2013, largely a function of one of the defining characteristics of the market environment overall from the 2008 crisis through to 2013: extremely low, and persistently low, interest rates.

Low rates for a long time

As equity markets started to improve in early 2009 and into 2010 there was a gradual shift back towards investors demonstrating a willingness to put principal at risk to receive a particular payout or yield. However, there remained a significant population of higher risk averse investors who were interested exclusively in principal-protected instruments (ideally with the FDIC insurance overlay) but sought the ability to participate in equity market upside gains or at minimum have the opportunity to outperform traditional fixed rates saving or deposit products. Many of these investors were attracted to the stock basket yield generator product, which remained one of the most popular products in the US retail market through 2011. In addition, the ability to structure yield possibilities far exceeding those available in traditional certificates of deposit made the range of rate-linked structured products highly attractive, resulting in the growth in interest-rate-linked products from about 150 in 2008 to over 800 by 2011. This remained the case even as market interest rates continued to drop from 2010 into 2012, making it increasingly difficult to offer attractive terms on products and forcing providers to extend the tenor/maturities of these products to keep the principal protection affordable in such a low rate environment.

As 2012 and even early 2013 witnessed market interest rates continuing to decline, and the equity markets continued to see significant growth from 2009 lows, many investors began to re-evaluate the mechanisms by which they were seeking yield. Whereas from 2010 into 2011 most investors had demanded full principal protection, in the latter part of 2012 and into 2013 many investors began shying away from longer and longer dated principal-protected products (as well as moving away from purchasing those same products from issuers with lower and lower credit ratings) and exhibiting a willingness to invest in principal-at-risk products linked to equity underlyings with deep downside-buffered protection (often as much as 50% of initial spot levels) with shorter maturity, better credit and higher yield possibilities. These products came in many flavours, but often contained some form of knock-out buffered protection (short knock-out put) and in many cases even worst-of equity exposure (with deep downside protection) to maximise the yield possibilities. By early 2013, worst-of equity-linked products with this downside buffer and linked to index, ETF and single stock products were once again being offered by virtually every large provider in the US structured products market.

Media and regulatory focus

Like many financial products in the post-crisis era, structured products became the object of increasing external focus from 2010 onwards, both from media sources and from various regulatory bodies. Much of the media, particularly in the more mainstream publications, focused specifically on poor product performance with highlights on certain single stock linked principal-at-risk structures with negative returns. There was also significant coverage of investor losses related to the bankruptcy of Lehman Brothers with some of the investor claims and litigation related to the Lehman Brothers bankruptcy lasting for many years after 2008. Specifically, many claims included allegations of unclear disclosure and/or sales practices around principal-protected notes that ultimately returned cents on the dollar to purchasers. One direct impact of this was increasingly robust disclosure around the credit risk inherent in all structured notes, including that attached to certificates of deposit for investment amounts in excess of applicable FDIC insurance limits.

From a regulatory perspective, the post-crisis period ushered in an era of increased attention from a variety of regulatory agencies on a range of topics related to structured products. Many of the enquiries were focused specifically on the reverse exchangeable product, in large part due to its status as the most frequently issued/purchased US structured product (especially in the period prior to 2008) as well as its single-stock-linked payout profile that could, and in some cases did, result in significant losses for investors who purchased products linked to stocks that performed poorly. (Although in all cases it should be noted that the investor's payout under the reverse exchangeable would have exceeded the return had the investor bought the stock outright due to the payment of the guaranteed coupon stream.) Enquiries focused on a variety of different aspects of the reverse exchangeable and were initiated in this period by the regulatory bodies of several US states, the US Securities and Exchange Commission as well as the Financial Industry Regulatory Authority, and received by many of the primary providers and distributors of structured products in the US.

While there were a variety of regulatory-driven structured products enquiries in this period (focused on both reverse exchangeables and other aspects of the market) probably the most meaningful and long-term influential action from a regulator since the Securities Offering Reform in 2005 was the dialogue that the SEC initiated with most of the key US structured products issuers in mid-2012 around their disclosure practices and, specifically, seeking a level of standardisation in what had increasingly become a diverse and in some cases inconsistent approach from issuer to issuer. The SEC initiated the dialogue by requesting feedback from these principal issuers on a variety of disclosure related matters, with a particular focus on internal valuation methodologies both at the time of pricing/issuance and post issuance in the secondary market. Over the course of approximately 12 months the SEC communicated with this group of issuers regarding these points, and more generally about other specific disclosure practices and improvements, culminating in early 2013 with a promulgation to these institutions that the SEC would begin expecting the specific disclosure of an estimated value of the structured notes.

Overall, the stated goal of the SEC in this dialogue and published guidance was to increase consistency between issuers and transparency to investors across the structured products market. Practically, the SEC mandated that issuers begin disclosing the "fair or estimated value" of their products in their disclosure materials and that such a number, in general, had to be net of any adjustments of fees incurred. (In many respects this requirement to publish a "mid-market" value overlapped in important respects with mandates from the Commodities Futures Trading Commission guidance under the Dodd–Frank Act to provide a "mid" value pre trade for inscope swaps, although obviously the regulators involved and industries affected were quite distinct.) The SEC's guidelines began appearing in the revised disclosure of most structured products issuers in the early to middle part of 2013.

Commoditisation and the drive for efficiency

As the US structured products market rebounded from 2010 into 2011 and beyond, approaching its pre-crisis volumes by 2012, trends towards product standardisation and in some cases outright commoditisation that had first appeared in 2007–8 (which had been interrupted by the crisis in late 2008) began to reappear. In many respects this was the logical outgrowth of patterns that had been developing since the market's inception, most significantly:

- the arrival of new issuers and distributors and their abilities to offer a complete product suite;
- saturation of market payouts due to industry maturity and the limitation of market environment/pricing parameters; and
- the rise in cross-selling across distribution channels driven by open architecture.

While the efficiency of product offering and speed to market had always been significant considerations for both product providers and purchasers (recall, for instance, the revolutionising impact of the 2005 Securities Offering Reforms), the drive for maximum efficiency and streamlined issuance reached a new height from 2011 onwards.

For many key players in the US market there was an opportunity to leverage platform development work that had already been completed, often before the crisis, in European and especially Asian markets, where the drive to product commoditisation was much further along. Specifically, these initiatives focused on the ability to offer auto-pricing solutions to (at a minimum) distributor clients and to test a variety of investment possibilities and a streamlined issuance process to deliver prospectus disclosure to clients once a particular product had been selected. Frequently this required a degree of document automation on the part of the product provider, which while improving delivery speed also kept legal fees to a minimum. Ultimately, issuers sought a streamlined issuance platform which allowed clients to click-to-trade customised structured product offerings in very small notional size while maintaining requisite profitability. In this respect, these endeavours can be viewed as a trend towards a model (at least for popular, standardised products and payouts) increasingly characterised by low notional and high volume, maintaining a profitable margin net of expenses.

US INSURANCE MARKET AND ANNUITY PRODUCTS

The US insurance market has experienced a remarkably similar pattern of growth since the early 1990s. Over this period there has been a dramatic increase in the aggregate volume, overall ability and variety of annuity products offered by insurance companies. Generally, there are two different varieties of annuities – fixed and variable – widely sold in the US. Each of these broad categories is further divisible into a much wider variety of individual products with specific characteristics. The available terms under these products have, like structured products generally, changed substantially since 2008.

In the fixed annuity market, the product most closely related to a structured product is known as an equity indexed annuity. Compared with a standard fixed rate annuity which typically pays a guaranteed and fixed interest rate, the return on an indexed annuity is tied to the performance of an underlying reference asset. While these products were (in the early 2000s) and still are most often tied to a major US market index, such as the S&P 500, it is possible to find a fairly diverse range of underlying reference assets. However, these products are not viewed as securities by US regulators and are therefore subject to a different external scrutiny and oversight process. This includes but is not limited to different standards and/or requirements about disclosure practices and also requiring product rating and approval.

Purchasers of equity indexed annuities typically seek to increase the yield in their investment portfolios by introducing some equity market exposure. These products began emerging in the mid-1990s when ordinary investors began opting to sacrifice some guaranteed/fixed yield for the opportunity to participate in the stock market booms. Additionally, these products are covered by insurance from the various US state guarantee funds up to various thresholds, thereby offering some type of guaranteed minimum return. Most equity indexed annuities pay an annual return based on the performance of the underlying but can also introduce averaging calculation on the return or monthly resetting coupons (where each of the monthly return is capped and added together for an annual payment, although monthly negative returns can reduce any positive performance – commonly known as a cliquet). For many investors the main attractions of this product are the ability to defer tax payments until the maturity of the contract, as well as the ability to roll investments from one annuity to another without incurring a taxable event.

While similar to the fixed annuity market in some important ways (tax deferred growth, insurance product not subject to securities law regulation), the variable annuity market is far larger, more complex and statistically more diverse than the indexed annuities described above, as well as traditionally being much longer in investment tenor (often 30 years or more). Variable annuities are often compared to a mutual fund structure, since the holders of a variable annuity generally have their lump sum investment held in a separately managed account with some degree of direct ownership interest in the underlying assets. Variable annuities became one of the mostly widely offered and purchased investment products for US retail clients in the years preceding the crash of 2008. Originating in the early 1990s, and driven by the general pursuit by investors of the massive gains in the equity markets in the late 1990s, by 2006–7 variable annuities were offered by every sizeable insurance company in the US.

The wide variety of variable annuity products available for purchase by the mid-2000s, as well as the highly positive economic environment and expectations prevalent in that era, meant that the terms available on many of these annuity contracts became more and more favourable to the purchasers. In addition to typically including different options around payments to estate beneficiaries in the event of a holder's death, variable annuities sold in this period offered guaranteed rates of return reflective of the booming market environment of that period.

However, as the market slowed and eventually culminated in the dislocations of late 2008 and early 2009, many insurance companies began realising that the variable annuities they had written, and specifically some of the guaranteed returns they were now obligated to pay, were becoming increasingly expensive as equity market values collapsed and interest rates plummeted. As this remained problematic for much of the late 2000s and into the early 2010s (perpetuating even as the equity market rebounded, primarily due to the persistently low interest rates in those years), insurance companies largely responded by reducing the terms offered in any new variable annuity contract. Predictably, this reduction in what had previously been very attractive terms available in the years prior to 2008, especially when combined with the market performance in those years, resulted in net sales of variable annuity contracts dropping dramatically from a high of around US$180 billion in 2007 to less than US$120 billion by 2009. This drop was also magnified by the diminished practice of rolling existing investments from a current contract to a new one, which had become very prevalent in the pre-crisis era especially as issuers continually competed in offering the best product pricing. Despite the drop after 2008, in 2012–13 sales had rebounded and stabilised somewhat at about US$150 billion (although still considerably less than the pre-crash high watermark in sales).

CONCLUSION

The US structured products market, including the retail insurance product segment, has grown massively in both breadth and depth since its early days in the mid-1990s to a status by the middle of 2013 where issuance volumes are once again approaching record amounts. From a relatively small universe of providers and purchasers at inception (and its earliest focus predominantly on large issuances sold infrequently to institutional buyers) by the first half of 2013 there existed a large range of product offerings covering every payout characteristic and every asset class (as well as many proprietary index linked and/or hybrid underlyings) offered by virtually every large bank, and some of the small ones, in the US. Additionally, these products have grown from being available to only a limited number of high-net-worth private banking and large-scale wirehouse distributor clients to being available in essentially every large investment service network across the country.

The overall pattern has been one of dramatic growth, albeit with a few notable interruptions. This is the case for the overall product mix, although retail insurance products, especially variable annuities, have yet to rebound to their pre-crisis levels both in products/terms available as well as overall annuity sales. Most notably, the crash of 2008 set the whole industry back several years in terms of growth and development, with market volumes and investor appetite only really rebounding fully as we entered 2012. The maturity of the industry has also been positively influenced by the activities of US regulators – most importantly the SEC in the 1998 plain English reforms, the 2005 Securities Offering Reform and once again with 2013's guidance around consistent and transparent disclosure among product issuers of the estimated value of their offerings.

The structured products industry in the US today rivals hedge funds for the amounts of rolling assets under management, and has (as of yet) not suffered the dramatic underperformance and liquidity concerns roiling the hedge fund industry in the past several years. At this stage, all signs point to the continued growth and maturity of the structured products market in the US and their ever-increasing role in the US market as a valuable tool for individual retail clients to customise and diversify their exposure across an ever-increasing array of product, payout and provider options.

1   DTC is the central securities settlement system for the US. This is where all security settlements occur and client positions are housed and tracked.

2   All data in this section was obtained from StructuredRetailProducts.com.

REFERENCES

Ackerman, A., 2012, "SEC Wants Clearer 'Notes'", *Wall Street Journal*, April 17, URL: http://online.wsj.com/article/SB10001424052702304818404577350213355950268.html.

AKA Insurance Services, 2012, "A Basic Introduction to Annuities", URL: http://www.akingagency.com/Annuities.pdf.

Armstrong, F., 2012, "Structured Notes Buyers Be Warned", *Forbes*, URL: http://www.forbes.com/sites/greatspeculations/2012/11/30/structured-notes-buyers-be-warned/.

Bhullar, J. S., M. Byrnes and P. S. Singzon, 2013, "Variable Annuity Market Trends: Strong Market to Lift 3Q13 Results, Low Returns and Tail Risk Long-Term Concerns", JP Morgan North America Equity Research. Category Archives: Structured Notes, (2009–2013), URL: http://www.investorprotection.com/blog/category/structured-notes/.

Bloomberg, 2013, "Structured Notes", Bloomberg Briefs, URL: http://www.bloomberg briefs.com/structured-notes/.

Colesanti, J. S., 2012, "Demanding Substance or Form: The SEC's Plain English Handbook as a Basis for Securities Violations", *Fordham Journal of Corporate & Financial Law* 18.

Ferry, J., 2008, "Structured Products: Keeping It Simple", *Euromoney*, URL: http://www.euromoney.com/Article/1924298/Structured-products-Keeping-it-simple.html.

FINRA, 2011, "Structured Notes with Principal Protection: Note the Terms of Your Investment", Financial Industry Regulatory Authority, URL: http://www.finra.org/Investors/ProtectYourself/InvestorAlerts/Bonds/P123713.

Hays, J. R., and R. A. Dulisse, 2004, "Introduction to Annuities", in *Essentials of Annuities*. The American College.

Hintzke, D., and C. S. Brown, 2011, "FATCA's Impact on Structured Products", *Journal of Structured Finance* 17, pp. 17–22.

Kim, J. J., and B. Levisohn, 2010, "Structured Notes: Not as Safe as They Seem", *Wall Street Journal*, URL: http://online.wsj.com/article/SB10001424052748704804504575606843404836032.html.

Koh, P., 2008, "Equity derivatives: Investors Fear Structured Note Counterparty Risk", *Euromoney*, URL: http://www.euromoney.com/Article/1899724/Equity-derivatives-Investors-fear-structured-note -counterparty-risk.html.

Maxey, D., 2013, "Structured Products Are More Available, but Awfully Confusing", *Wall Street Journal*, URL: http://online.wsj.com/article/SB10001424127887324323904578368410157355812.html.

McCann, C., and D. Luo, 2006, "An Overview of Equity-Indexed Annuities", Securities Litigation and Consulting Group, Inc.

Rieger, M. O., 2012, "Why Do Investors Buy Bad Financial Products: Probability Misestimation and Preferences in Financial Investment Decision", *Journal of Behavioral Finance* 13, pp. 108–18.

Telpner, J. S., 2004, "A Survey of Structured Notes", *Journal of Structured and Project Finance* 9, pp. 6–19.

Zweig, J., 2013, "How Apple's Fall Bit Bondholders, Too", *Wall Street Journal*, January 25, URL: http://online.wsj.com/article/SB10001424127887323854904578263941939124314.html.

9

A Regulatory Perspective

Jeremy Jennings-Mares

Morrison & Foerster (UK) LLP

How do we define a structured product? The term means different things to different people. For some it evokes thoughts of the structured credit products, such as collateralised debt obligations, that were so prevalent in the financial markets in the years leading up to the global financial crisis. This chapter focuses mainly on investment products whose return is linked to the performance of one or more of a reference index, price or rate, which we will refer to generally as an "underlying asset".

Unlike many structured credit products, the link to the performance of the underlying asset is not created through a security interest or a proprietary interest in the underlying asset itself, but is typically achieved through the use of embedded derivatives, such as options. Indeed, some people refer to these types of structured products as "securitised derivatives". They may or may not be listed on an exchange, and in terms of legal structure (or "wrapper") they may be issued in the form of a bond, certificate or other kind of security, a warrant, a deposit, a life assurance contract or a trust instrument.

A key characteristic of the kind of structured product discussed in the rest of this chapter is that its return is determined not by the active investment management of investor funds, but instead by a pre-specified formula or set of contractual terms, which will prescribe how the product will perform in a given financial scenario.

Defining structured products, far from being a purely esoteric exercise, is a very real issue when it comes to the question of how they are (or should be) regulated. A typical structured product may be structured as a bond or other type of security, but the link to the underlying asset is essentially a derivative contract, and yet the underlying asset that will provide the return on the product may be a single share. Therefore, should regulators approach the product as a debt security, as an over-the-counter (OTC) derivative contract or as a share?

The lack of a consistent, harmonised definition of a structured product therefore leads, as we shall see, to a wide differentiation in the features that regulators in different countries, and in different financial sectors, will concentrate on. The result is that this leaves opportunities to exploit not only geographical differences in regulatory approach, but also sectoral – for instance as between the securities industry, the fund management industry and the insurance industry.

Before any regulators who may be reading this chapter start to get too concerned, the rest of the chapter does not set out ways of exploiting those differences, but looks, among other things, at what approaches regulators are (or should be) adopting with regard to structured products.

The purpose of regulation

Before regulators can decide which are the most salient features of structured products on which to focus their scrutiny, they should first take a step back and ask "what is the purpose of financial regulation in this context?".

Most people would agree that the protection of investors should be a key focus of financial regulation, particularly so-called "retail investors", who may be less sophisticated or less able to bear losses (or both) than professional investors such as banks, asset managers, investment firms, insurance companies and pension funds. But what should investors be protected from? Should they be protected from losses arising from an investment simply not performing as well as they had hoped? Or alternatively, if the structured product was an appropriate product to be sold to them, and one for which they understood fully the possible risks and returns and the circumstances in which the risks and returns would be triggered, then is the better view that any losses suffered are merely unfortunate and simply part and parcel of investing in financial products – some you win, some you lose?

While some legislators and regulators may be inherently averse to any retail investor suffering a loss on a financial product, most would probably say that their role was not to prevent retail investors from losing money. However, they would point to the large disparity between the information and financial experience possessed by the manufacturer of the structured product on the one hand, and by an average retail investor on the other hand, and would ask "could such disparities be exploited by the manufacturer in a way that is unfair and detrimental to the interests of retail investors?".

Modes of regulation

In Europe and the US, the regulation of financial products as a whole has traditionally focused on what happens at the point of sale of the product – in terms of both what information has been disclosed to the potential investor at or before the point of sale and whether the conduct of the market participant at and before the point of sale has been fair and appropriate.

In terms of disclosure, regulators ask, "has there been disclosure of all information that an investor could reasonably be expected to need in order to make an informed investment decision? Has that information been disclosed fairly such that it is reasonable to expect that it would be capable of being understood by the investor?".

In terms of conduct of business, regulators, certainly in Europe, ask, "has the structured product provider or distributor dealing with the client acted honestly, fairly and professionally in accordance with the best interests of their clients?"

Under the Markets in Financial Instruments Directive (MiFID), investment firms in Europe that sell structured products are required to carry out an analysis of the "appropriateness" of the product for a particular retail investor. This requires them to obtain information from the retail client regarding their knowledge and experience in relation to the type of product being sold, so that the firm can assess whether the product is appropriate for the particular client.

Complexity

MiFID, however, allows firms to dispense with the appropriateness test where the product is being sold on an "execution-only" basis at the initiative of the investor. This exemption applies only to certain types of investment, such as listed shares, money market instruments, bonds (expressly excluding bonds that embed a derivative), units in regulated Undertakings for Collective Investment in Transferable Securities (UCITS) funds and other financial instruments which are considered non-complex.

This is intended to be a non-exhaustive list of financial instruments that are considered sufficiently simple that they can be sold to retail investors without having to assess their appropriateness. Secondary MiFID legislation provides further specific conditions that, if satisfied by a product, will qualify that product as an additional non-complex product for the purpose of the execution-only exemption. These criteria are, broadly:

- it is not a derivative product;
- there are frequent opportunities to sell the instrument at publicly available prices;
- the investor cannot lose more than the amount they invest in the instrument; and
- there is publicly available, sufficiently comprehensive information on the product that is likely to be readily understood by an average retail client, to enable them to make an informed investment decision.

We can see therefore that complexity is specified by MiFID as one key factor in deciding whether a financial product is able to be safely sold to retail clients without an appropriateness test.

A couple of points are worth noting, though. First, it is clear that neither OTC derivatives nor securities that embed a derivative will be considered non-complex for the purposes of this execution-only exemption (and therefore that the sale of structured products to retail investors will usually require an appropriateness test in Europe). However, in contrast, for the time being, an investment in a fund governed by the UCITS Directive is automatically considered a non-complex instrument, despite the fact that very many UCITS funds use derivative products as part of their strategy. This particular anomaly is due to be addressed by changes to MiFID which will not designate so-called "structured UCITS funds" as automatically non-complex, and later on we discuss the issue of sectoral inconsistencies in the context of the proposed Packaged Retail Investment Products (PRIPs) Regulation.

Second, although the above criteria supposedly define what is regarded as non-complex, we can see that these criteria also consider issues such as the liquidity of the product, the risk of the product (in terms of whether a client can lose more than they have invested) and the disclosure or availability of information which is comprehensible to an investor.

Risk

Let us look first at the risk associated with a product, and its relationship to the product's complexity. The first thing to note is that complexity and risk are two completely separate concepts, and also concepts that may bear no relationship to each other in the context of a structured product. They may even be diametrically opposed to each other.

For instance, we might say that a product which by its terms will pay the investor no less than 100% of the amount originally invested (ie, is fully principal-protected) is at the less risky end of the spectrum. However, this does not mean that the product is not difficult for an average retail investor to understand.

In fact, often in a principal-protected structured product, it is the very mechanism that delivers the principal protection that can be one of the features of the product that is the hardest to understand for a retail investor. But this raises the question as to what extent an investor actually needs to be able to understand everything about a structured product. Does the investor simply need to understand the essential risk–reward profile and, for instance, whether or not principal protection is provided and what percentage of its initial investment is covered, which entity is providing the protection and in what circumstances the protection will be available?

Different jurisdictional approaches

At this point it is worth looking at which features of structured products and their related sales processes are the subject of regulatory focus in different jurisdictions.

Belgium

In August 2011, the Belgian Financial Services and Markets Authority (FSMA) launched a consultation on the appropriate regulatory framework for the distribution of structured products to retail investors. This followed on from a so-called "voluntary" moratorium designed by the FSMA to be observed by Belgian financial institutions on the retail distribution of structured products. Most Belgian distributors decided to comply – a not insignificant development, given the size of the Belgian structured products market (FSMA had estimated that at that time there were approximately US$112 billion worth of outstanding structured products in the hands of Belgian investors).

Two of the intended objectives of the FSMA in regulating structured products are to enhance transparency for investors in relation to sales of structured products and to reduce the complexity of structured products being sold. The consultation focused on the relationship between these two objectives, including considering the question of whether, irrespective of how much information was provided or available to investors, and however good that information, there are certain financial products that should be regarded as too complex for certain investors to understand.

The FSMA also consulted on the concept of a "risk threshold" for retail structured products, as well as the concept of mandating the inclusion of uniform risk classifications/indicators and on the minimum standards for the organisation of a secondary market for the structured product in question.

Italy

In Italy, there has been greater focus by the regulators on the liquidity of the financial product, and particularly whether there are opportunities for the investor in the structured product to sell the product, based upon a publicly available market value. In terms of disclosure to investors, they have focused on the detailed disclosure of the "fair value" of each component of the product (eg, the zero-coupon bond part and the option part), as well as an overall liquidation value of the product and the likelihood of the investor being able to sell or redeem the product (prior to maturity) at a "market price". They have also required the disclosure of a comparison of the risk–return profiles of retail structured products with more traditional, well-known, low risk financial products.

Denmark

Since April 2011 Denmark has required that investment products sold or advised on by investment firms must contain so-called risk labels (commonly known as "traffic lights"). These traffic lights are determined by a combination of the risk associated with the product and the complexity of the product. A green traffic light indicates that there is a small risk of losing the entire capital investment, and also that the product type is not considered to be difficult for retail investors to understand. A yellow traffic light indicates that there is a risk of losing some or all of the capital investment, but again the product type is not considered difficult for retail investors to understand. A red traffic light indicates that there is either a risk of losing more than the capital invested or that the product type is considered difficult for retail investors to understand. The selling of, or advising on, products in the red category is limited by regulation to those persons who have undertaken specific training and obtained certain qualifications.

France

A 2012 position paper from the French Financial Markets Authority (AMF) on the marketing of complex products focuses on both complexity and principal protection, and details four criteria which the AMF considers suggest a higher risk of a client not understanding the risks involved with the product. These are

1. the poor presentation of the product's risk/payout profile,

2. the investor's lack of familiarity with the assets underlying the structured product,

3. the payout profile of the product being dependent on the occurrence of several conditions across different asset classes simultaneously, or

4. the product involving a high number of mechanisms (three or more) in order to determine the overall return on the product.

If any of these four criteria exists, and the product offers less than 90% principal protection (in other words if the investor may, by the terms of the product, lose more than 10% of their investment), then the marketing materials for the product must contain a prominent warning as to its complexity and/or its possible unsuitability for inexperienced investors.

United States

The US also has a very active structured products market, with the Securities and Exchange Commission (SEC) estimating US sales of retail structured products in 2010 of US$45 billion, and in 2012 the Financial Industry Regulatory Authority (FINRA) published a guidance notice to investment firms on its intended heightened supervision of complex products. Complex products are not exhaustively defined, but specifically include products containing complicated or intricate derivative-like features. For such products, investment firms are required to put in place product governance processes including appropriate approval procedures, sales force training, reviews and determinations of suitability of the product for individual customers. Firms are also required to consider whether simpler products could be offered to investors as a reasonable alternative to the structured product.

In the context of whether a product is sufficiently complex to warrant the heightened level of supervision in the US, FINRA considers that any product with multiple features that affect its returns differently under various scenarios is potentially complex, and the question must be asked whether it is reasonable to expect an average retail investor to understand the basic manner in which the features of such a product interact to produce the return.

United Kingdom

A later section (page 248) will explore, separately, the approach to structured products regulation of the UK, this being perhaps the most active jurisdiction for the "manufacturing" of structured products, and the UK's authorities being at the forefront of discussions on structured products regulation.

The right regulatory approach?

We can see that complexity is considered by regulators as an important basis for determining their regulatory approach. Regulators' main problems with complexity are that it can make it more difficult for an investor to understand the products and this in turn leads to a number of concerns:

- it is thus more difficult to be certain that an investor is capable of understanding the proposal sufficiently well to make an informed investment decision;
- complexity can make it more difficult for the investor to compare the features of a complex product with those of other, simpler products that provide a similar commercial exposure to the underlying asset (an issue that is discussed in the context of the proposed PRIPs Regulation);

- more broadly, complexity makes regulators worry that there is a greater likelihood of investors being exploited by the product manufacturers or distributors, in relation to products that are more difficult for them to understand.

However, if we were to use complexity as the sole basis for regulation, this could give rise to some unexpected consequences. For instance, it could mean that a structured product that provided the investor with full principal protection and exposure to a broad-based equity index would be more heavily regulated than a direct investment by an investor in the shares in one of the companies constituting that index. This result may be considered justifiable in terms of the ease of an investor's understanding, but is not justifiable in terms of comparable risk, given that the latter investment exposes the investor to a much greater level of risk of losing their investment.

So where should the risk profile of a structured product fit into an ideal regulatory framework? One of the possible concepts on which the Belgian FSMA consulted was whether it would be appropriate for structured products that were fully principal-protected to be governed by a regulatory regime that was less stringent than the regime applicable to other types of structured products. The lower risk of detriment from an investment in such a product arguably means that the investor does not require such a deep understanding of so many features of the product, and in particular exactly how the mechanics of the principal protection are constructed.

Alternatively, how should other features of a product such as its liquidity (or illiquidity) affect how the product should be regulated? Some regulators, such as those in Italy, feel that if there is a ready, liquid, secondary market for structured products (which might often require commitments from structured products' originators or distributors to provide a secondary market in the product), then the level of additional investor protection required should be lower than for illiquid products. This is on the basis that, with a liquid product, an investor has more of an opportunity to exit early from a product that turns out not to be suitable or appropriate for them or one where they are not happy with the actual product performance.

IOSCO

In April 2013 the International Organisation of Securities Commissions (IOSCO) issued a consultation report on the regulation of retail structured products. The report contained feedback on various consultation questions posed earlier to the regulator members of IOSCO, as well as proposing a regulatory toolkit of potential regulatory responses in respect of retail structured products.

IOSCO focused on five main areas.

Overall regulatory focus

IOSCO suggested that an ideal approach to structured products regulation should consider the entire "value chain", ie, the relationships involved in the entire life of the product. It also advocated a "horizontal" approach to regulation that is not determined by the base instrument or "wrapper" of the product, or by the type of underlying reference asset for the product. We will see that this is an approach which forms the basis of the proposed PRIPs Regulation in Europe.

Product design and issuance

Product issuers could be encouraged or made to be responsible for identifying and assessing the types, classes and features of their target investor base. This would involve a thorough analysis of investor needs (such as the target investors' risk profile, tolerance for loss of capital, investment objectives and investment time frame), in order to promote investment products in a way that can be easily understood, based on the financial experience and education of the target market. The rationale behind this thinking is that if products are designed with a particular class of investors in mind, they are more likely to be suitable for an average member of that class.

These recommendations complement the earlier recommended IOSCO suitability standards for the distribution of advice on structured products, which outlined principles for financial intermediaries to, among other things:

- distinguish between retail and non-retail customers when distributing complex financial products;

- verify that the structure and risk–reward profile of a financial product is consistent with a particular customer's experience, knowledge and investment objectives; and

- have a reasonable basis for any recommendation or advice to a customer when distributing complex financial products.

IOSCO also proposes the use of financial models, including so-called "value for money" tests, in order to stress-test a product and inform any internal product approval processes.

As part of focusing on the development stages of the value chain, IOSCO recommends the development by product manufacturers of an effective internal governance process, to ensure adequate safeguards and controls are in place to protect investors.

Product disclosure and marketing

IOSCO recommends aligning disclosure standards to ensure consistency with an investor's ability to understand the disclosure, including the need for short-form or summary disclosure, possibly based on a template short-form disclosure document. As we shall see in a later section, this recommendation again very much mirrors the approach being taken in Europe pursuant to the proposed PRIPs Regulation.

Other recommendations are a requirement for full disclosure of fees and costs levied in the context of retail structured products and the disclosure to investors of the estimated fair value of a product upon issuance. This particular proposal follows the position set forth by the US SEC in February 2013 that the offering documents for registered offerings of structured notes should contain the issuer's estimated value of the instrument. IOSCO also recommended imposing requirements to set out hypothetical scenarios, using formulas to give examples of the way in which a particular product may generate a return.

Product distribution

IOSCO suggests that product manufacturers could be made responsible for the way in which products are distributed to consumers, at least insofar as putting in place distribution strategies tailored to an intended target market, and obtaining undertakings from intermediaries to ensure structured products are only sold upon recommendations from highly competent and highly qualified distributors.

Post-sales practices

Finally, IOSCO's toolkit also outlined a number of regulatory measures intended to cover the post-sale period of a retail structured product. These include:

- keeping investors informed of key information during the life of a structured product, such as financial performance statistics, details of key events and past performance;

- performing regular product reviews for use during product design for new products or to take action with respect to an existing product;

- where issuers make a secondary market in a structured product, disclosing to investors of the relationship between the sale price and the secondary market value of the products;

- disclosing of certain information at the time of a product's maturity, including detailed calculations of how the final return was determined;

- providing a right to retail investors to walk away from a contract for a structured product within a specified period after the sale;

- ensuring that investors have a user-friendly mechanism for channelling complaints after purchase of the product;

- providing a formal dispute resolution process in respect of retail structured products; and

- introducing product intervention powers, including the potential ability to either ban outright, or mandate changes to, certain features of structured products.

Having looked at some of the geographical differences between regulatory approaches to structured products, we shall turn, in a later section (page 260), to some of the differences that exist by virtue of what can be termed "sectoral" differences, such as the industry sector of the issuer of a structured product, or the legal form of the product.

UNITED KINGDOM
Retail distribution review
Prior to its abolition at the end of March 2013, the UK's Financial Services Authority (FSA) had for many years been pursuing an initiative designed to ensure that investment advice provided to retail customers in relation to retail investment products was of a high quality and, where presented as independent advice (as opposed to restricted advice), was genuinely free from bias towards any

particular solutions or from any restrictions that would limit the range of solutions that could be recommended to the retail client. Investment advice is particularly relevant to the sale of structured products to retail investors, since the complexity of many products will render them unsuitable for non-advised sales to retail clients. This initiative is commonly known as the Retail Distribution Review (RDR). In the RDR, the definition of a retail investment product was drafted so as to be intentionally consistent with the then draft of the PRIPs Regulation. Since the PRIPs legislation is still subject to fluctuation, it is expected that the definition of retail investment product in the RDR may similarly change to fall in line with the eventual regulation.

In broad terms, the RDR involved three main changes in relation to the sales of retail investment products. First, it introduced a new standard for the quality of advice provided by financial advisers on retail investment products, including the need for advisers to describe themselves as providing independent advice or restricted advice, with independent advice requiring much higher levels of care owed to the retail investor.

In June 2012, the FSA published its final guidance on independent advice, which essentially states that independent advice in relation to a retail investment product must be based on a comprehensive and fair analysis of the relevant market and must be unbiased and unrestricted. Restricted advice in this context is any advice which does not meet the requirements for independent advice.

Second, the RDR introduced enhanced requirements for the professional qualifications and standards required for retail investment advisers themselves.

Third, as from January 2013, the RDR prohibits the payments of fees or commissions from third parties to investment advisers in relation to advised sales of retail investment products. The reason behind this third change was to put an end to the inherent bias that retail investment advisers might have towards recommending a product to retail clients based on the commission payable to them, rather than purely what was in the best interests of the retail client. For many years, the FSA has had concerns (some would say well founded) that retail investment advisers have been motivated to recommend structured products (and also other investments, such as endowment mortgages) to retail investors, rather than simpler "alternatives", based mostly or entirely on the amount of commission payable to the adviser, rather than the products' suitability for the retail client.

As a result of the RDR, many manufacturers and distributors of retail structured products are revising their charging structures to reflect the new regime in the UK. It is worth noting that the latest draft of the proposed MiFID II Directive also prohibits the receipt by investment advisers of fees and commissions from third parties, although only in relation to the provision of independent advice. Third party fees and commission for restricted advice are currently not subject to the same restrictions as in the UK.

Regulatory intervention

This is the third, and most controversial, "pillar" of structured products regulation, alongside the other two pillars of pre-sale disclosure and point-of-sale business conduct. The first two pillars are likely to remain a staple feature of most structured product regulatory regimes in developed countries, but in the years since the Lehman collapse, regulators in many jurisdictions have become more focused on the fact that the first two pillars only allow regulators to address detriment caused to investors as a result of breach of the various regulatory requirements. In other words, the point-of-sale disclosure and conduct-of-business regime does not allow regulators to prevent investor detriment – only to deal with the aftermath. As a result regulators have become much more interested in the concept of regulatory intervention at an early stage in the life cycle of a structured product, in order to prevent investor detriment arising in the first place.

The FSA (now the Financial Conduct Authority (FCA)) of the UK was one of the lead regulators in this regard. In January 2011, the FSA signalled its intention to become much more interventionist and intrusive in its approach to the regulation of structured products. Although the FCA continues to believe that point-of-sale regulation is a critical element of regulatory focus, it also considers that product design and decisions about how products will be developed, and to whom they will be marketed, play an important role in determining outcomes for investors. Therefore, its regulatory approach will focus on issues such as the product governance processes employed by firms, whether there is effective competition in the structured products market for the benefit of consumers and whether firms are exploiting consumer behaviour. The particular focus of the FCA is likely to be on complex products (including those with structures which the FCA considers to be opaque), products which carry an inherent conflict of interest, products with secondary charges or layers of charges, as well as products where the consumer is attracted by a teaser rate and then tied in. The FSA previously accepted that, as part of formulating its new interventionist regime, it will need to balance its possible actions against the scale of possible detriment to be prevented and the number of consumers potentially affected, since it recognises that heavy-handed intervention could have a damaging effect on the market for structured products.

Although the new FCA is in the process of finding its feet on structured product regulation, it is useful to look at some of the possible product intervention options which the FSA previously highlighted, since the same options could generally be available to any regulator of structured products.

Possible product intervention options for regulators

The following sets out the possible regulatory intervention options outlined by the FSA, starting with the most radical options and ending with the least radical.

- **Pre-approval/pre-notification of products:** this is likely to be considered by regulators as the option of last resort, given the resources that would be required by regulators in certain jurisdictions to be able to examine and investigate the features of a new product. It also potentially places the regulator in the difficult position of being seen to endorse the safety of a product which has been pre-approved by it, or which has been pre-notified to it and in relation to which it has not intervened. The danger here is therefore that investors would be less likely to exercise their own due diligence in relation to a product considered to have the regulators' stamp of approval. The FSA itself all but ruled out the general pre-approval of products but did not rule out the possibility that this approach might be used in the future for certain products or certain markets.

- **Banning products or banning/mandating certain features of the products:** the FSA believed that, where products, or product features, have the potential to cause significant detriment to consumers, it could choose to exercise the right to ban products or product features, and the FCA now has this power. In June 2013, the FCA made use of its banning powers for the first time in banning the promotion of unregulated collective investment schemes, and close substitutes, to ordinary (as opposed to high-net-worth or sophisticated) retail investors in the UK, even where such investors had received specific financial advice in this context.

- **Price interventions:** the FCA can intervene in relation to the pricing of products, including looking at the relevant charging structure and making pricing comparisons with other appropriate (low-charging) products or in the most extreme cases imposing a cap on the overall level of charges. The FSA indicated that it continued to regard price interventions as useful in certain circumstances, in particular where it considered that competition in the market was lacking.

- **Mandating consumer and industry warnings:** including publishing lists of products considered to be generally unsuitable for the mainstream retail market. In addition, the FCA could in future consider mandating "wealth" warnings, requiring product providers and distributors to include a prominent specified risk warning, similar in concept to the warnings required to be printed on cigarette packets in many countries.

- **Prohibiting the non-advised sale of certain products to certain categories of clients:** although this remains an option for the FCA, it has the potential to severely limit the retail market for products that are targeted. This is because many retail investors may be dissuaded from seeking advice in relation to financial products, particularly in the light of the requirements under the RDR in the UK, and the proposed MiFID II changes at EU level, whereby investment advisers will no longer be able to receive fees from third parties and therefore in many cases will seek to charge fees directly to clients seeking their advice.

- **Adding new competence requirements for advisers:** including more specialist professional qualifications for advisers in relation to certain non-mainstream products. Under the RDR advisers will be subject to increased requirements, both in terms of initial qualifications and in relation to ongoing competence qualifications.

Staying in the regulators' good books – what is required?

In conjunction with its statements of possible early intervention options to be utilised to prevent consumer detriment, the FSA, in March 2012, published finalised guidance for the providers and originators of retail structured products, in terms of the development and governance of such products, so as to minimise the risk of poorly designed products and mis-selling. Their main recommendations were as follows.

- **Product approval procedures:** firms should have transparent and auditable product approval processes which provide for clear roles and responsibilities for the individuals involved in the approval processes, and which should "embed the delivery of fair outcomes for customers". The FCA also expects firms to have strict criteria for when a "light touch" approval process may be used and when the full, robust approval process is required.

- **Product development:** firms should identify their relevant target market for the product, in particular identifying customer needs and objectives and designing the product to cater for them. In this regard, consumer research should be specifically designed to help assess the risk tolerance of the target market, such as that market's willingness and ability to bear loss. It should also be designed to help assess the investment objectives of the target market, such as whether consumers are looking for capital growth or return, and their attitude towards risk, measured against reward.

- **Design and development of product features:** firms should ensure that product features that are visible to consumers are likely to be understandable by them so that they can see where their return is designed to come from, can assess the likelihood of receiving it and, where applicable, can understand that they may receive no return at all, or may lose some capital. The design process should take account of factors such as how the gross return of the product is divided up between the different stakeholders and whether the division (including fees and charges) is "fair" from the consumer's perspective.

- **Firms should undertake sufficient due diligence in relation to the counterparty (eg, the issuer or the guarantor of the securities):** such as examining credit default swap spreads and other market information, rather than simply relying on external credit ratings of the counterparty. In addition, the terms of structured products should be clear and fair and accurately represent the features contained in the product design.

- **Stress-testing and modelling:** firms should ensure products are routinely tested under a variety of conditions, including the product performing within its design parameters and a failure of a design feature. The stress-test should be forward-looking, as well as involving backtesting.

- **Marketing, distribution and communications:** firms are expected to take care in their use of non-advised sales of products containing complex features which are difficult to explain. In addition, firms are expected to carry out due diligence on the distributors of the product, both initially and on an ongoing basis, including ensuring products are in fact being sold to their target market. They are also expected to act on their assessments of distributors, as necessary, which could include amending the product literature for future distribution, providing further training for distributors or limiting distribution to specific channels.

- **Information to distributors:** distributors should be given sufficient information on the structure of the product, its implicit charges and the market conditions needed to generate a particular outcome so that they can:

  - understand the details of the product and its target audience;

  - compare the product with other available retail products;

  - understand the risk and reward aspects of a product and the cost–benefit analysis of capital protection;

  - understand all the conditions in which the product will perform as expected.

The FCA strongly encourages the use of training for the purpose of informing distributors appropriately.

- **Information to consumers:** firms should take action to ensure that information supplied to consumers is clear and is provided before, during and after the point of sale. Firms are expected to assess the nature and complexity of a product and the financial capability of the target market, and tailor the information accordingly. The information should promote the product features in a fair and balanced way.

- **Post-sales responsibilities:** in order to facilitate the ability of consumers to change products or submit claims or complaints after a sale has completed, firms are expected to periodically review their products in order to ensure they still meet the needs of the target audience, and to ascertain whether they are on course for the performance originally expected. Firms are also encouraged to develop a strategy for contacting consumers if the performance of a product begins to deviate substantially from what consumers had been led to expect. The FCA considers that firms have a responsibility to treat consumers fairly throughout the life of the product and to endeavour to provide easy methods of early redemption.

LEHMAN BROTHERS

The Lehman collapse in 2008 provides a good example of a case of sales of structured investments which necessitated regulatory intervention, in respect of the so-called "Minibonds" which were sold in various Asian jurisdictions for several years before the collapse of Lehman.

The key features of a typical issue of Minibonds were as follows.

- Although Lehman entities acted in many roles in relation to the Minibonds, such as arranger, dealer, swap counterparty, calculation agent and market agent, the Minibonds were securities issued not by a Lehman entity, but by a special purpose company incorporated in an offshore jurisdiction, such as the Cayman Islands, and not part of the Lehman Group.

- Thus, investors in the Minibonds were not entitled to any recourse against a Lehman entity in respect of any losses they might suffer on their Minibonds, and had access only to those assets of the special purpose issuer that were specifically ring-fenced for the benefit of the investors in the particular issue of Minibonds.

- The Minibonds were structured so as to pay a fixed rate of interest which was significantly higher than prevailing rates of interest that were otherwise available to investors.

- Repayment of the principal amount of the Minibond on the specified maturity date, however, would take place only if at such a date there had occurred no credit event (eg, a bankruptcy or other insolvency event) with respect to one or more specified entities. If such a credit event did occur prior to the specified maturity date of the Minibonds, then a certain amount would, under the terms of the Minibonds, be deducted from the principal amount of the Minibonds that would otherwise have been due to the investor, based upon agreed procedures regarding valuation of the debt obligations of the reference entity. The investor was thus exposed to the credit risk of the underlying credit reference entities.

The above features are fairly common to issuances of credit-linked structured products generally, but particularly noteworthy in the case of the Lehman Minibonds were the provisions for the security provided for the benefit of the investors in the Minibonds, as follows.

- Whereas it would be normal for a credit-linked note issued by a special purpose vehicle to give investors the benefit of security over assets such as government or corporate bonds with a low default risk, the security for the Minibonds consisted of so-called synthetic collateralised debt obligations (CDOs). These synthetic CDOs were themselves collateralised by debt securities, in many cases issued by a member of the Lehman Group. Therefore when the Lehman entities filed for bankruptcy, not only were no more payments made to the issuer by the Lehman entity acting as swap counterparty, but the debt obligations ultimately acting as collateral for the Minibonds were also in default.

- Therefore, despite their innocuous-sounding name, the Minibonds were sufficiently complex to cause many a professional investor to scratch their head. However, these Minibonds were widely sold in various Asian jurisdictions to ordinary retail investors, including a high proportion of retired investors.

In Hong Kong alone, it is estimated that approximately HK$20 billion (US$2.6 billion) worth of Lehman structured products were sold to over 50,000 retail investors. As at the end of 2008, the Hong Kong Monetary Authority alone had received details of nearly 20,000 complaints linked to Lehman structured products, of which nearly 13,000 related to Lehman Minibonds.

In many cases, the Asian regulators investigating claims related to the Lehman Minibonds have chosen not to release comprehensive details of the complaints received, or of alleged misconduct surrounding the sales of the Minibonds. However, anecdotal evidence abounds of pensioners being encouraged to invest in these Minibonds with promises of the opportunity of winning televisions, fridges, cookers, etc, if they did invest.

The Lehman Minibond saga caused various Asian regulators to examine not only breaches of existing regulations affecting the sales and distribution of structured products, but also whether additional regulation, or a new approach to regulation, was required.

In Hong Kong, the HKMA concluded that the existing regime was structured in a very similar way to the regimes of other major developed economies, including Europe and the US. The regulatory regime centred, similarly, around the twin concepts of adequate disclosure of information to potential investors and adherence to various conduct-of-business principles including an assessment of suitability of a particular financial product for a particular investor and the principle of dealings with investors being carried out in a fair and professional manner.

Inevitably, though, in the aftermath of such a financial scandal, any regulator would be compelled to at least give thought to whether certain products should be restricted or banned, either altogether or for certain categories of investor. Similarly, the HKMA considered whether to propose these sorts of restrictions on structured product sales to retail investors, but they noted that none of the other regulatory regimes they had surveyed contained such restrictions.

The recommendations of the HKMA were as follows.

- Not to institute a ban on certain structured products, favouring the retention of the existing disclosure-based system rather than removing the freedom of choice of investors.

- To focus on investor education, as an adjunct to the disclosure-based regime, and in particular the undertaking of public education programmes to help educate investors as to the purpose of disclosure – to enable them to make informed investment decisions, but also to be able to take responsibility for those decisions and recognise that whether to invest or not to invest was ultimately their choice, based on an adequate understanding of the information provided to them regarding the nature and risks of the relevant product. The regulatory framework should be strengthened to take into account the complexity of investment products being sold to retail investors, the change in the expectations of the public as to the level of protection afforded to them by regulation and the risk tolerance of investors.

- Acknowledging that few retail investors are likely to read a full prospectus, the introduction of a requirement for a uniform short-form disclosure format for retail structured products (and possibly for other retail investment products) should be considered. The intention of such short-form disclosure would be to set out the key benefits and risks of a product, giving equal prominence to both, with such disclosure being given to an investor prior to any sale. Key issues to be covered would be whether the product was principal-protected, the major risks that could be suffered by the investor (including the potential maximum loss that could be suffered), limitations on any secondary market for the product and the total costs attached to the product. In addition, the HKMA envisaged the distributor providing a statement of key facts surrounding the sales process, including issues as to the capacity in which the institution was acting and any fees and commission it received, together with a statement as to whether or not the product was covered by any deposit protection scheme and a reference to any complaints procedure or dispute resolution scheme applicable to the product. The HKMA also considered adopting a health-warning system for retail structured products which contained embedded derivatives, along the lines of a large-print warning, alerting investors to the potential risks of the product.

- To focus on better disclosure, rather than more disclosure.

- To introduce restrictions on the use of gifts as a marketing tool in the promotion of financial products to retail investors.

The HKMA also found that there was significant potential for customer confusion where products were sold to them at their retail bank. For example, if the customer's initial intention was to place or roll over a simple fixed term deposit, then a structured product sold to them at that time may cause confusion as to whether the structured product was similarly protected by a deposit protection scheme, which in most cases it would not be. The HKMA concluded that allowing the same sales staff to conduct both ordinary banking business and retail investment product business, coupled with the ease with which a depositor could become an investor, tended to reinforce the perception that there was little difference in principle between a structured product and a fixed term deposit. Therefore they concluded that segregation of retail structured products business from traditional retail banking business should be considered.

In terms of how far such a segregation should extend, the HKMA considered subsidiarisation – ie, not allowing the same legal entity to conduct both businesses – as well as the less-disruptive method of physical segregation of the two different activities within a branch, coupled with investor education regarding the different functions of the investment business, and the prominent placement of warning signs. It recommended also that there be a complete separation between information on a customer's deposit account and on their investor account and a prohibition on the institution making use of deposit-related information to target customers for investment activity.

Further recommendations included the following.

- Separating a customer's risk profile from the sales process and for the risk profiling to be carried out by non-sales staff, to minimise the chance that the risk profiling could be tainted by the desire to sell financial products to that investor.

- The audio recording of the sales process and ancillary arrangements, to act as possible evidence in any future dispute about mis-selling of a product.

- Where a distributing institution decides to change the risk-rating of a product, it should be required to notify customers to whom it had previously recommended and sold the product. Despite there not necessarily being any easily accessible secondary market for the product, the HKMA considered that the customer should be informed at an early stage in case they were able to take steps to offset the perceived increased risk.

Separately, the Hong Kong Securities and Futures Commission made new regulations in the aftermath of the Lehman Minibond scandal. These included mandating the retention of complete documentation of the reasons why the customers had invested in the product in cases where the risk rating applied to the product does not match the customer's risk profile.

It also recommended, similarly to some European jurisdictions, as well as Singapore and Australia, the introduction of a cooling-off period in relation to the sale of certain financial products, during which customers could decide to cancel their investment without penalty.

The SFC also considered introducing the concept of "mystery shoppers", who would verify the information available to potential investors in a distribution venue, such as a bank branch, as well as the quality of advice offered in relation to the sale. Another option considered was the conducting of customer interviews and surveys to observe how the sales process was working.

Where disputes arise between investors and intermediaries, the SFC recommended the establishment of a focused, specialised organisation (along the lines of a financial services ombudsman) to adjudicate or settle such disputes.

The SFC also recommended increased scrutiny of remuneration packages of sales staff, in order to ensure that staff were not being inappropriately incentivised to sell products which might not be suitable for the investor.

Many of the recommendations by the HKMA and the SFC are echoed in the PRIPs Regulation in Europe, discussed in the following section.

THE REGULATION OF PRIPS IN EUROPE

In October 2007, the European Commission decided to try to adopt, across Europe, a coherent approach to the transparency and conduct-of-business requirements for "substitute" retail investment products.

Originally their principal aim was to seek greater consistency and a more level playing field, in regulatory terms, for financial products that offer investors similar financial exposures, irrespective of how they are structured or "packaged". While this remains an important objective of the PRIPs initiative at the time of writing, there is now much more focus on investor protection through increased transparency and product comparability.

The initiative concentrates on pre-point-of-sale disclosure to investors and point-of-sale conduct-of-business principles (rather than product intervention powers).

The PRIPs regime focuses on the fact that an investor who desires exposure to, say, the FTSE 100 Index could invest in a number of different products that would provide that exposure. These include a structured note linked to that index, an investment fund that tracks that index, a unit-linked life insurance policy that tracks it and a structured bank deposit which pays interest calculated by reference to the performance of that index. Yet, the regulations governing the sale of such products diverge tremendously, and in respect of structured bank deposits there is no specific regulation at all. Some of the concerns of the European Commission stemming from this fact are the lack of a level playing field for some financial industry sectors, and the possibility of regulatory arbitrage that could ensue from such regulatory differences. Their goal, therefore, was greater conformity of regulations concerning disclosure and conduct of business across all sectors, though the regulations for each sector need not be identical.

In selecting their blueprint for the harmonised regime, the European Commission decided to model the regulatory disclosure obligations on those of the UCITS regime, which is the directive governing the establishment, operation and investment in mutual funds intended to be sold to retail investors in the European Union. What the European Commission found particularly attractive was the UCITS requirement for a Key Information Document (KID). As part of the review of the existing UCITS Directive in 2009, the European Commission decided to mandate the production of a KID in respect of every UCITS fund, with this document constituting a short aid to investor understanding, to be made available to investors in addition to the "full" prospectus required for each fund. The concept of the KID is that it should be a concise document, written in plain, easily intelligible language, summarising for investors the key information points concerning the fund.

One of the particular concerns of the structured products industry in modelling the aid to disclosure on the UCITS KID was that the degree of structural difference between structured products and UCITS funds would make it very difficult to shoehorn key information items for structured products into the format used by UCITS funds. For instance, unlike structured products, UCITS funds are subject to product regulation. In other words, the UCITS directive and related legislation dictate, in great detail, matters such as the assets in which a UCITS is permitted to invest, restrictions regarding the management of the fund, the safeguarding of its assets and the investment policies of the fund. As a result, a UCITS fund is a very homogenised product, whereas in contrast a structured product is by its nature a bespoke product, designed with the intention of achieving a specific economic effect, given particular factors. As such, structured products vary from structured product to structured product much more than from UCITS fund to UCITS fund, making it difficult to achieve a description of all key information elements in a two-page document, as required in respect of a KID for a UCITS fund.

In addition, whereas a UCITS fund generally relies on the performance of its fund manager for its returns, a structured product typically has no manager and achieves its economic results purely as a result of its contractual terms and the return that those terms provide for in the particular prevailing economic circumstances. As a result, a summary of certain items, such as the total costs associated with the investment, cannot be stated meaningfully in the same way as for an investment in a managed fund. Whereas, in the case of a fund-based investment, the costs of various service providers and intermediaries will affect the ultimate return on a fund-based investment because that return is not pre-defined, in contrast, the return of a structured product is pre-defined and therefore fees and costs paid by the structured product provider in assembling the structured product will not affect the return on the investment. However, the European Commission views such disclosure as essential for allowing the investor to make a meaningful comparison of the different investment products available to them across the different sectors.

In July 2012, the European Commission finally published a draft regulation, dictating the content and format of disclosure of the key information relating to a product to investors. The European Parliament was due to consider the draft legislation in its plenary session on November 18, 2013, with the final legislation possibly becoming operative in mid-2015.

To begin with, in drafting the PRIPs Regulation the European Commission encountered a similar problem to that outlined at the beginning of this chapter: how to define exactly what they are purporting to regulate.

Originally the proposed definition of a PRIP was "a product where the amount payable to the investor is exposed to fluctuation in the market value of assets or payouts from assets, through a combination or wrapping of those assets, or other mechanism other than a direct holding". This definition focused on the product either combining various different elements to form a composite, or alternatively containing an element of packaging or wrapping of an underlying asset so that it became a different thing from a direct investment in the underlying asset.

What the definition did not contain, however, was any reference to the retail investor element of the product offering.

In the final draft of the regulation published by the European Commission, the definition of PRIP had changed significantly and was now defined as "an investment where, regardless of the legal form of the investment, the amount repayable to the investor is exposed to fluctuations in reference values or in the performance of one or more assets which are not directly purchased by the investor". The draft regulation makes it clear that the obligation to produce a key information document only applies to the sale of such a product to retail investors. The definition is intended to cover all investment funds (including UCITS funds), all structured products (whether these are packaged as insurance policies, funds, securities, bank deposits or otherwise) and, possibly, any derivative contract. The reference to packaging or combination of different elements has been removed and the focus of the KID requirements is now very much on any instrument whose return fluctuates against the value or performance of other assets. Previously the reference to the need for some form of packaging would have excluded bilateral over-the-counter derivative contracts, whereas arguably it now does not.

The European Commission had originally considered prescribing a non-exhaustive list of products which expressly fell inside or outside of the regulation. Although this list is not specified, there is an express exclusion of certain types of product from the scope of the regulation, including:

- bank deposits with a rate of return determined by reference to an interest rate;
- "vanilla" securities that do not embed a derivative;
- insurance products that only offer pure protection insurance or non-life products which provide no surrender value that is exposed to fluctuations in the performance of underlying assets or reference values;
- certain occupational pension schemes;
- pension products for which a financial contribution from the employer is required by national law and where the employee has no choice as to the pension product provider.

The draft regulation provides for certain specific content requirements for the KID, as well as the general requirements that the KID must be accurate, fair, clearly laid out and not misleading, that it must be short (although with no specific length limit) and use clear, succinct and comprehensible language.

At the time of writing in autumn 2013, the draft regulation is still subject to ongoing negotiation before it is agreed by the European Parliament and some of the particular provisions which may be subject to change are the requirement for a simple risk indicator (given concerns as to a simple indicator giving an over-simplified measure of risk for a complex product, and thereby leading to a risk of over-reliance on the indicator by certain investors), as well as the liability for a KID which does not comply with the terms of the regulation. In this regard, the first draft of the regulation provided that a retail investor could claim damages for losses suffered as a result of reliance on a KID which did not comply with the regulation and that in this regard the burden of proof would be on the product manufacturer to show that the KID did in fact comply with the content requirements. This constituted a reversal of the normal burden of proof, and may end up being re-reversed in the EU legislative negotiations.

Conduct-of-business requirements for PRIPs

In relation to the point-of-sale conduct-of-business requirements, the European Commission felt that MiFID represented the "gold standard", although at the time of writing it does not apply to insurance products or to bank deposits. The MiFID Directive is being reviewed, and a MiFID II Directive and a Markets in Financial Instruments Regulation are expected to be finalised during 2014. As part of these changes, structured bank deposits are proposed to be brought within the scope of the MiFID regime for the first time. In relation to insurance products, the Insurance Mediation Directive is undergoing a similar review and is proposed to be amended to introduce rules consistent with those in MiFID, particularly in relation to conflicts of interest and conduct of business. In addition, the UCITS framework is proposed to be amended to ensure that direct sales of fund investments by UCITS asset managers are subject to the MiFID regime, as well as sales by intermediaries (which are already subject to the regime).

MiFID conduct-of-business obligations

When the MiFID II regime comes into effect, intermediaries selling any PRIP will be subject to the following existing MiFID conduct-of-business obligations:

- to act honestly, fairly and professionally in accordance with the best interests of the client;
- to conduct an assessment, based upon information provided by the potential client, of whether the PRIP is appropriate for that particular client, based upon the client's knowledge and experience in investments of that type;
- when executing orders, to obtain the best possible result for the client in terms of price, costs, speed and any other consideration relevant to the execution of the order;
- to take all reasonable steps to identify conflicts of interest with their clients and to manage those conflicts of interest so as to ensure with reasonable confidence that the risk of detriment to the client will be prevented or, if that is not possible, to disclose the conflict to the client.

In the context of the duty to act honestly, fairly and professionally in accordance with the best interests of the client, the MiFID regime provides that fees or commissions paid by third parties must be clearly disclosed to the client. Exceptions to this rule include circumstances where the fee or commission is designed to enhance the quality of the service to the client, or where the fee is necessary for the provision of investment services and by its nature cannot give rise to conflicts with the firm's duty to act honestly, fairly and professionally in accordance with the best interests of its clients.

CONCLUSION

In the low-interest-rate environment at the time of writing, it seems that many investors regard a high yield on an investment as more important than full capital protection (it generally being rare for a product to be able to offer both). Alarm bells should therefore be ringing for producers and distributors of structured products. Where retail investors have incurred capital losses on financial investments, the recent trend has been for them to "give it a go" in terms of claiming that the product was mis-sold to them, whether that claim has any merit or not.

For their part, structured products providers and distributors will continue to have to comply with existing point-of-sale conduct requirements (such as those imposed by the MiFID directive in Europe) and 2013 publications from regulatory bodies such as IOSCO indicate that compliance with both the letter and the spirit of the existing standards will be carefully scrutinised.

Existing pre-sale disclosure requirements are going to be "enhanced", at least in Europe, under the forthcoming PRIPs Regulation, and liability of product manufacturers for non-disclosure, or mis-disclosure, will become easier for investors and regulators to establish.

However, in addition to the existing regulatory principles, structured product manufacturers will have to show regulators that their products have been conceived, designed, developed, marketed, sold and monitored in a manner designed to reduce the possibility of detriment to the retail investors to whom they are sold. The flip side of this focus on the entire life cycle of a product is that regulators are also sharpening their weapons of early product intervention, for use where they consider that the risk of possible investor detriment from a type of product outweighs the benefit to be derived from it.

Nevertheless, a structured product represents one of the best ways of meeting an investor's specific investment needs, because it can be tailored to achieve the specific economic result desired by the investor. Therefore, hope remains that regulators will develop approaches to the regulation of structured products that appropriately balance investor protection and investor choice and that the use of any product intervention powers will be proportionate to the risk being addressed.

10

Risk and Modelling

Clarke Pitts

This final chapter tries to identify and explain some of the key problems that structured products have caused, in particular, large losses with recognised risk and also, more worryingly, unexpected losses from previously unrecognised risk. We will examine the shortcomings of the popular local volatility model and the generic problem of crowded trades and the consequences of their hedging.

The first generation of structured products was simply established derivatives combined and packaged for the convenience of investors. These components were separable and could be evaluated using the financial models that have been adopted by the banks for these component contracts. For the option parts, this generally meant the Black–Scholes option model or Merton's binomial model. I will not assume any knowledge of these in this chapter and instead seek to give the reader an intuitive feel for what these models do and how the flaws in the approach have led to some colossal losses. If you have no patience or appetite for such arcane or technical discussions then it may not be for you but it is an interesting and important issue. There remain some substantial problems with the financial modelling of structured products (and other complex derivatives), which, in the wake of the global financial crisis, should give the reader food for thought.

Conventional option pricing theory rests rather heavily on the premise that the probability distribution of the returns of the market is continuous and lognormal. Rather than examining what this means, let us move swiftly on to whether it is true or not and if that matters particularly.

In short, there is abundant reason to believe that market returns are not lognormally distributed. This can be seen by looking at the historic behaviour of shares, exchange rates, interest rates and indexes. Moreover, the market recognises this quite explicitly by

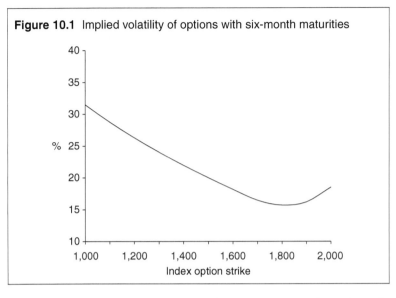

Figure 10.1 Implied volatility of options with six-month maturities

having very different implied volatilities for options where the only difference between them is the strike price. That is to say, a put option on the S&P 500 index with a strike price of 1,500 expiring in three months might have, say, 15% implied volatility, while another with the same expiration date but a strike of 1,400 will usually be priced such that the implied volatility is significantly higher. If the market returns were, in fact, lognormal, then we should expect all the options of a given maturity to have about the same implied volatility.

In Figure 10.1 we see a graph showing the implied volatility of options with six-month maturities.

With such a clear contradiction of the premise of lognormal returns it might seem obvious that new models should be adopted but this has not happened. There are good reasons for this. Market participants have learned to cope with the shortcomings of the models by using different implied volatility for different strikes and can compensate for some of the misleading risk management results. This may be hard to comprehend so I will try to elucidate with an example of how practitioners mitigate the failings of their models on an everyday basis.

When a professional option trader is hedging their risk against a move in the market, they use a model to measure how much the price of the option should change if the market price of the asset on which the option is written changes by a small amount. This gives them a sensitivity for the value of their position known as "delta". First, they price the option using the market as it is now then move the spot price by a small amount and reprice. The change in value in the option divided by the change in value of the underlying asset is the delta. The simple (and usual) approach is to assume that all other considerations (interest rates, dividends, volatility, time to maturity) are not going to change. However, when the proximity to the current price of the strike is important for deciding what the volatility is, that assumption starts to fail.

By way of an example, an option trade has a call option on the S&P 500 that expires in three months. The strike is at-the-money, which is to say at the current level of the index. Let us decide that the index is 1,500 today and that is the strike of the option, too. It is a call option so the expected payout (in statistical or probabilistic terms) rises as the market goes up and falls if the market declines. If today's at-the-money options are trading at 15% implied volatility, then let us say that the delta is 50% for this at-the-money option. Then if the stock market rises by one index point, their option will increase in value by 0.5 points. However, now the stock market is above the strike and, as illustrated above, in-the-money (ie, options with strikes below the current market level) have higher implied volatility than at-the-money options. So they could anticipate that the option will appreciate by more than the 0.5 points (the gain attributable to the sensitivity to the underlying asset price). There will be an extra gain associated with a small increase in implied volatility. This incremental change is called the "smile delta" and that impact can be offset by hedging with a short position in S&P 500 futures in just the same way as the ordinary delta would be.

These "workarounds" function sufficiently well to allow the trading and risk management of straightforward options. The traders, their management and the control functions know the models and recognise their shortcomings. Auditors and regulators observe that the process is established and done quite consistently from firm to firm and the necessity of using this approach to satisfy all parties is almost absolute.

However, the same "fact" pattern has been observed for very similar situations in the past. After Black and Scholes published their paper in 1973, very little skewness was observed in option prices (implied volatilities). That is to say that low strikes were not

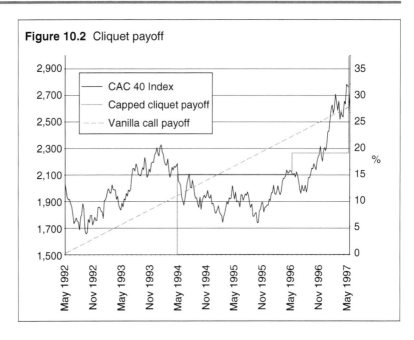

Figure 10.2 Cliquet payoff

CAC 40 Index

Capped cliquet payoff

Vanilla call payoff

materially more expensive (higher implied volatilities) than at-the-money or high strikes. After the crash in 1987 the market learned and subsequently the difference has been so marked that it is very hard to explain the high prices of low strike options with models that do anticipate skewness, eg, jump models without implausible parameters such as monthly drops of 10%.

In the early 1990s the French market was quite turbulent, particularly around the various referendums on the Maastricht Treaty which were necessary for the switch from using the French franc, Danish kronor and other currencies to the euro. Many investors found themselves in products where the embedded call options were far out-of-the-money so when the market rallied they were not benefitting much (such options have a low market delta). So rather than promoting the (now) old fashioned zero-coupon bond with a call option, they offered the capital guarantee (through the zero) for five years and a strip of call options, each lasting a year. The idea being that if the market fell in the first year then the option that year would yield nothing but the client would get a second bite at the cherry as the next option would start at the beginning of year two with a strike price of the then current (lower) level. This product is called a cliquet, a French word that means a ratchet. It is a compelling idea and has many merits. However, this innovation did present some major problems. First, five one-year call options are much more valuable than one five-year call option. The pricing of options rises as a function of log time if we exclude interest rate, dividend and volatility effects. So in order to make the structure work the providers had to cap the payout of each year by making each option a call spread rather than a simple call. This means that the investor can receive the capital appreciation of the market each year up to a certain amount, say 20%, and any gains beyond that are forgone. Figure 10.2 illustrates the ratchet effect.

These products proved immensely popular and were sold in very large amounts. The investment banks and brokers providing the risk management came to rue the day cliquets were ever conceived of. They had materially mispriced them, and to their own detriment. How and why this happened is worth examining, not least as the explanation points to the possibility of such mishaps occurring in the future.

LOCAL VOLATILITY

The products that had early redemption terms (callable, autocallable (ie, knock out)) or where the payout depended not just on the terminal value of the index at the end of the life of the investment but also on how it had got there, required pricing tools much more sophisticated than the Black–Scholes model or other similar technology, which had been used to value and hedge conventional (in market parlance, "vanilla") options. The French, who often lead from the front in terms of innovation in this industry, came up with a very clever solution called local volatility. Bruno Dupire of Société Générale and Emanuel Derman of Goldman Sachs adopted this technique to price more complex derivatives. An elegant explanation of the concept can be found on Emanuel Derman's own website.[1] The author cannot improve on that and will not try to do so.

Instead, let us look at the crux of the model and why it failed so dramatically while the users naively assumed all was well. When there is a reasonable universe of observable option prices for a given asset, such as the S&P 500 or gold (for example) then option traders can create a volatility surface that can be used to price any conventional option, using extrapolation and interpolation (usually nonlinear). One thing that all the observable options are likely to have

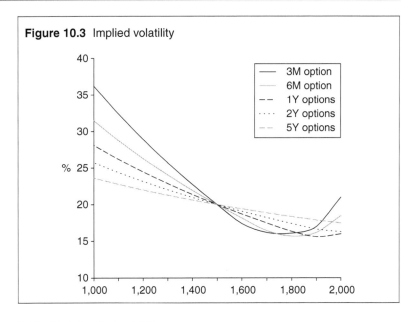

Figure 10.3 Implied volatility

Table 10.1 Implied volatility

| | Strike (%) | |
Maturity	100	120
One year	20.0	18.0
Two years	20.0	19.0
One year (in a year's time)	20.0	20.0

in common is that they start "now" ie, with a "strike" price that is already determined. These are called "spot" starting. Essentially all market traded options are spot starting. Using local volatility, users can determine the volatility for any time and strike, whether spot starting or not, so long as they have sufficient input from observable vanilla options to which they can calibrate their functions.

In Figure 10.3, the implied volatility for options with longer and shorter maturities is included. We can see that shorter dates (such as 3M) have steeper and more curved features and long dates (eg, 5Y) express less skewness and curvature. This term structure is very important in the example below. It is nearly always the case that shorter dated options have steeper (and more curved) implied volatilities across strikes.

If we take a highly simplified version of this information and examine it (Table 10.1), we can see why a local volatility model is too naive.

For this purpose, we shall ignore interest rates, dividends and other important but irrelevant factors. If a one-year option is priced such that it implies volatility of 20% for the next year and simultaneously a two year option is priced such that it implies volatility of 20% for the next two years, what then should we expect volatility to be in a year's time (for the following year)? Without recourse to sophisticated mathematics we can see that it ought to be 20% for the second year.

However, if out-of-the-money calls (in this case 120%) are priced with 18% volatility for one year and 19% for two years (a plausible scenario), then what should a 120% call option for a year, starting in a year's time, be priced at? It seems it should also be 20%, though the averaging is of the variance (ie, the square of the volatility)[2] so in fact it works out at 19.95%, which is roughly the same. Now the important thing to recognise is that the skewness (the difference between 100% strike option implied volatility and 120% strike option implied volatility) for one-year options seems to be 2% but in a year's time it is "expected" to fall to nothing. However, traders are unlikely to anticipate that skewness (ie, the difference in implied volatilities attributable to differences in strike price) will disappear and if they had been asked to price "forward starting" options, then they might have centred their expectations around the then current levels or historic average levels of skewness. Traders were using this new tool to price complicated combinations of forward starting and other "path dependent" structures that could not be broken down into conventional spot starting options so they did not appreciate the error being made. When traders and various control functions such as auditors checked that the local volatility-based models priced options for which they had observable prices (ie, spot starting vanilla options) they found a high level of accuracy. With this modest amount of due diligence various banks and brokers wrote colossal amounts of capped cliquets and other exotics.

The most sophisticated houses check new models by using simulations and other techniques. Some houses realised this shortcoming of the local volatility model fairly quickly; others took longer (years) to catch on and by virtue of being the cheapest offer, these firms had done a great deal of business before they discovered that their success was less to do with the brilliance of their sales or trading and was mainly a consequence of the fundamental error in their pricing. Losses ran to hundreds of millions of US dollars for individual houses. Such numbers might seem modest in the context of the carnage later inflicted by credit derivatives but in the late 1990s this was a huge blow and removed many individuals and some firms from the industry.

We might imagine that this was the end of the road for local volatility. However, it is still the main model used for pricing and risk managing exotic equity derivative options (and other derivatives, particularly commodity linked). The error in pricing for forward skewness is a known flaw and existing usages adopt a conceptually crude adjustment to compensate for the mispricing of forward skewness. Other models have killed their keepers but live on. An interesting account of the Gaussian copula (widely used for pricing and managing CDOs) by Donald MacKenzie and Taylor Spears of the University of Edinburgh tells a similar story with far more spectacular consequences (McKenzie and Spears 2012).

It is a contentious topic. The local volatility model is well established and familiar to traders, management, control functions, auditors and regulators. It reproduces observable vanilla options prices accurately and works quickly enough to be practical for everyone. On the other hand, it relies heavily on assumptions that are demonstrably wrong (particularly lognormal returns) and has led users to disaster (cliquets, volatility swaps and others). Why then does it persist?

In the natural sciences, the quality of a model is measured by its predictive qualities. In microeconomics we seem to be less demanding. Local volatility fails to predict the smile delta, term structure of skewness and forward skew. Jump-based models do pick up these observable features of the market and so a good case can be made for incorporating "jumps" into the models. However, they are not without issues of their own and we should not expect a migration anytime soon.

Many would say that local volatility is not really a model at all and this point of view has some merit but has not discouraged the industry adopting it wholeheartedly. Readers who would like a more technical but still accessible explanation of this issue might find various papers published by a specialist financial engineering consultancy, Ito 33, useful.[3]

The conclusion then is only that the prevalent models are fragile, inadequate and known to be materially wrong at a fundamental level while they calibrate well. We like to paraphrase this as "exactly right and completely wrong". They are used to price and risk manage hundreds of billions of exotic derivatives despite their known shortcomings.

CONCLUSIONS: CONCEPT OF COMPLEXITY

In Chapter 1, various merits and shortcomings of derivatives and structured products were identified. The issue of complexity was alluded to and that needs a little further examination. If we consider an ordinary option on a share, the models for pricing it use the prevailing interest rates, a forecast of volatility of the share price, likely dividends, share price, strike price and maturity to determine a value. If we look at an option on a bond, then it is the interest rate (yield) of the bond that is assumed to be stochastic (ie, variable). The reason for this apparent contradiction is that, while interest rates do change over time, the effect on most share options is very modest and can be ignored. Making both variables will not change the theoretical value of the share option so long as it is reasonably short dated, ie, the life of the product is less than five years. (How short dated depends on what degree of change in value is considered significant, how volatile interest rates are and how correlated are the changes in interest rates with changes in the stock price.)

However, when interest rates came down to very low levels the tenors (maturities) of structured products were increased to make the transactions marketable. If you recall the example in Chapter 1, a five-year zero-coupon was worth 71% with interest rates of 7%. When five-year rates are just 2% the zero-coupon bond is much more valuable – about 90.5%. Once friction costs such as distribution, legal and licensing costs have been paid this does not leave much money for options and the product would be unsaleable. In some cases, the industry responded by making the tenor much longer – up to 30 years, in fact. Some banks producing these products blithely continued to ignore interest rate volatility when offering very long-dated equity options and with this rather rash approach they won very high market share and apparently large profits. By excluding

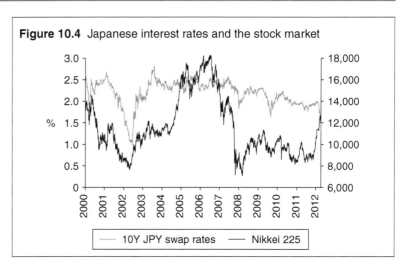

Figure 10.4 Japanese interest rates and the stock market

the possibility of interest rates changing from the model the risk reports for their businesses showed no sensitivity to this possibility, ie, should interest rates become volatile then it would not affect the values of their inventory at all.

It might be argued that they were unlucky, the bond market remained very low and so volatility and covariance of long-term yields did not affect their portfolios for quite a long time. Then, in 2003, there was a vicious jump in the bond market and the volatility shot up. By this time, the banks and brokers had built a large inventory of long-dated structured products and started to report very large losses. The products have first-order exposure to the covariance of the interest rates and the stock market returns. In 2003 that proved to be disastrous but, as you can see from Figure 10.4, 2008 and 2009 were even more dramatic. The hedging of the Japanese Power Reverse Dual Currency had a seismic impact on exchange rates and long-term swaps market too (Kaminska 2011). While the numbers were even larger there, the natural liquidity in bonds and exchange rates is greater too.

Figure 10.5 shows how dramatically the covariance[4] has jumped. The covariance was very low and largely ignored but the exposure was real and when the markets became turbulent the spike was very large in 2004 and enormous in 2009, causing colossal losses for the investment banks which had issued Enman bonds.

A short explanation of the mechanics of the dynamic hedging in interest rates may help the reader understand what has happened.

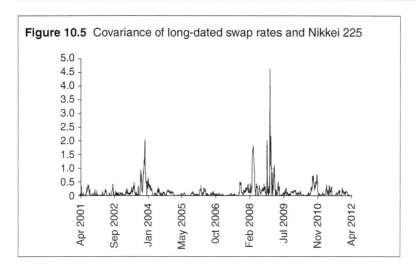

Figure 10.5 Covariance of long-dated swap rates and Nikkei 225

At the end of Chapter 7 there is a reference to Enman bonds, which were sold in colossal amounts. In this product, which typically had a 30-year maturity but regular knock-out events to make the expected life much shorter, typically three years or so at the outset. The knock-out events were triggered by the Nikkei 225 appreciating a modest amount above the level at the inception of the deal. It pays a fixed coupon, which the trading desk that is managing the position will "buy" a coupon stream through a swap to match their "expected" (according to the model) liability. If the Nikkei 225 depreciates, then the chance of the knockout event decreased, this makes the expected life of the deal longer and the trading desk has to buy more coupons for the extension in the expected life. This is akin to buying bonds, and if the market then recovers the life shortens and they have to unwind the extra fixed coupons (selling bonds). These re-hedges are achieved through swaps and the transaction costs and are quite modest as long as the price of the coupons (ie, the prevailing interest rates) has not changed while the Nikkei is going up and down. By ignoring interest rate volatility the desk have implied that they will not incur any losses from volatility of interest rates. The Japanese bond market was very stable for a long time and while the desks did suffer modestly the impact was quite modest in relation to the large margins demanded by firms to create such complicated and long-dated products.

To make matters worse for the staff involved, these losses arose from risks that had not been reported; management take a dim view of losses generally but when they are large and from risks that had not previously been known, then their indignation is greatly magnified. This was not a problem for every company nor even all the businesses in the culprit firms, but several hitherto stars of the industry had their careers curtailed.

Another important risk management problem: crowded trades and the impact of hedging them

All structured products created by banks and brokers are hedged. Most require continuous rebalancing of those hedges, so-called dynamic hedging. This is completely benign and normal until the impact of that dynamic hedging starts to move the market. In order to understand this properly the very process by which derivatives are hedged needs to be understood. This author does not propose to go into the gory details or any of the mathematics required to do this.

Consider a share whose price is US$100, and a one-month call option with strike price of US$10 and another one-month call option with a strike price of US$1,000. If the share price moves up by US$1, then the US$10 call will go up by US$1, too (or, more precisely, the present value of US$1). At the same time the US$1,000 will not move from a value of almost zero. This is because the US$10 call option is nearly certain to be in-the-money at expiry while it is vanishingly unlikely that a US$100 share will rise above US$1000 in a short period of time. The "delta" for the US$10 call is about 100% and for the US$1000 call it is zero. This "delta" is the ratio of shares to options required to hedge the options trader. It will be nice and stable in the example above so the trader will not have to rebalance their portfolio to remain hedged unless the stock falls 90% or rises by a factor of 10, neither of which are at all likely. The situation changes if the option strike is "at-the-money" ie, the strike price is US$100. In this case small moves in the share price are significantly changing the chances of the option being in-the-money at expiry. It is at roughly 50:50 at the outset but if the stock rallies significantly, then the delta will rise towards 100% and, conversely, if the stock prices fall, the delta will drop until it reaches zero. As the share price moves the option trader will buy shares (rising market) to hedge a short call option position and then sell shares (when the market falls back). As the market moves up and down they expect to realise a loss on these

Table 10.2 Share prices delta

Option strike (US$)	Share price (US$)	
	100	101
10	100%	100%
100	50%	52%
1,000	0%	0%

rebalancing trades and the magnitude of the expected losses are anticipated in the option price by the implied volatility. If the actual volatility of the share is markedly above the "implied" volatility when the trader entered into the position, then they will (on average) suffer a loss on the portfolio of options and shares over the life of the option. Obviously the converse is true: should volatility be lower than that which was implied, then they will enjoy a profit.

The models (of substantially all types) implicitly assume that the re-hedging they prescribe will not affect the market price of the assets. If the rising stock price causes the option trader to buy more shares, then it may be the case that this new demand will provoke a further rise in the share price, necessitating their buying more and so forth. This key assumption has proved the undoing of many derivative traders over time and is demonstrably wrong in the cases where the total derivative inventory that is being "dynamically" re-hedged is very large in relation to the natural liquidity in the asset that is being traded. It is startlingly commonplace for assets to become enormously volatile (or near static) and/or highly correlated with seemingly unrelated assets due to the colossal volumes of dynamic hedging required by the derivative desks, who are manfully trying to minimise the net/aggregate risks they have according to the approved models of their organisation.

The structured products industry tends to be concentrated on fashionable payouts and on popular underlying assets; these two features combine to cause problems for all the participants and sometimes for innocent bystanders.

Among the best examples of crowded trades are the Enman and PRDC issues from Japan mentioned above. There is no particular reason for Australian dollar versus yen to be so highly correlated with long-term interest rates other than the existence of a colossal amount of structured products. When markets are incited to vicious volatility and sudden spikes in correlation are observed, market pundits and supposed experts rush to give plausible and intuitive explanations as to how market "news" has precipitated these moves; educated and articulate people invent a narrative trying to make sense of what they see while being unaware of the major currents under the surface that are entirely mechanical in nature. This problem arises partly from ignorance of the scale and scope of the structured product markets and partly from a lack of understanding of the dynamic hedging process.

Other, simpler, examples include reverse convertibles on single shares. Preparing a paper to present to clients a while ago, we did some research, the results of which startled not just the audience but the author and the author's colleagues. There were structured products on 30 days' trading volume for one major company (Nippon TV) and about 10 days' volume for another (Sony) at the time. The hedging related to those deals was clearly very strongly influencing the behaviour of the share prices, both in direction (down) and in volatility (diminished) in these cases.

For Nippon TV, it became very straightforward to predict the trajectory of the shares and we profited significantly from this insight. The necessary information was available but the market was oblivious. We only noticed as the data had been collected for unrelated purposes.

Although these examples are from Japan, a market that was a major focus of the author's career in the early 2000s, other instances of the same phenomena exist all over the world. It might be said that the tail is wagging the dog in these cases.

We might observe that every trade has two sides, the buyer of a structured product has the reverse risk and exposure to that of the firm that has engineered and sold the product. However, the two sides of the transaction manage this risk very differently; the investor usually does no hedging of any sort and enjoys or suffers the consequences accordingly. This means that this is not a zero-sum game after all; the investor can profit from a rising market and the bank can profit from producing something for the client and hedging it to recover more than the gain achieved. Not all the trades work out so nicely. PRDC again affords a wonderful illustration of how the opposite can also be true: both the investors and the banks lost huge sums on what was ostensibly a zero-sum trade!

The magnitude of risk both systemically and to individual firms is very much a function of the aggregate risk in the system, yet neither market participants nor regulators make any substantial effort to monitor this. In the author's view it is a colossal failure of all parties and one that may end badly.

1   See http://www.ederman.com/new/docs/gs-local_volatility_surface.pdf.

2

$$\sigma_{t,T} = \sqrt{\frac{T\sigma_{0,T}^2 - t\sigma_{0,t}^2}{T - t}}$$

3   See http://www.ito33.com/publications/technical.

4   The volatility of the Nikkei multiplied by the volatility of long-dated swaps rates again multiplied by the correlation of the Nikkei/Swap Rate.

REFERENCES

Kaminska, I., 2011, "PRDCs, the 30-Year Swap Spread and Japan", FT Alphaville Blog, March 17, URL: http://ftalphaville.ft.com/2011/03/17/518081/prcs-the-30-year-swap-spread-and-japan/.

MacKenzie, D., and T. Spears, 2012, "'The Formula That Killed Wall Street'? The Gaussian Copula and the Material Cultures of Modelling", Working Paper, University of Edinburgh, URL: http://www.sps.ed.ac.uk/__data/assets/pdf_file/0003/84243/Gaussian14.pdf.

Index

(page numbers in italic type relate to tables or figures)

A

ABN AMRO, 209
accumulators, 99–102
  "I kill you later" nickname of,
    104–5
Advanced Information and
    Communications Network
    Society, 186
AIK Group, 90
Al Dente 7, 92
Alternea, 90
ARC Capital and Income, 59, 60
Arkea Mutual, 91
Asian market, 95–117, *97, 102,*
    105, 107, 108, 109, 110, 113, 114
  China, 114–16
  Dual Currency Investment in,
    111
  financial crisis in, 96, 111
  Hong Kong, 95–106
  Japan, 95, 119–61, *121, 125,*
    133, 135, 136, 144, 145, 148,
    151, 153, 154, 158, 163–205,
    167, 173, 176, 198–9, 203
    beginning of history of
      structured products in,
      120–34; *see also individual*
      countries
    beginning of "lost 20 years",
      134–43
    biggest investors in, 124–7
    and collapse of asset bubble,
      123, 184–6
    dual-currency structure in,
      128–31; *see also*
      dual-currency structure,
      Japan
    history of retail products in,
      182–204
    life insurance companies in,
      124–7

    and Lehman Brothers, 257–9
  Singapore, 95–106
  South Korea, 106–11, *107*
  Taiwan *110,* 111–14

B

Bank of China, 129
Bank for International
    Settlements (BIS),
    introduction of, 136
Bank of Japan (BoJ), 119, 123,
    136, 145, 179
Bankers Trust, 25, 26
Banque Populaire, 91
Barclays, 43, 93
Bear Stearns, 102
Bel20, 89
Belgium, 88–90
  approach of, to regulation,
    241–2
  see also European markets
Benefic, 92
Benson, Dr Robert, 79
Black–Scholes, 32, 155, 269, 271,
    273
BNP Paribas, 80, 91
Bolton, Anthony, 65
Bradford & Bingley, 51
branch networks, products
    retailed through, 16–17
  see also structured products

C

Cac49, 91
Caisse D'Epargne, 91, 92
callable bull–bear certificates
    (CBBCs), 17, 103
Canadian Bank, 210
capital-at-risk FTSE 100 autocall
    products, annualised
    performance of, 74
  see also UK market

capital-at-risk FTSE 100 linked
    digital growth products,
    annualised performance
    of, 74–5
    see also UK market
capital-at-risk FTSE 100 linked
    structured products,
    annualised performance
    of, 73
    see also UK market
capital-at-risk FTSE 100 linked
    "super-tracker" (geared
    growth) products,
    annualised performance
    of, 75
    see also UK market
capital-at-risk structured
    products, annualised
    performance of, 74
    see also UK market
capital-guaranteed note, 2
capital-guaranteed product, first
    trade in, 25–6
Capital Markets Daily, 80
"captive customer bases", 46
Cardia, Lamberto, 82
Carrefour, 92
Cedel, 23
Census and Statistics
    Department, Hong Kong, 97
Central Provident Fund (CPF), 98
CGER Assurances, 89
Charles Schwab, 212
Cheung Kong (Holdings)
    Limited, 103
China, 114–16
    see also Asian market
China Insurance Regulatory
    Commission, 115
China Securities Regulatory
    Commission (CSRC), 115
Chiyoda Life, 185
"Circular of the People's Bank of
    China on the Relevant
    Matters Concerning the
    Pilots of RMB Interest Rate
    Swap Transaction", 114
    see also Asian market: China

Cirio, 82
Citibank, 106
CITIC Pacific Limited, 103–4
Client Advisor Competency
    Standards (CACS), 106
Closed-End Investment
    Companies (CEICs), 42, 43
CMG First State Asset
    Management, 98
CMS spread structure, Japan,
    139–41
    characteristics, 140–1
        major investors and their
        motivation, 140
        pricing and
        risk-management issues,
        141
        reasons for success of, 141
        regulation, accounting
        background, 140
        structuring and distribution,
        140–1
    description, 139–40
        investor's payout, 140
        transaction form, 140
        typical terms, 139–40
    outcome, 141
Commerzbank, 86, 90
Commodities Futures Trading
    Commission, 230
contract-for-difference (CFD),
    18–19, *19*
covered warrants, 23
Credit Suisse, 14–15, 87, 93
crowded trades, impact of
    hedging, 280–3

D

David Aaron, 51
Davis Palk & Wardwell, 209
DAX, 2–3, 30, *30*, 86
DBS, 104
decumulators, 102–3
    "they kill you later" nickname
    of, 105
Denmark, approach of, to
    regulation, 242–3

Depositary Trust Clearing
Corporation (DTC), 212
derivatives, structured products
as, 1
Derman, Emmanuel, 273
Deutsche Bank, 18, 86, 93
Deutsche Zentral-
Genossenschaftsbank,
86
Deutscher Derivate Verband
(DDV), 83–4, 86
distribution dynamics in UK
market, 35, 45–8
see also UK market
Dodd–Frank Wall Street Reform
and Consumer Protection
Act, 230
DRL, 59
Dual Currency Investment,
popularity of, in Asia, 111
dual-currency structure, Japan,
128–31
characteristics, 130–1
major investors and their
motivation, 130
reasons for success of, 130
regulation, accounting
background, 130
risk pricing and
management issues, 130–1
structuring and distribution,
130
description, 129–30
investor's payout, 129–30
transaction form, 129
typical terms, 129
outcome, 131
see also Japan; reverse
dual-currency structure,
Japan
Dupire, Bruno, 273

E

"easy products", 47
Ecureuil Europe 2003, 92
Ecureuil Gestion, 92
EMEA, 210
EuroClear, 23, 25

European markets, 79–94, *80, 85*
Belgium, 88–90
early days, 79–81
France, 81, 91–3
Germany, 81, 83–6
Italy, 81–3
and PRIPs regulation, 260–5
and product maturity, 93
Spain, 81
Switzerland, 83, 86–8
UK, 81; *see also* UK market
see also individual countries
European Security and Markets
Authority, 80–1
EuroSTOXX 50, 55, 81
Eurotunnel, 24–5

F

Fannie Mae (Federal National
Mortgage Association), *see*
Federal National
Mortgage Association
Federal Deposit Insurance
Corporation (FDIC), 216
Federal National Mortgage
Association (Fannie Mae)
129
Fidelity, 65, 212
Financial Advisors
(Amendment) Bill, 2012
(Singapore) 106
Financial Conduct Authority
(FCA), 250–1
as successor to Financial
Services Authority, 63
Financial Industry Regulatory
Authority (FINRA) 243–4
Financial Instrument and
Exchange Act (Japan),
165–6
Financial Markets Authority
(AFM), France, 243
Financial Services Authority
(FSA), 249, 250
"Capital-at-risk products" fact
sheet of, 57
largest fine by, 51

Lehman Brothers findings of, 58–61
and Norwich & Peterborough, 62–3
and precipice bonds, 49, 57
and SCARPs, 55
structured-deposits guidance of, 63
"Thematic Review" announced by, 58
"Wider Implications Review" of, 58
Financial Services Compensation Scheme (FSCS), 56, 60, 64, 69
Financial Services and Markets Authority (FSMA), Belgium, 90, 241–2
Financial Supervisory Commission (FSC), Taiwan, 111
Financial Supervisory Service, 108
Financial Times Lexicon, 1
"formula-driven", 38
Fortis, 89, 90
Fortis/BNP, 88
France, 81, 91–3
approach of, to regulation, 242
see also European markets
FTSE 100, 18, 41, 43, 50, 53–4, 81
and EuroSTOXX, 55
and UK product dynamics, 68–75
FTSE 100 linked structured deposits, annualised performance of, 73–4
see also UK market
FTSE 100 linked structured products, annualised performance of, 72–3, *73*
see also UK market
FTSE MIB, 81

G

Gadd, Alan, 41, 42
Germany, 81, 83–6
see also European markets

Great East Japan Earthquake, 180

H

"halos versus shadows", 65–6
Hang Seng, 81, 96, 97
Hargreaves, Peter, 4
Hashimoto, Prime Minister, 145
HKMA, *see* Hong Kong Monetary Authority
Hong Kong, 95–106
and Lehman Brothers, 257–60
more stringent regulatory regime in, 105
see also Asian market
Hong Kong Monetary Authority (HKMA), 104, 257–8
Hong Kong Stock Exchange, 18, 103
HSBC Asset Management, first equity-linked accounts launched by, 41
Hypo Vereinsbank, 86

I

"I kill you later", 104–5
implied volatility, 11–13, 29–30, 270–2, *270*, 274–5, *274*, 281
ING, 88
Internal Revenue Service (IRS), 212
International Monetary Fund (IMF), 106
International Organisation of Securities Commissions (IOSCO), 245–6
International Settlements regulatory framework, 136
Invesco Perpetual, 65
Investment Management Association (IMA), 3, 67
Iraq, Kuwait invaded by, 28
Irish Life, 26–7
Italy, 81–3
approach of, to regulation, 242
see also European markets

J

James Capel, 41
Japan, 119–61, *121, 125, 133, 135, 136, 144, 145, 148, 151, 153, 154, 158,* 163–205, *167, 173, 176, 198–9, 203, 278*
  biggest investors in, 124–7
  and collapse of asset bubble, 123, 184–6
  ENMAN bond:
    and Lehman impact, 202–4, *203*
    terms, characteristics, 201–4
  Great East Japan Earthquake in, 180
  history of retail products in, 182–204
    background, 182–3
    chronological development, 183–204
    collapse of asset bubble, 184
    Plaza Accord, 184
    revised Securities and Exchange Act, 191
  knock-in/knock-out NKY-linked note, 196–201
    major buyers and their motivation, 197
    reasons for success of, 197, 200–1
    regulation, accounting background, 197
    structuring and distribution, 197
    terms, 196
  and Lehman crisis, 179–82
    background, 179–80
    and market movement and impact on each party, 180–2
  life insurance companies in, 124–7
  and mark-to-market (MTM) accounting:
    introduction of, 164–6; *see also* mark-to-market (MTM) accounting and expansion of user base
    investor type and product particulars, 166–9
  and mark-to-market (MTM) accounting and expansion of user base, 164–79
  and power reverse dual currency (PRDC) structure, 143–60; *see also* power reverse dual-currency structure, Japan
    background, 143–6
    and long-dated foreign-exchange products, first generation of, 146–50
    product particulars, 150–5, 157–60
    second generation of, 150–5
  structured products in, beginning of history of, 120–34
    asset price bubble, corporate behaviour behind, 120–2
    background, 120–3
    and dual-currency structure, 128–31; *see also* dual-currency structure, Japan
    Koala loan, 131–4
    product history, 124–8
    product particulars, 128–34
  structured products in, beginning of "lost, 20 years", 134–43
    product history, 137–9
    product particulars, 139–43
Japan Capital Guaranteed Trust (CGT), 112
Jardine Fleming, 96, 112
Jubilee Notes, 104
Julius Baer, 87

K

KBC, 88, 89
Keio University, 174
Key Information Document (KID), 261–2, 263, 264

Keydata Investment Services, 49,
  61–4
  regulatory stance and actions,
    63
knock-in–knock-out (KIKO),
  107, 196–201
Koala loan, Japan, 131–4
  characteristics, 132–4
    major investors and their
      motivation, 132
    pricing and
      risk-management issues,
      134
    reasons for success of, 133
    structuring and distribution,
      132–3
  description, 131–2
    borrower's payout, 132
    typical terms, 131–2
  outcome, 134
KorAm Bank, 106
Korea Financial Investment
  Association (KOFIA) 107
Korea First Bank, 106
Korea Stock Exchange, 107
KOSPI 200, 107
Kuwait, invasion of, 28
Kyoei Life, 185

L

Landesbank Hessen-Thüringen, 86
Lawson, Nigel, 42
Legal & General, 43
Lehman Brothers, 9, 17, 35, 39,
  40, 49, 56–61, 65, 82, 104,
  112, 224, 228
  Asian markets drawn closer
    by, 116
  and Japan, 179–82, 202–4, 203
    background, 179–80
    and market movement and
      impact on each party,
      180–2
  and regulation, 255–60
  regulatory review findings
    concerning, 58–61
    advisory firms, 58–9
    providers, 59–60

UK's low exposure to,
  compared with other
  markets, 58
Leonteq, 87
Libor, see London Interbank
  Offered Rate
liquid and listed products,
  17–19
  see also structured products
Lloyds TSB, 51
London Interbank Offered Rate
  (Libor), 74, 98, 112
LPL Financial, 212

M

M&G Investments, 36, 76
Maastricht Treaty, 31, 272
MacKenzie, Donald, 276
Major, John, 41
Maldonado, Bill, 41, 42
mark-to-market (MTM)
  accounting:
  introduction of, background,
    164–6
  investor type and product
    particulars, 166–9
  listed companies, 168–9
  local financial institutions,
    167–8
mark-to-market (MTM)
  accounting and expansion
  of user base, 164–79
  and cost reduction by
    converting existing
    fixed-rate coupon liability
    to floating rate, 169–71
  and debt assumption, 170
  description and terms,
    169–70
  reasons for success of, 170
  regulation, accounting
    background, 169
  structuring and distribution,
    169
  and unlisted companies,
    170–1

cost-reduction swap by taking
leveraged
foreign-exchange risk,
171–2
major users and their
motivation, 172
reasons for success of, 172
regulation, accounting
background, 172
terms, characteristics, 171–2
user's payout, 172
and Financial Instrument
Exchange Act,
introduction of, 165–6
investment swap, with
leverage foreign-currency
risk, 174–6
characteristics, 175–6
description, 174–5
investor's payout, 175
major investors and their
motivation, 175
pricing and
risk-management issues,
176
reasons for success of, 176
regulation, accounting
background, 176
structuring and distribution,
176
transaction form, 175
and schools, religious
organisations and
foundations, 174–9
local authorities, 177–9
structured note/loan structure
for local authorities, 177–9
borrower's payout, 178
major borrowers and their
motivation, 178
outcome, 179
regulation, accounting
background, 178
structuring and distribution,
178
terms, characteristics, 178–9
marketing materials, 56, 64

Markets in Financial
Instruments Directive
(MiFID), 82, 239–40, 265–6
conduct-of-business
obligations for, 265–6
Master Agreement on the
Trading of Financial
Derivatives on the
Inter-bank Market, 115
media and commentators'
impact on UK market,
64–8
Meoli, Carmine, 86
Merrill Lynch, 80, 104, 208, 209
Meteor Asset Management, 59
MI Security EMU Consumers 1,
89
Midland Life, 26–7
MiFID, *see* Markets in Financial
Instruments Directive
Millennium 3, 92
Minibonds, 4, 104, 255–60
see also Lehman Brothers
Minter-Kemp, Robin, 41, 42
Mitsubishi UFJ Financial Group,
145
Mizuho Financial Group, 144–5
Monetary Authority of
Singapore, 104, 106
Morgan Stanley, 104, 208–9
"Morgan Stanley reading room",
208

N

National Association of
Financial Market
Institutional Investors, 115
Natixis, 90
NDFA, 59
"New Normal", 64
Nigiri, 122, 123
Nikkei, 81, 96, 123, 184–5, 191–2,
279
Nippon Credit Bank, 143
Nippon TV, 282
non-performing loans (NPLs),
134, 143
Northern Rock, 40

Norwich & Peterborough, 62–3
"Notice on Issues Regarding
     Expanding Designated
     Banks' Forward Sale and
     Purchase of Foreign
     Exchange Business to
     Customers and Launching
     RMB Swaps against
     Foreign Currencies", 114
  see also Asian market: China
Notice on the Issues of Business
     Scope of Derivatives
     Product Transaction by
     Domestic Commercial
     Banks, 115

O

Oman, Ron, 79
Open End Investment
     Companies (OEICs), 43

P

Packaged Retail Investment
     Products (PRIPs)
     Regulation, 240, 246, 247,
     249, 260–5
  conduct-of-business
     requirements for, 265
Parmalat, 82
PEA, 91
Peel, Siegfried, 84
People's Bank of China, 114, 115
PEPs, *see* Personal Equity Plans
Pershing, 212
Personal Equity Plans (PEPs),
     41, 42–3
  Single Company version of, 43
Pinnacle Notes, 104
Plain English Prospectus
     Mandate (SEC), 208
Post, La, 91
Poste Italiene, 81
Poste Vita, 82
power reverse dual currency
     (PRDC), 278
power reverse dual currency
     (PRDC) structure, Japan,
     16, 143–60

and long-dated
     foreign-exchange
     products, first generation
     of, 146–50
  notes, 149–50
  product evolution and
     market dynamics, 146–8
  selling options, 148–9
  product particulars, 150–5
  choosers *150*, 151
  PRDC, 152–4, *153*
  PRDC, capped, 153–4, *154*
  second generation of, 155–60
  callable, 155
  principle risk, 156
  product particulars, 157–60
  update on client segment,
     155–6
precipice bonds, 49–56, 65
  "distribution" aspects of, 55–6
  "manufacturing" aspects of,
     51–5
PRIPs, *see* Packaged Retail
     Investment Products
     (PRIPs) Regulation
Private Banking Code of
     Conduct, Singapore, 106
privately placed and
     individually negotiated
     transactions, 13–16
  see also structured products
product intervention options for
     regulators, 251–3
  see also regulation

Q

Qualified Domestic Institutional
     Investor (QDII) scheme,
     115

R

Raymond James, 212
regulation:
  and Bank for International
     Settlements, introduction
     of, 136–7
  in Belgium, 241–2
  complexity of, 239–41

in Denmark, 242–3
and derivative size, 113
different jurisdictional
approaches to, 241–4
discussed, 237–67
in France, 243
in Hong Kong, 257–60
and International
Organisation of Securities
Commissions (IOSCO),
245–6
overall regulatory focus,
245–8
post-sales practices, 247–8
product design and
issuance, 246–7
product disclosure and
marketing, 247
product distribution, 247
and issuance of convertible
bonds, warrants and
commercial paper, 121
in Italy, 242
and Lehman crisis, 255–60
media, and US
structured-products
industry, 228–30
modes of, 239
and Packaged Retail
Investment Products
(PRIPs) 260–5
purpose of, 238–9
right approach to, 244–5
and risk, 241
in South Korea, 106
in UK, 248–55
and due diligence, 254
and information to
consumers, 255
and information to
distributors, 254
intervention, 250–1
and marketing, distribution
and communications, 254
and pleasing the regulator, 253
possible product
intervention options, 251–3

and post-sales
responsibilities, 255
and product approval
procedures, 253
and product development,
253
and product features' design
and development, 253
Retail Distribution Review
(RDR), 248–50
and stress testing and
modelling, 254
in US, 243–4
see also Dodd–Frank Wall
Street Reform and
Consumer Protection Act;
Financial Conduct
Authority; Financial
Services Authority;
Markets in Financial
Instruments Directive;
Securities and Exchange
Commission (SEC);
Securities Offering
Reform; Undertakings for
Collective Investment in
Transferable Securities
Regulation D, 214
Regulation S, 214
"Regulations on
Over-The-Counter
Trading for Securities
Companies", 115
regulatory perspective, 237–67
Resona Bank, 185, 191, 205
Retail Distribution Review
(RDR), 9, 46, 63, 68, 76,
248–50, 252
Retail Note Issuance
Programme, 103
reverse dual-currency
structure, Japan,
141–3
characteristics, 142–3
major investors and their
motivation, 142
reasons for success of, 143

regulation, accounting
background, 142
structuring and distribution,
143
description:
investor's payout, 142
typical terms, 142
see also dual-currency
structure, Japan
risk and modelling, 269–83, *270,
272, 274, 278, 279, 281*
and complexity, 277–83
and crowded trades and
hedging, 280–3
and local volatility, 273–7
RJ Temple, 51

S

S&P 500, 81
Saddam Hussein, 28
Sal Oppenheim, 84
Salomon Brothers, 23–6
Samurai bonds, 129
see also Japan
Sanpaol, 81
Saunders, Richard, 3–4
Schiro, Vito *85*
Scottish Widows, 53–4
Securities Act, 213
Securities Association of China,
115
Securities and Exchange Act
(Japan), 123, 146
revised, 191
Securities and Exchange
Commission (SEC), 17,
208–9, 213–15 *passim*, 243
Securities and Futures
(Amendment) Bill, 2012
(Singapore) 106
Securities and Futures
Commission of Hong
Kong, 99, 104, 260
Securities Offering Reform, 213,
220, 229, 230, 234
Seoul Central District Court, 107
severe acute respiratory
syndrome (SARS), 99

SG, 91
Shanghai Stock Exchange, 115
short volatility, 12, 28
Singapore, 95–106
Chinese as large part of
resident population of,
97–8
see also Asian market
SMI, 81
Smith, Terry, 3
Société Générale (SocGen), 18,
79, 91, 209, 273
Sogeposte, 92
South Korea, 106–11, *107*
export dominance of, 107
see also Asian market
Spain, 81
see also European markets
Spears, Taylor, 276
SPR, *see* StructuredProduct
Review.com (SPR)
Standard Chartered Bank, 103
Korea First Bank acquired by,
106
State Administration of Foreign
Exchange, 115
Straits Times index, 96, *97*
structure capital-at-risk products
(SCARPs), 49, 51, 55
structured products:
as derivatives, 1
explained and discussed, 1–21,
5, 14, 19
"formula-driven", 38
history and evolution of,
23–33, *29, 30*
capital-guaranteed product,
first trade in, 25–6
market evolution, 28–33
hypothetical deal to explain, 2
as investment, pros and cons
of, 6–13
complexity, 10–11
currency protection, 8
lack of costs/charges
transparency, 8–9
liquidity, lack of, 9
market access, 7

market distortions, 11
payoff transformation, 7–8
risk, extra layer of, 9
tax efficiency and avoidance,
    7
in Japan, beginning of history
    of, 120–34; see also Japan
regulatory perspective on, see
    regulation
reported annual sales of, 17
and risk and modelling,
    269–83, 270, 272, 274, 278,
    279, 281
and complexity, 277–83
and crowded trades and
    hedging, 280–3
local volatility, 273–7
types of, 13–19
liquid and listed, 17–19
privately placed and
    individually negotiated,
    13–16, 13
retailed through branch
    networks, 16–17
UK market in, 35–77; see also
    UK market
absolute versus relative
    measure of, 44–5
fundamental positives of,
    36–40
January 1996, 41–2
late, 1990s to, 2000s, 43–4
relative versus absolute
    measure of success of,
    44–5
retail, fast progress of, 40–1
through 2000s, 44–5
in US, see US structured
    products
see also individual countries,
    regions
Structured Products Association,
    17
StructuredProductReview.com
    (SPR), 68, 72
StructuredRetailProducts.com,
    79, 80
subprime mortgages, xiii, 102

Sumitomo Mitsui Financial
    Group, 145
Swiss Association of Asset
    Managers (SAAM), 87
Swiss Bank Corp (SBC), 79
Swiss National Bank, 86
Swiss Stock Exchange, 88
Swiss Structured Products
    Association, 86
Switzerland, 83, 86–8
    see also European markets

T

Taisei F&M, 185
Taiwan 110, 111–14
    see also Asian market
Tax Exempt Special Savings
    Accounts (TESSAs), 41–3
Technology, Media and
    Telecommunication (TMT)
    Guaranteed Fund, 98
TESSAs, see Tax Exempt Special
    Savings Accounts
"they kill you later", 105
Tokkin funds, 121, 122, 123
turbo certificates, 17

U

UBS, 79, 87
UK market, 35–77, 70, 73
distribution dynamics in, 35,
    45–8
first significant breakthrough
    in, 41
investment in, 36–7
media and commentators'
    impact on, 64–8
product dynamics in, 68–75
and structured product
    performance data for
    products in UK
    professional adviser
    channel, 68–75
professional adviser channel
    in 73
capital-at-risk FTSE 100
    autocall products,

annualised performance
of, 74
capital-at-risk FTSE 100
linked digital growth
products, annualised
performance of, 74–5
capital-at-risk FTSE 100
linked structured
products, annualised
performance of, 73
capital-at-risk FTSE 100
linked "super-tracker"
(geared growth) products,
annualised performance
of, 75
capital-at-risk structured
products, annualised
performance of, 74
FTSE 100 linked structured
deposits, annualised
performance of, 73–4
FTSE 100 linked structured
products, annualised
performance of, 72–3, 73
underlyings, 72
and regulation, 248–55
and due diligence, 254
and information to
consumers, 255
and information to
distributors, 254
intervention, 250–1
and marketing, distribution
and communications, 254
and pleasing the regulator,
253
possible product
intervention options,
251–3
and post-sales
responsibilities, 255
and product approval
procedures, 253
and product development,
253
and product features' design
and development, 253

Retail Distribution Review
(RDR), 248–50
and stress testing and
modelling, 254
specific events and issues
affecting, 48–64
Keydata Investment
Services, 49, 61–4
Lehman Brothers, 49, 56–61,
65; see also Lehman
Brothers
precipice bonds, 49–56, 65;
see also precipice bonds
structured products in:
absolute versus relative
measure of, 44–5
entry of, 37
equity-linked deposit
accounts, launch of, 41–2
fundamental positives of,
36–40
HSBC Asset Management's
first equity-linked
structured deposit
accounts, 41
January, 1996, 41–2
late 1990s to 2000s, 43–4
PEPs and TESSAs, 41–3
relative versus absolute
measure of success of,
44–5
retail, fast progress of, 40–1
through, 2000s, 44–5
Undertakings for Collective
Investment in Transferable
Securities (UCITS),
239–40, 261–2
Unicredit, 81
United Capital Guaranteed
Funds, 98
United States:
approach of, to regulation,
243–4
insurance market and annuity
products in, 231–3
structured products in, see US
structured products
UOB Asset Management, 98

US structured products, 207–34
  growth era and industry
      maturity, 210–22
  client channels, 210–13
  distribution wrappers and
      market impact, 213–15
  key products, 215–19
  industry reception and early
      years, 208–10
  industry shake-up, 222–31
  2010–13, 225–7
  commoditisation and drive
      for efficiency, 230–1
  low rates for a long time,
      227–8
  media and regulatory focus,
      228–30
  September, 2008–March,
      2009: the plunge, 222–4
  signs of rebirth: 2009, 224–5
  yield generators and
      proprietary algorithms,
      225–6

and insurance market and
    annuity products, 231–3
USD/JPY, 96

V

Volvo, 26
Vontobel, 87

W

well-known seasoned issuers
    (WKSIs), 215
Woodford, Neil, 65
World Bank, 137
World Federation of Exchanges,
    95
wrappers, 1, 43, 91, 237
  and market impact, 213–15

Z

Zaiteku (*zaimu tekunorojii*), 120–1
Zhengzhou Commodity
    Exchange, 114
ZKB, 87